Listening to Killers

Listening to Killers

LESSONS LEARNED FROM MY TWENTY YEARS
AS A PSYCHOLOGICAL EXPERT WITNESS
IN MURDER CASES

James Garbarino

UNIVERSITY OF CALIFORNIA PRESS

University of California Press, one of the most distinguished university presses in the United States, enriches lives around the world by advancing scholarship in the humanities, social sciences, and natural sciences. Its activities are supported by the UC Press Foundation and by philanthropic contributions from individuals and institutions. For more information, visit www.ucpress.edu.

University of California Press
Oakland, California

Library of Congress Cataloging-in-Publication Data

Garbarino, James, author.
    Listening to killers : lessons learned from my twenty years as a psychological expert witness in murder cases / James Garbarino.
        p.   cm.
    Includes bibliographical references and index.
    ISBN 978-0-520-28286-5 (cloth : alk. paper)
    ISBN 978-0-520-28287-2 (pbk. : alk. paper)
    ISBN 978-0-520-95874-6 (ebook)
    1. Murderers—United States—Psychology.   2. Murder—United States—Psychological aspects.   3. Trials (Murder)—United States.   4. Evidence, Expert—United States.   I. Title.
    HV6529.G37 2015
    364.152'3019—dc23   2014032693

24   23   22   21   20   19   18   17   16   15
10   9   8   7   6   5   4   3   2   1

In keeping with a commitment to support environmentally responsible and sustainable printing practices, UC Press has printed this book on Natures Natural, a fiber that contains 30% post-consumer waste and meets the minimum requirements of ANSI/NISO Z39.48-1992 (R 1997) (*Permanence of Paper*).

Cover photo: Mark Wragg/istockphoto.

To the public defenders and mitigation specialists who seek to understand, protect, and, if possible, care for America's killers. And to the victims, who bear the brunt of America's failures to protect and nurture children and youth at risk in their homes and their communities.

CONTENTS

ACKNOWLEDGMENTS

I would like to thank the many individuals and institutions that have supported me and my work over the last twenty years. These include my academic homes during this period: Loyola University Chicago, Cornell University, and the Erikson Institute for Advanced Study in Child Development. I also must thank all the lawyers, mitigation specialists, and mental health professionals with whom I have worked as an expert witness. And I acknowledge the "killers" who are at the core of this book. They shared their stories with me as we sat in jails and prisons around the country. As Truman Capote found in the writing of his masterpiece *In Cold Blood,* hearing these stories can open the way for complicated relationships. For reasons of confidentiality and because some of the cases that I report in this book are still in the appeals process, which can last decades, I have used pseudonyms (marked by an asterisk) and altered the details of crimes in most cases.

In addition, I want to offer my appreciation to several people who facilitated the writing of this book. My thanks to Judy Jones for seeing the value of the proposal and steering me to Roger Levesque. He shared Judy's enthusiasm and put me in touch with Maura Roessner at the University of California Press, who immediately became an advocate for the book. I appreciate the efforts of all three.

I also appreciate Joshua Garbarino's input on legal issues dealing with expert witnesses, as well as his friendly editorial suggestions. Thanks to Diane Geraghty of Loyola University Chicago's Child Law Program for her suggestions on how to treat the development of juvenile justice in the United States. Thanks also to my colleagues in the Psychology Department at Loyola University Chicago—Fred Bryant, Rebecca Silton, and Laura Stockdale—for sharing their knowledge in ways that strengthened the book. Special appreciation to Robert Zagar for generously sharing his work on predictors of violence. Finally, I wish to thank two reviewers of the preliminary manuscript—Jose Ashford and Kathleen Heide—whose constructive criticism and suggestions enabled me to improve the book before it went into final production with the University of California Press team.

An earlier version of some of the material presented in chapter 1 appeared as an article: Understanding criminal "choices" in context. American Journal of Orthopsychiatry, 81 (2011), 157–161.

Introduction

BECOMING AN EXPERT WITNESS

June 30, 2010: Images of the movie *Dead Man Walking* flood my mind as I sit in a small interview room on death row in Alabama's Snake River Correctional Institution. Across from me sits a very dangerous man, hands and feet shackled, a chain anchoring his belt to a bolt on the floor. Clad in an orange prison jumpsuit, his name is Danny Samson* and he is thirty-four years old. Danny is so threatening that when he appears in court, six corrections officers are present on the chance that he might erupt violently, as he is prone to do. I am here because Samson is going to trial for the third time for the murder of motel clerk Marney Johnson during a robbery on Christmas Eve in 1981. He was tried and sentenced to death twice before, but the death sentence was appealed successfully both times and a new trial granted. My job is to help a jury and judge make sense of his violent, troubled life and thus give them a rationale for seeing him with compassion and sparing him from execution. He has the bulging muscles and tattoos so common among men who have been incarcerated for a long time, and he has a long record of repeated violent assaults on other inmates and prison guards. This includes murdering another inmate, twenty-seven-year-old Timothy Roberts, in 1999. Samson has been in and out of prison since he was fifteen years old and is a very damaged person emotionally, morally, and spiritually. At the end of the interview, I ask him a final question: "What can you tell me about yourself that people would be surprised to hear?" He pauses a moment, then replies, "I cry myself to sleep at night." Afterwards, I check out his story: he does. Inside this big, scary, dangerous man is a frightened and hurt little child. You wouldn't know that by seeing him. You wouldn't know that by looking at his prison records. You have to listen to him.

I listen to killers. I listen for the human story behind the monstrous act. I do this as an expert psychological witness, so that I can testify in court about

*Throughout this book, asterisks indicate case studies in which I have used pseudonyms and altered identifying information.

how these killers came to travel a path from childhood innocence to adult depravity and violence through the accumulation of emotional and moral damage. I listen to these killers talk, I review their records, and sometimes I interview family members to identify and understand the psychological, social, cultural, and biological forces that have brought them to a criminal court, accused of murder.

I do this so that when I talk to a judge and jury, they can take this story into account in making their decisions, sometimes about guilt or innocence, but more often about what penalty to impose—mostly execution or life in prison. I usually tell of a life forged in a history of child abuse that affected emotional stability and intelligence, of neurological issues that affected judgment, of pervasive mis-socialization that undermined moral development—forces at work in a killer's life that make the crime more "understandable" as a human act.

The goal is never to excuse or justify the crime, only to explain it psychologically and socially. Once guilt has been established, the prosecution seeks to document "aggravating" factors to justify the harshest possible punishment, while the defense's goal is to explain the defendant as someone worthy of compassion despite the horror of his actions, to highlight the "mitigating factors" in his case—and "his" is typically the right pronoun. I have worked with a few female defendants, but the overwhelming majority of defendants in murder cases are male, and about 98 percent of those sentenced to death are male. According to Amnesty International, since 1930 about four thousand men, but only about forty women, have been executed.

Given the nature of the crimes involved, this differentiation between the humanity of the person and the inhumanity of his actions requires the judge or jury (in legal terminology the "trier of fact") to be able to separate the origins of the defendant's behavior from the nature and consequences of that behavior. I usually seek to explain the defendant (not typically the crime itself) through an analysis of the experiences in childhood and adolescence that eventually led him to "choose" violence over nonviolence (I put the word *choose* in quotation marks because often there is only limited choice involved, as we will see in chapter 1).

Thus, I am not trying to use my professional expertise to justify violent crime, only to illuminate the reality of how one's past pain can lead to one's present infliction of pain on others. In a sense, then, my work is an exercise in developmental depth psychology: to give depth and developmental nuance to something that seems to have no depth and that seems to be straightforwardly evil.

The "best" legal outcome in most of these cases (from the defendant's perspective) is life in prison, often with no possibility of parole. Immediate release is never an option, so the message that the defense hopes to elicit is not "Go forth and sin no more." Rather, the message that the defense strives to obtain from the court is "We recognize how the suffering of your life distorted your development. Now take the rest of your life to make your peace with the hardship that you experienced and, even more so, the terrible suffering that you inflicted."

My job in these cases is to provide a framework within which the judge and jury can make sense of the wide range of information presented to them by social workers, psychiatrists, other psychologists, teachers, and "lay people" such as family members and neighbors who know the defendant and can report on his life experiences. These reports include information about the defendant's childhood conditions, schools and other institutional settings, family history, and the social context in which the crime in question occurred.

CRIME AND PUNISHMENT IN THE UNITED STATES

Each year about fifteen thousand murders occur in the United States, according to the Centers for Disease Control and Prevention. As of 2014, thirty-two states (and the federal government) offered the death penalty as part of the menu of legal responses to murder. Research reviewed by Death Penalty Focus demonstrates the variability with which it is applied; biases of race and gender, misunderstandings by jurors, and arbitrariness by prosecutors all play roles in this variability. Because of the complexities of legal appeals and the reticence of some states to enforce the death sentences that have been imposed, the actual number of executions is small compared with the number of inmates living under death sentences. In 2011, for example, there were forty-three executions, compared with seventy-eight death sentences handed down by courts. *But more than three thousand individuals sit on death rows around the country, according to the Death Penalty Information Center. Only 2 percent of the counties in the United States account for a majority of the actual executions, according to an analysis by Richard Dieter for Deathpenaltyinfo.org.*

The United States currently has about 5 percent of the world's population but more than 25 percent of the world's incarcerated population, according to a compilation prepared by Solomon Moore for *The New York Times*. While most of the inmates in America's jails and prisons are there for nonviolent crimes (mostly drug-related offenses), more than seven hundred thousand are currently imprisoned for violent crimes alone, including "murder, non-negligent manslaughter, manslaughter, rape, other sexual assault, robbery, assault, and other violent offenses."

In states where the death penalty is not legal, the most severe sentence a criminal can receive is life imprisonment. But a sentence of life imprisonment can mean different things in different states. In six states, all life sentences are imposed without the possibility of parole. In the other forty-four states, life sentences can be given with or without parole. In 2003, there were approximately 128,000 inmates serving life sentences, and nearly 34,000 of them had been sentenced to life without parole. There is a similar trend among juveniles. In 2008, according to The Sentencing Project (www.sentencingproject.org), there were 6,807 juveniles serving life terms, 1,755 without the possibility of parole—although a 2010 U.S. Supreme Court decision (*Graham v. Florida*) declared this unconstitutional in cases that did not involve murder (and as a result, many of these cases are being reviewed).

How did these inmates come to receive such harsh sentences? What led them to commit these crimes? What are the psychological repercussions of life imprisonment and living on death row? And how can we learn from these cases to prevent others from following in the footsteps of these inmates? All these questions arise for me because my professional mission goes well beyond serving as a psychological expert witness for individuals.

As a researcher, a scholar, and a human rights advocate, I am concerned with the "big picture" of criminal violence in America. I am concerned with the tension between understanding the damaged individuals who commit murder and the right of society to protect itself. But I am also concerned with the ways in which social factors such as racism, economic inequality, and poverty contribute to the damage individuals incur *and* with the way society responds to those individuals. In this book I will address these "big picture" issues. But first, I think it is important to explain why I find myself in the role of psychological expert witness in the first place.

THE PATH FROM STUDENT TO EXPERT

I didn't start out to become an expert psychological witness in murder cases. In fact, I didn't even start out planning to become a psychologist. When I graduated from high school and started college at St. Lawrence University in 1964, I planned and expected to be a lawyer. By the time I finished college and started graduate school in 1968, however, things had changed, and I planned and expected to become a college professor teaching political science and history. When I changed my focus in 1969 and left my graduate program in government at Cornell University, I planned and expected to become a junior high school teacher (and switched over to the Education Department). Even when I serendipitously stumbled into a graduate program in human development in 1970, I only planned and expected to become a college professor and to teach developmental psychology to generations of students.

I hoped I might become enough of an expert in matters of child development that I could follow in the footsteps of my mentor, Urie Bronfenbrenner—a famous figure in the field of child development who was one of the founders of Head Start—and influence public policy about children as he had done. That was where things stood when I walked to the stage in 1973 to receive my PhD from Urie's hand (as a faculty member of the Cornell University Board of Trustees, this was one of his perks, to hand over doctoral degrees to his students).

But now, more than forty years later, here I am, an expert psychological witness specializing in murder cases, particularly death penalty cases (in addition to being the college professor teaching generations of students about human development that I had planned and expected to be those many years ago). I think that explaining how I got to this point is a good place to start my reflections on what I have learned in the process.

The first step was becoming an expert in matters of child abuse and neglect. My first research publication in this field appeared in 1976 in the journal *Child Development,* and it was only the first of many. By 1986, my career had developed to the point that I was awarded the first C. Henry Kempe Award by the National Conference on Child Abuse and Neglect. Kempe is recognized as the "founder" of the field of child abuse prevention and treatment. Although others had made important contributions before, it was physician Kempe who stimulated passage of the first major national child abuse prevention and treatment legislation in 1974. Receiving the award named in his honor marked my arrival as an "expert" psychologist, but it was not until six years later that I entered the world of the expert psychological *witness.*

The legal system has a complicated, love–hate relationship with expert witnesses. Two precedent-setting cases provide the foundation. In 1923, *Frye v. United States* established that expert witness testimony was admissible as evidence if it was based on a scientific technique generally accepted as reliable in the scientific community. This led to experts being accepted by courts after being vetted through testimony and cross-examination as to their credentials, experience, skill, and reputation.

In the years after 1923, the *Frye* test became the standard. The various subtleties were worked out so that by 1975, it was codified in the "Federal Rule of Evidence 702," which states that "A witness who is qualified as an expert by knowledge, skill, experience, training or education, may testify in the form of an opinion or otherwise, if: (a) the expert's scientific, technical, or other specialized knowledge will assist the trier of fact to understand the evidence or to determine a fact in issue; (b) the testimony is based upon sufficient facts or data; (c) the testimony is the product of reliable principles and methods; and (d) the expert has applied the principles and methods reliably to the facts of the case" (updated to reflect the current version of FRE 702: www.law.cornell.edu/rules/fre/rule_702).

In 1993, the U.S. Supreme Court decision in the case of *Daubert v. Merrell Dow Pharmaceuticals* addressed the issue of "novel scientific evidence." In what came to be known as the "*Daubert* rule" (which is not followed in all states), the court ruled that testimony that relied on "innovative or unusual scientific knowledge" was acceptable only if there was evidence that it had been subject to the regular process of scientific vetting to assess reliability and validity. In the *Daubert* case, the responsibility for assessing whether or not particular evidence (and thus particular expert witnesses) met this standard fell to the trial judge, which turned the trial judge into a "gatekeeper" for the evidence.

The term used to describe what was to be avoided was *junk science*. Like so many principles, it sounds simple in the abstract but is often hard to demonstrate in reality, as I found out when I was called upon to make the transition from academic "expert" in the classroom, the conference lecture hall, and the professional journal to "expert witness" in the court room. The first two times I answered the call, I was rejected by the legal system, once in a case that went all the way to the U.S. Supreme Court. It was not until the third attempt to use me as an expert psychological witness that my testimony was accepted by the courts despite the objections of the other side (the prosecution in that case).

THE BABY LOLLIPOPS CASE

My first case as an expert witness did not play a big role in forging the understanding of the emotional and moral damage that has become the central theme in my work, so I will only describe it briefly. In 1992, I was called upon to testify as an expert witness on child abuse in a grisly child murder case in Florida. The case was known in the media as the "Baby Lollipops Case" because it started with the finding of a dead three-year-old in the bushes of a home in Miami—a child identified only by the white T-shirt he wore, with an array of lollipops on the front. Eventually, the child was identified as Lazaro Figuero. His mother, Ana Maria Cardona, was apprehended and tried for causing his death. The details of his abuse were gruesome in the extreme.

The prosecutor in the case asked me to testify as an expert on child abuse to help the jury understand how it was possible that one child in a family could be singled out for abuse (the two other children in the household had not been abused). I did so and then returned to Chicago. Ana was convicted and became the first woman sentenced to death for the murder of her child in Florida history. I learned of Ana's death sentence only later, from a newspaper account. Since an expert witness is testifying as a "disinterested, objective party on the basis of scientific knowledge" (as the rules make clear), personal feelings and beliefs should not be at issue. Thus, my personal feelings and beliefs about the death penalty in 1992 are not the issue here, nor were they then (nor are they when I testify now, because as a professional expert I am bound to analyze the data objectively rather than in service to any ideological bias). But I will say that I was surprised to read that Ana had been sentenced to death, because when I testified in her case I had been unaware that the prosecutor was seeking the death penalty.

THE FELICIA MORGAN CASE

The second time I was asked to serve as an expert witness involved the cause to which I have devoted the past twenty years of my life: applying knowledge from the field of developmental psychology to understand the pathway that leads from childhood maltreatment and social deprivation to murder. It is an approach that did not win easy acceptance because, following the *Daubert* rule, the legal system did not yet see the validity of this novel approach—a fact that became clear in the case of Felicia Morgan.

On October 26, 1991, seventeen-year-old Felicia Morgan shot and killed another teenager, Brenda Adams. The case had elements that immediately made it high profile: at a time when youth violence among Black kids was escalating, both shooter and victim were Black teenagers. What is more, it seemed particularly "senseless" (the word used by the Wisconsin Supreme Court in a ruling on the case when it was appealed) because it stemmed from an attempt by Morgan to steal the coat Adams was wearing at the time.

I was approached by Felicia's lawyer to serve as an expert psychological witness in the case. Attorney Robin Shellow is a crusading lawyer who specializes in representing youthful violent offenders, underdogs from the underclass in which community violence and child abuse and neglect are rampant, alongside poverty and social deprivation. Since 1994, more than thirty of her clients have either been murdered or killed themselves. She contacted me because she had become aware of the work I was doing in Chicago to explore the impact of living in "the urban war zone" on the development of the "war zone mentality" among children and youths.

The Urban War Zone

I had taken on this topic when I arrived in Chicago in 1985, as president of the Erikson Institute for Advanced Study in Child Development. Students there included many individuals who were working in preschools, kindergartens, and elementary schools serving poor, violent communities. These students came to me with stories of how the young children they taught were affected by the violence they experienced in the community, and sought my help in making sense of it.

At the same time, I was beginning to visit war zones around the world—initially focusing on the Palestinian–Israeli conflict. I was struck by the similarities (and differences) between kids facing violence in conventional war zones organized around political conflicts and kids facing the chaos of gang violence in Chicago. Out of this work came the idea of "the urban war zone."

In 1991, my colleagues Kathleen Kostelny and Nancy Dubrow and I published our book *No Place to Be A Child: Growing Up in a War Zone,* in which we considered the experience of children and youths in five places: Nicaragua, Mozambique, Cambodia, Israel–Palestine, and Chicago. In 1992, we were joined by Carol Pardo in publishing *Children in Danger: Coping with the Consequences of Community Violence,* which focused on the experience of young children in the urban war zones of Chicago and other cities.

Our most important conclusion was that the effects of living in any war zone are magnified by living in families that themselves are violent, traumatic, abusive, and neglectful. We came to see that the double whammy of violent trauma at home and in the community was particularly destructive of normal emotional and moral development. This described Felicia's life, and it was why Robin Shellow wanted me to participate in her defense.

Felicia seemed to be a classic example of a poor, abused, and neglected child who grew up in a community that was flooded with violence that left her traumatized and morally disoriented. Robin and I agreed that if a jury understood this, it would help transform her "senseless" killing of Brenda Adams into a terrible event with two victims, not just one. Although I never used the term, the press started to call this "the urban psychosis defense," and as we will see, others adopted the term.

Rejected by the Court

When the day of the trial arrived, I anxiously boarded the train in Chicago for the ninety-minute trip to Milwaukee, where the proceedings were being held. When the time came for my testimony, the prosecutor objected on the grounds that anything I (or anyone else) had to say about Felicia's development as an abused child and a traumatized adolescent was irrelevant. Judge Michael Goulee listened as Robin guided me through what I would say if permitted to testify; then the prosecutor had his turn with me. After listening to both sides, the judge ruled that he would not allow the jury to hear what I had to say, so I got back on the train to return to Chicago. My testimony was rejected.

Felicia was convicted. However, during the "victim impact" phase of the sentencing hearing, when Brenda's father was given a chance to speak about Felicia's actions in killing his daughter, he spoke movingly about how hearing about Felicia's experiences as a traumatized and abused child allowed him to have compassion for her. He told the court, "I want to beg the court and really plead with the court to give this kid a second chance."

Mr. Adams went on to say that he wanted Felicia to have a chance for parole if she succeeded in getting a college education while in prison. In response, the judge obliged, by ordering that Felicia be eligible for parole in thirteen years (the minimum time legally possible—sixty years was an option) and added, "You can change, and we are going to give you that opportunity." This was progress of a sort, giving the judge and the victim's family a way of understanding Felicia Morgan as something more than a monster, and the murder she committed as something more than "senseless."

Moving beyond Post-traumatic Stress Disorder

Looking back on my proposed testimony (in light of what happened later when Felicia's conviction was appealed), I think that one mistake we made was allowing what I had to say to be couched in the somewhat limiting language of *post-traumatic stress disorder*. This was the term that dominated the psychological discussion at that time, but it doesn't really capture the dimensions of what I was talking about—and would talk about for the next twenty years as I fine-tuned my analysis of the war zone mentality (a matter that I will take up in detail in chapter 3).

Robin appealed Felicia's conviction, in part on the grounds that I was not allowed to testify. From my perspective, the relevant questions addressed in the appeal were these two (of the four questions raised):

Did the trial court erroneously exercise its discretion by excluding expert psychiatric and psychological testimony on post-traumatic stress disorder and expert and lay testimony on Morgan's psychosocial history?

Did the trial court violate Morgan's constitutional right to present a defense by excluding the expert testimony of a psychologist from the responsibility phase of her bifurcated trial, on the grounds that it was irrelevant and cumulative to evidence already presented?

When the case reached the Wisconsin Court of Appeals, the three-judge panel ruled two to one in favor of the trial judge and against including my testimony. I was told that one judge agreed with the trial judge, one judge disagreed, and the third disagreed with the content of the trial judge's ruling but thought that it was the judge's decision to make and therefore voted to uphold it. The ruling read, in part: "After a careful review of the arguments presented by the parties and our own review of the applicable law, we conclude that there are no grounds for reversing Morgan's judgment of conviction. Accordingly, we affirm." So wrote the court. That was 1995. The Wisconsin Supreme Court denied review.

Robin then appealed to the U.S. District Court for the Eastern District of Wisconsin and won. But then the State of Wisconsin appealed to the U.S. Court of Appeals for the Seventh Circuit, and the state won (i.e., the court of appeals reversed the district court judge's ruling). That was in 2000. The problem in this case was that the courts ruled that what I had to say about Felicia's developmental pathway being rooted in family violence, child abuse, deprivation, community violence, and trauma was irrelevant to questions of her guilt. Their legal view was that this line of evidence about how a defendant *grew up* did not bear on what he or she *did*. But this perspective was changing, at least in the thinking that was guiding the higher courts conceptually in the mid-1990s.

SHIFTING THE GROUNDS FOR EXPERT TESTIMONY

In 1996, Cleveland-Marshall Law School Professor Patricia Falk published an article titled "Novel Theories of Criminal Defense Based upon the Toxicity of the Social Environment: Urban Psychosis, Television Intoxication, and Black Rage" in the *North Carolina Law Review*. In the introduction, she wrote that "in recent years, defendants have proffered a multitude of novel theories of criminal defense in seeking to explain their criminal behavior in terms of internal and external influences beyond their control, including biological processes, chemical reactions, intra-psychic dynamics, social conditions, and cross-cultural stresses. This article focuses on one subset of this burgeoning class of defenses: those based upon the central premise that the defendant's criminal conduct was caused, or significantly influenced, by his exposure to social environmental factors or, if you will, toxins affecting his mental functioning."

She went on to argue that "While a wide panoply of toxins exist within the fabric of our social environment, three of the most pervasive and damaging are: the daily reality of violence in our nation's homes, neighborhoods, and communities; the incessant barrage of graphic depictions of violence presented in the media; and the persistence, if not resurgence, of racism despite the guarantee of legal equality. It is not a coincidence, then, that defendants have raised defenses based upon these same three social conditions—urban psychosis, television intoxication, and black rage."

In 1994, I had published my book *Raising Children in a Socially Toxic Environment,* so I was quite familiar with the concept of "social toxins" to which Falk referred (citing my book in her article). Falk linked the term *urban psychosis* to the Felicia Morgan case—although, as noted earlier, I never used that term in defending Felicia Morgan. Leaving that aside, Falk's article signaled a shift in focus, away from the dismissive and insulting characterization of these lines of defense as "the abuse excuse," as if the experience of child abuse were unimportant or irrelevant in understanding human development. Imagine if individuals who were suffering from the consequences to their health and behavior of having malignant cells in their bodies that caused a tumor were dismissed and ridiculed as offering an explanation that was called "the cancer excuse."

Instead, Falk moved the discussion forward, toward an appreciation for the actual interplay of psychological, social, and biological influences in the pathway that takes a child through adolescence and into adulthood. She argued that the kind of legal extension of scientific advances represented by the study of social toxins like traumatic violence that we argued for in Felicia Morgan's case is warranted (and can be extended to issues of violent television programming and racism). This was not surprising on Falk's part, since she was the product of a graduate program in Psychology and the Law and had professional degrees in both fields.

The Relationship between Science and the Law

Falk cited a 1946 U.S. Supreme Court case (*Fisher v. The United States*) in the introduction to her analysis. In that death-penalty murder case, the lower courts had ruled against permitting expert psychological and psychiatric testimony because it would have supported a verdict somewhere between "not guilty by reason of insanity" and "fully culpable of first-degree murder," and the law at that time did not permit such an intermediate position. The Supreme Court's majority affirmed the lower court's ruling barring the expert testimony. But Justice Murphy was joined by Justices Frankfurter and Rutledge in a dissenting opinion arguing that "Only by integrating scientific advancements with our ideals of justice can law remain a part of the living fiber of our civilization." One can hear in this statement the kind of thinking that would lead to the *Daubert* rule fifty years later.

These Justices were speaking on behalf of expanding the integration of psychology and the law, as Falk was in her article. Although in Felicia

Morgan's case the 1946 *Fisher* majority view prevailed, this expansion to reflect new knowledge and concepts of psychological development can and does happen. It had happened in the half century since the *Fisher* case. I witnessed it happen in 1995, in a state courtroom in Denver, Colorado, when my brand of "social toxicity" defense was accepted in the case of *Colorado v. Rivas,* and a precedent was set that paved the way for my work in "forensic developmental psychology" over the next two decades, which continues today.

THE LEONEL RIVAS CASE

A member of the North Side Mafia gang, 19-year-old Leonel Rivas had spent his short life surrounded by and immersed in traumatic violence at home and in the community. As an abused and neglected child, he had watched his mother being raped. In his neighborhood there were few alternatives to aligning himself with a gang. Thus, by the time he was a teenager, he had been shot and stabbed and beaten up himself (and had been involved in the assault and violence that is the currency of life in a street gang). He had friends who had died on the mean streets of his neighborhood.

The incident that brought him before the court was one in which he and another young man entered into an escalating confrontation that started with the flashing of rival gang signs as Rivas drove around in his neighborhood. There was aggressive posturing, and the confrontation reached a crisis when Rivas believed he saw his opponent reach for a gun under the dashboard of his car.

In the context of gang life in the community (including the fact that under the dashboard was the usual spot for keeping guns hidden but ready), it was for Rivas a reasonable assumption that this was the precursor to violence. In this he resembled a soldier patrolling a village in Afghanistan or Iraq during the wars there who saw imminent attack in the suspicious movements of a local who could be an enemy. In an act of preemptive attack, Rivas fired his own weapon into the other car and killed the driver. Prosecutors Bill Robbins and Lamar Simms charged him with first-degree murder.

Public defenders Nancy Holton and Susan Fish countered with an attempt to prove self-defense. Under Colorado law at the time, a person who felt that he or she was threatened with imminent lethal attack was entitled to use force—even lethal force—in an act of self-preservation. The key is that this perception of threat was to be understood *given that individual's life experience*. This was the opening for my testimony in the case. (The "stand your ground" elements of this defense received national attention twenty years later in the 2013 trial of George Zimmerman for the shooting of Trayvon Martin on February 26, 2012, in Florida.)

Holton and Fish argued that because of his life experience, Rivas *did* feel he was in imminent threat of losing his life in this confrontation. They called upon me to explain how his history of traumatic violence at home and in the community, coupled with his own cognitive and emotional issues, could indeed cast Rivas's actions as self-defense. They chose to call this "urban survival syndrome" (preferring this term over what the media had called "urban psychosis" in the Felicia Morgan case and what I term the "war zone mentality").

The Judge Rules to Allow My Testimony

When the prosecution filed a motion to exclude my testimony, the decision to allow or disallow this defense fell to the trial judge, Murray Richtel. To his credit, he allowed the defense to make this "urban survival syndrome" argument, and I was permitted to testify. After hearing the testimony, the jury rejected the prosecution's request for a first-degree murder conviction (with a possible life sentence) and instead convicted Rivas of "illegal discharge of a firearm" and "reckless manslaughter." The judge sentenced him to the maximum sentence, thirteen years.

Overall, given the circumstances of the case, we believed that we were successful: although the self-defense argument was not accepted, the verdict reflected an appreciation for our analysis. It acknowledged that the developmental pathway of Leonel Rivas's life had set him up *both* to feel lethally threatened in a situation that would not have been such for others with a more "normal" childhood and adolescence *and* to respond recklessly when he did feel threatened (shooting into a car that in fact contained not just Leonel's supposed antagonist, but a young child as well). We had cleared the *Daubert* rule's hurdle.

Whatever else it accomplished, the Rivas case set a precedent, and precedent is vitally important in the legal system, because a decision like this could (and, as it turned out, would) open the doors for other courts to admit my brand of testimony (whether by me or others). What I had to say about the developmental psychology of killing in America was now accepted in at least one state court—whether it was called "urban psychosis," "urban survival syndrome," or "war zone mentality."

Although it was not binding on other states, this decision seemed to open the door for me as an expert psychological witness. I was ready to confront the awful reality of homicide in the United States by offering my emerging understanding of how emotional and moral damage accumulates to form the war zone mentality and what significance it has for judging the "choices" made by violent offenders. My life's work had begun, and in the two decades that followed I have been involved as an expert in more than fifty murder cases. I have served for the defense in all these cases, not because I have refused to appear for the prosecution, but because I have not been asked by the prosecution. This is presumably because what I have to say does not fit with the message they are trying to send to the jury about the defendant. I have offered to share my perspective with prosecutors when the occasion has arisen, but they haven't taken me up on it. This, I think, is a feature of the adversarial nature of the criminal justice system.

Having spent the first twenty years of my career seeking to understand how trauma, abuse, social deprivation, and exposure to violence affected children and youths, I spent the next twenty years testifying as a psychological expert witness and honing my understanding of the lives of killers. To that I turn next.

THIS BOOK

Part I, "Getting Close to Killers," focuses on what we can learn about killers if we are willing to take on the distressing and often distasteful task of entering into their world. In the first chapter, I explore the issue of "choice" in the criminal justice system. The simple idea of choosing between right and wrong, good and evil, gives way to an appreciation for the complexities of criminal choice, including the role of unconscious forces and brain issues in executive function and emotional regulation. Chapter 2 addresses the difficult challenge of finding emotional and social connections between "us" and "them." Compassion for the untreated traumatized child that inhabits and often drives the adolescent or adult killer is essential for understanding why they kill and can provide the bridge from us to the killers among us. Chapter 3 explores the experiences that produce moral damage in killers, how they learn to live by the dictates of the war zone mentality in which acts of violence "make sense." Chapter 4 considers the other primary ingredient of the developmental psychology of killing, namely the emotional damage that arises from untreated trauma in childhood and adolescence as a result of abuse, neglect, and social deprivation.

Part II, "The American Way of Killing," explores the cultural and social factors that underlie our American understanding of killing and how we respond institutionally and politically. Throughout these discussions the issue of racism is a common theme: no understanding of murder in America can be complete without such a focus, as we will see. Chapter 5 focuses on the way we view and treat juveniles who commit violent acts. It does this by dissecting the slogan that guides much of our policies and practices: "If you're old enough to do the crime, you're old enough to do the time." Chapter 6 explores the processes of change that can improve the lives of killers and, thus, the safety of society. The focus is on rehabilitation, transformation, and redemption. Chapter 7 takes on the critical role of American attitudes and beliefs about guns in the cultural, social, and psychological dynamics of killing. Like chapter 6, this chapter goes beyond a common slogan (in this case, "Guns don't kill people") to demonstrate a more realistic understanding of social and psychological realities, namely that "people with guns kill people." The book concludes with an attempt to bring together all I have learned about killing to address issues of policy and practice in matters of prevention and intervention. Chapter 8 is titled "Making Sense of the Senseless: Understanding and Preventing Killing in America."

PART I

———

Getting Close to Killers

The Concept of Choice in the Criminal Justice System

October 5, 2010: Robert Tallman* tells me that he estimates he has been in sixty one-on-one street fights. He reports that he will smile through anything but he won't let anyone take advantage of him. He says, "I smile at them. But I've been through too much to let anybody take advantage of me. I don't mind getting beat up if that's what it takes. . . . I will do anything to respond to what you do." *He made the choice to fight and never give in to intimidation by others.* On August 26, 2009, he shot and killed two teenagers who he thought had been part of a group that assaulted his stepbrother.

March 27, 2012: Junior Mercedez* tells me that as a child, "fear and anticipation of violence seemed like the norm to me. Later, when I started visiting other kids' houses I could see what's really normal. . . . I never told anyone about my home life. I just lied about it. . . . The Code is you have to take care of things yourself and don't involve outside people." *He made the choice to keep the abuse and neglect he experienced at home a secret.* On November 15, 2011, in a case of fatal child abuse, he beat to death his girlfriend's two-year-old child out of frustration with the boy's misbehavior.

Two bad choices. Two fatal outcomes. Is it really that simple? The criminal justice system runs on the principle that people choose what they do, and thus the principal issue in most cases is the matter of "good" versus "bad" choices. It all sounds so clear-cut: Human beings have free will, and therefore they should be held accountable for the choices they make. Some individuals make good choices, and they should be rewarded for those good choices. Others make bad choices, and they should be punished for those bad choices. Simple.

However, the more I listen to killers, the more I think it is quite the opposite of simple. This is particularly true in cases that involve juveniles and young adult offenders who are not yet mature adults, but it applies to adults as well. You can't understand these boys and girls, these men and women, unless you are willing to dig deeply into the processes by which people in general make choices. You have to look at the way in which the social and psychological environment that killers inhabit shapes the options they have to choose from, and the processes they use to make those choices, particularly the bad ones. Then you have to look at what modern neuroscience tells us about how brain functions affect the choices people make.

In most cases, you must do this if you want to respond with justice based on an accurate understanding of what happened. But in *every* case, it is essential if you are to respond with compassion, not just for the victims and their families, who naturally are almost always the beneficiaries of our compassion, but for the murderers themselves, toward whom it is usually more challenging to feel compassion.

The issue of choice is always present in the courtroom, but rarely as baldly as it was when the attorney representing convicted serial killer Jorge Susindo* asked me this question: "Can the experience of prolonged, severe trauma affect a person's ability and motivation to make 'good choices' in life?"

I answered, "Yes, it can and does."

The attorney continued the examination: "Can you explain that?"

In the courtroom, I could give only a brief answer along these lines: All choices are made in a particular context, a particular place and time. Who you are and where and when you live plays a role in shaping the range of choices open to you and, thus, the choices you make. Both internal issues (such as knowledge of options, understanding social realities, internalized cultural values, unconscious forces, and brain functions) and external issues (such as the rewards and punishments meted out by the social environment) can affect an individual's perception of the available choices and the consequences of one choice versus another. That's the short answer. This chapter is the long answer.

DO THEY MEET THE LEGAL GROUNDS FOR INSANITY?

The killers I have listened to made a choice to kill someone, often for reasons that seem utterly "crazy" to an outsider. However, none of them met the strict legal criteria for an insanity plea. That is, none of them maintained that at the time they committed their crime they did not appreciate the nature or the wrongfulness of what they were doing. In the strict and narrow terms employed by the legal system, they were not so impaired by a mental illness or "mental defect" that they were totally disconnected from reality (for example, hallucinating). Also, while they often justified what they did in terms of the "war zone mentality" that I mentioned in the introduction and will examine in detail in chapter 3, they were aware that what they were doing was illegal (in the sense that it violated mainstream norms), even while it might be consistent with the rules of engagement in the war zone in which they lived.

Sometimes, and in some jurisdictions in the United States, it is possible to assert that a killer was suffering from a mental condition or mental defect that created an "irresistible impulse" to kill. This generally doesn't apply to "my" killers but is used in the rare case of an ordinarily "law abiding" citizen who goes crazy because of some extreme situation, like "normal" parents who kill the person who molested their child. This happened in Shiner, Texas, in June 2012, when a father walked into his house during a social event to find his four-year-old daughter being sexually abused by a man who was a casual acquaintance of the father. The father was so enraged that he beat the man to death. In the wake of the incident, every person CNN interviewed in the town—including the sheriff—approved of his action and believed he shouldn't face any criminal charges. Ultimately the local prosecutor agreed, and no charges were filed. In what is, I think, a related phenomenon, since 1976 Texas has executed more people than any other state—four times as many as its closest rival for this dubious honor. Violent retribution is—in Texas at least—a "good" choice, whether it is made by an individual or by the state, when the grounds for that choice are culturally validated.

An insanity defense seeks to get the defendant acquitted of his crime by saying, in effect, "my client was not operating within a normal moral framework at the time of the killing because he was so crazy he didn't know what he was doing, or didn't know it was wrong, or couldn't help himself from doing something that he wouldn't ordinarily do and would not do again in the future." By and large, the killers to whom I have listened don't meet these criteria for the legal definition of insanity.

This is not surprising, given the rarity of such pleas succeeding in American courts. A study commissioned by the National Institute of Mental Health and reported by PBS found that the insanity defense is raised in less than 1 percent of all felony trials (about half being for crimes of violence, 15 percent for murder), and successful in only about 25 percent of those instances (thus, one-quarter of 1 percent of all felony trials). Typically, such cases involve plea bargains for defendants who had already been diagnosed with a mental illness, so it is still rarer for an insanity plea to succeed in a trial. For example, as an analysis conducted by Robert Buettner found, according to the New York State Division of Criminal Services, of the 5,910 murder trials completed from 2003 to 2013, in only seven cases was the defendant found not guilty for reason of mental disease or defect (that is, "legally insane").

NOT LEGALLY INSANE, BUT CRAZY NONETHELESS?

Most of the killers I listen to commit their crimes in states of mind that mimic the conditions that define legal insanity: they believe that *in their world* what they are doing is necessary and therefore right. They are so emotionally damaged that *in their minds* they have lost sight of the relevance of "right and wrong." They are responding to powerful emotional forces—often unconscious forces—over which they have little if any control, at least *in the moment of their violent action*. It is in this sense that they make "crazy" choices.

The more than fifty murder cases in which I have been involved over the past twenty years have included many different explanations for the violent choices made. When looked at from the outside observer's point of view, many seem crazy. However, each makes sense when looked at from the inside of their minds (and hearts in some cases). What follows is not a standardized system for classifying these choices, but it does make sense to me as a representation or typology of choices to kill that I hear from men and boys (and some women and girls).

A Typology of Crazy Choices to Kill

Survival. We are programmed to survive. When faced with a threat, we respond to ensure our survival. However, as we will see in chapter 3, some of us learn lessons that predispose us to choose preemptive violence when we feel threatened. When Leonel Rivas saw a rival gang member reach under the dashboard of his car, he thought his opponent was grabbing a gun and would shoot him if he didn't protect himself. *He chose to shoot first.*

Lust for power. What the philosopher Friedrich Nietzsche called "the will to power" is strong in many of us. In the violent world that some of us live in, this seeking for power leads us to choose violence as a means to that end. Daniel Wellington* sought to uphold his "image" in the neighborhood and gain power by carrying a gun, behaving recklessly, engaging in numerous "stickups," and taking a role in drug dealing. *In explaining his choice to shoot a rival drug-gang leader, he says, "If you cut off the head, the body dies."* He says that these actions were essential to garner resources and protect himself in a "dog eat dog" world.

Monstrous narcissism. Narcissists are dominated by their egotism, pride, vanity, selfishness, and drive for prestige (usually at the expense of others). When it becomes extreme, it can reach the level of a clinically diagnosed personality disorder. Researchers, including Joshua Foster and his colleagues, have observed that narcissism is generally higher, on average, in males than in females and in African Americans than in other ethnic groups in the United States (and generally higher in individualistic cultures like ours). Georgia Calhoun and her colleagues have found that it is prominent among violent juvenile delinquents. While awaiting trial for charges of robbery, burglary, and aggravated assault, twenty-four-year-old Nate Barrington* invaded the house of sixty-five-year-old Melanie Hampton and her seventy-year-old husband, Thomas Hampton, intent on robbing them. *To silence them so that he could get away with his crime, Barrington chose to beat and stab the couple until they died. He then burned their bodies and their home.*

Existential honor. As we will see in chapter 3, the "culture of honor" increases the risk that individuals will choose to respond aggressively when they feel humiliated or disrespected. Even beyond this culture of honor lies the foundation for violence in the feeling that without honor there lies the prospect of "psychic annihilation"—a fear that one will cease to exist as a person, as psychiatrist James Gilligan puts it. Eighteen-year-old Jonny Angleson* shot and killed seventeen-year-old Shawn Berthson on September 15, 2004, after a verbal altercation. Jonny's sister had been threatened at gunpoint by the victim and his friends a week before the shooting as part of an escalating conflict with neighborhood peers. *Jonny chose to defend his family's honor by shooting neighborhood rival Shawn.* His sister testified that if he had not done so, she would be dead.

Retaliation for sexual abandonment. Fear of abandonment is a powerful motivator for action. Geraldine Downey and her colleagues have identified "rejection sensitivity" among men as a significant risk factor for domestic violence. When individuals high on rejection sensitivity believe that they are about to be rejected and abandoned, they "choose" to engage in preemptive violence. Simon Dalton* was distraught and enraged at the thought that his girlfriend had broken off their relationship and started seeing other men. *In response, he chose to kill her, her mother, her grandfather, and a neighbor who tried to intervene on their behalf.*

Panic. Fear is a powerful motivator. Some individuals choose to kill because they are in a state of panic and literally "can't think of anything else to do." This may involve killing to avoid being killed oneself, or reacting impulsively when in a state of intense emotional arousal because the brain's capacity for effective "executive functioning" is suppressed. Ron Richardson was being pursued by a police officer. *Since he was already on parole, Richardson knew that if he was arrested he would be going back to prison for a long time, so he chose to shoot at the officer in an attempt to discourage him from continuing the chase. The officer was hit by one of the bullets and died.*

Criminal practicality. Researchers have long differentiated between acts of violence committed because of strong emotions, with the intent to inflict pain ("hostile" aggression), and acts of violence committed simply to attain a particular concrete goal ("instrumental" aggression). Some killing is done simply as part of the "business" of crime (e.g., drug dealing). Ronald Garner* kills because he sees it as just a normal part of his business managing a large drug-dealing operation. *For him, killing is a practical matter of criminal enterprise. "I kill because it's good for business," he says.*

Curiosity or thrill. Some human beings are so disconnected emotionally from the rest of us that they don't "get it" when it comes to moral decency. Psychologist Robert Hare has called these individuals "psychopaths." They are prone to kill just for the enjoyment of it or out of a perverse curiosity. *Tim Bankovic wanted to see how it would feel to kill someone, so he chose to lure two sandwich deliverymen to a secluded location and killed them to find out.*

Each of these categories of choice represents a "bad" choice, although in some cases these boys and men (and in a few cases, girls and women) thought that it was not an immoral choice, at least at the time when he (or she) committed the act. Each caused the death of another human being. I recognize the fact that appreciating the norm that murder is ethically unacceptable does not require advanced moral judgment. And I recognize that not all killing is murder: most people believe in killing others, at least under some circumstances (such as in self-defense, in war, or in state-authorized executions, for example). But even murder is not simple most of the time.

Most murderous choices reflect the particular worldview of the perpetrator, and "my" murderers often have special circumstances that affect their worldview. Their tendency to overidentify serious threats to their survival and their justification for preemptive assault reflect their war zone mentality and, thus, an inability to be a part of the moral world that most of us inhabit. Their emotional damage undermines their emotional self-regulation, increasing the risk that rage and fear from unprocessed rejection, humiliation, and abuse in their past will spill over into the present in situations that evoke the original trauma (more on this in chapters 3 and 4).

There are individuals like Tim Bankovic who really do not have any moral sense and are totally disconnected from humanity, either because they have no empathy or because they don't embrace moral values that demand respect for life. We call these individuals "psychopaths." Like psychologist and researcher Robert Hare, I prefer this term to the more commonly used "sociopath." Hare has argued that most individuals whose behavior is not impeded by allegiance to the mainstream moral community and who thus demonstrate a chronic pattern of antisocial behavior are best understood not as psychopaths but as sociopaths. What differentiates them is that psychopaths have human disconnection at their core (whether originating from a congenital inability to connect or from a developmental reaction to brutality in childhood), whereas sociopaths have "simply" developed a bad habit of behaving antisocially. This pattern may result from destructive psychological experiences in childhood and adolescence but not be associated with the emotional disconnection and "lack of conscience" usually attributed to true psychopaths. I will return to this issue in greater depth in chapter 3.

Obviously, people who feel that normal morality is just an impediment to satisfying their wants and needs are a danger to society. This is true whether the individual is a corporate executive who sells contaminated products to consumers because it helps the bottom line or a rapist who preys on vulnerable girls and women, coercing their silence by threatening them and their families with death. As Jon Ronson points out in his book *The Psychopath Test*, it is not surprising that research on the prevalence of psychopathy among CEOs finds a rate four times the national average (4 percent versus 1 percent). It may also be more prevalent among successful politicians, businessmen, and lawyers, jobs in which allegiance to truth is often subordinated to self-interest. What is more, if these psychopaths have good social skills, high intelligence, and high socioeconomic status, they may be able to avoid detection if they commit crimes or if they exploit people without breaking the law. I have heard more than one cop say that "only the dumb criminals get caught." It's an exaggeration that contains a truth.

Most killers are neither psychopaths nor sociopaths, which means they can and do have some general moral appreciation that killing is wrong (or at least *could be wrong* in some situations, but not the one in which they did the killing). But is this the same as the free will implied in "good choices"? I don't think so.

THE CIRCLE OF CARING

In the mid-1990s, my partner Claire Bedard and I spent many hours interviewing teenage boys incarcerated for crimes of violence (mostly assault of one sort or another, but including some who had killed people, usually other teenagers). At Cornell University, where I taught at the time, we called this the "Making Sense of Senseless Youth Violence Project." In 1999, when I published *Lost Boys,* the book that grew out of this project, I was often asked the question "These boys, don't they have any moral standards?" It's perfectly understandable why people asked this question. Some of the things violently delinquent boys do seem obviously wrong. They steal, shoot, stab, beat, rape, threaten, and cheat other people.

At the time, I responded along these lines: These boys often have moral values, but they don't apply these values in the ways and in the situations that most people do. In general, their "circle of caring" is smaller than that of most people, so few of their decisions are conventionally moral. Most are logistical and pragmatic. Will this action make me safer? Will this action get me precious resources? Is this person someone I care about, someone for whom I am responsible? Will this action restore justice to my world? Within their small circle of caring, they often do make moral decisions; outside it, as they often put it, they "do what I had to do."

I think of this often when listening to killers in my role as psychological expert witness. They have a code of behavior, but their life experience has drawn them into small circles of caring, circles in which most of the rest of us don't count very much. They make choices that reflect that code, as they understand it. In this sense, they are not psychopaths as Hare defines the term, although some of them clearly are sociopaths. Their understanding of right and wrong reflects the moral damage of the war zone mentality and the emotional damage that has accrued from unprocessed trauma, abandonment, rejection, and abuse. It reflects their alienation from the mainstream community. And it predisposes them to live on the dark side of human experience, where evil flourishes.

GROWING UP ON THE DARK SIDE

Being the victim of sexual abuse (and other forms of maltreatment) in childhood and adolescence is a common theme in the lives of killers. I hear about it often and read about it in the case records still more often. Simon Dalton* exemplifies this. When he was five years old, he was molested by a male relative. When he was seven years old, he was sexually molested by a seventeen-year-old girl. And when he was twelve, he was involved sexually with a nineteen-year-old girl; this constitutes statutory rape because of the age discrepancy between them. It is not surprising that as a sexually abused child he had learned to seek relationship through sex. But she met his emotional needs as well. His records state that "his life revolved around her at the time."

Although research on the development of boys who are sexually abused by females is very limited, a study by David Lisak testifies to effects that include sexual confusion (and rage) of the sort evidenced by Simon Dalton, as has been noted in reports by clinicians who have seen him over the years. He made many "bad choices" when it came to his relationships with women as an adult.

Given the gross emotional damage he experienced in domains of his life beyond sex, I don't think we should be surprised that he committed acts of "crazy" violence when he felt he was abandoned by his girlfriend in adulthood. Sexual abuse in childhood and adolescence impairs the ability of many victims to make "good decisions" later in life. This is particularly true in adolescence, when aspects of the human brain involved in decision making are still immature.

RATIONAL DECISION MAKING AND
THE HUMAN BRAIN

In chapter 5, our attention will turn to the special issues involved in adolescent decision making, with examples from cases, issues that extend beyond age eighteen, the legal line marking adulthood in the criminal justice system.

Here, I will just note that developmental factors can shape the quality of decision making. According to psychologist Larry Steinberg and his colleagues, teenagers typically have special problems because of the immaturity of their brains; their relative lack of experience in making important decisions, particularly when they are impaired by drugs and alcohol; and their susceptibility to peer influences.

But young or old, people don't make even "rational" decisions as rationally as we, and they, might like to think. Unconscious forces can influence powerfully the range of behavior an individual may choose. For example, research on what psychologists call "confirmatory bias" reveals that most people will continue to "choose" to behave consistently with a position toward which they are predisposed even when the empirical evidence before them is inconsistent with that position, or is so mixed that no conclusion could be drawn objectively.

In a study not about killers but relevant to their lives and deaths, Charles Lord and his colleagues found that when proponents and opponents of the death penalty were given brief descriptions comparing murder rates in states with and without the death penalty, they were inclined to shift a bit in the direction of the study's conclusion. However, when the researchers followed up with a more detailed description of the studies, almost all the participants returned to their original belief *regardless of the evidence presented.* How? They focused on details that supported their original belief and disregarded contrary evidence in the data. They discounted the validity of methods and results that ran counter to their original belief and embraced methods and data that supported it. In a similar vein, in a 2005 study published in the journal *Law and Human Behavior,* psychologist Saul Kassin and his colleagues found that police investigators were worse than college students in differentiating between true and false audiotaped or videotaped confessions (by real prison inmates) but that the police investigators were more confident in their (false) judgments.

In the social context in which they actually think, conclude, and decide, people are often not conscious of the fact that they are making such "bad choices." Psychotherapists make their living off this reality. Often, a process of "bringing to consciousness" through cognitive–behavioral or psychodynamic therapy is required before a client can make good choices in a variety of personally and socially significant situations. These forms of psychotherapy are used to correct unconscious biases that predispose individuals to "bad choices" of friends and romantic partners, negative self-assessments that can result in self-defeating choices, and misperceptions that can lead to aggression toward seemingly hostile people.

ADDICTIONS AND FREE WILL

Addictions can undermine—in some cases even negate—the strength needed to choose to avoid poisons and self-destructive behavior. Like many issues in human behavior and development, the question "Is addiction a choice?" has no simple and universal answer. The conventional wisdom on one side is that addictions are diseases, embedded in the brain, that make a mockery of choice and free will. In this view, the addict may choose to go forward with his addiction, but this "choice" reflects not free will but compulsion. The conventional wisdom on the other side is that addiction is simply a choice, and addicts display some combination of weak character and weak willpower as well as immoral intent.

Not surprisingly, the emerging truth goes beyond both forms of conventional wisdom. Survey data are used to support the point that many, if not most, individuals who exhibit addictive behavior (psychoactive drugs being the main focus of this research) do in fact stop using at some point in their lives. For example, according to psychologist Gene Heyman's 2010 review of this evidence (in his book *Addiction: A Disorder of Choice*), 60 to 80 percent of drug addicts (people who have at some point met the criteria for long-term substance dependence) terminate their addiction by the time they complete their thirties. In Heyman's reading of this evidence and the firsthand accounts of former addicts, the addict stops when the costs are too great in relation to the benefits. This undermines the credibility of the second conventional view, because it indicates that the addicted person "chooses" to stop being a drug addict (or an alcoholic).

But there is evidence to support a modified version of the "disease" model as an alternative to the "weak character" approach. This includes the fact that when drug addicts have mental health problems in addition to their drug problem (comorbidity, as it is called), they are much less likely to be able to manage their drug taking and to quit altogether. As Heyman sees it, this group constitutes most of the classic drug addicts who are the focus of most clinical interest and research. But they comprise only about 15 to 20 percent of the young addicts who eventually become chronic problematic users into their forties and beyond.

Modern neuroscience is documenting differences in the brains of what might be called "hopeless" addicts versus those who can control their drug use—or at least can learn to control it. Some of the former may have special neuropsychological vulnerabilities (whether due to genetic predispositions or to brains that have adapted to drug use) that impair the process of "free choice." This suggests that some individuals may conform to the view that drug abusers "choose" to use, but that the choice is hardly made freely (that is, without powerful compulsions that are difficult to resist). And as New Zealand psychiatrist Doug Sellman points out in his 2010 review of the evidence, "Addictive behaviour appears to involve processes outside of the sufferer's personal consciousness by which cues are registered and acted upon by evolutionary primitive regions of the brain before consciousness occurs." This implies that any "choice" is channeled by unconscious processes in the brain.

Some addicts make profoundly bad choices in life. That much is clear. The origins of these bad choices may be diverse. For some, they reflect the powerful hold of an addiction, a hold so strong that it saps "free will" and creates such an intense craving that any and all forms of rationalization will come into play to make sense of the choices made. For some, bad choices represent a habit that is limited by time and place—for example, drug users who use only on the weekend or binge drinkers who stop after they graduate from college. For others, such choices are tied up in their mental health issues, which can arise from diverse circumstances, including abuse, abandonment, and trauma. For these individuals, drug use may represent a choice to dull their pain, a kind of self-medication that is particularly common among victims of unprocessed trauma. This phenomenon seems to have played a role in the following case.

THE DUKE JIMENEZ CASE

As a teenager, Duke Jimenez* told me, he did not attend school regularly because of his mother's alcohol use, and he began going to school under the influence of alcohol. Thus, problem drinking is an issue shared by him, his parents, and most of his extended family. It appears that Duke was engaging in self-medication to deal with his trauma-related symptoms (as do many victims of unprocessed and unresolved trauma). He "chose" to do so, but in the context of the messages sent by his family's behavior regarding substance abuse. However the choice was made, his drinking and drug taking, combined with his trauma-related dissociation and other psychological symptoms, reduced his ability to manage his intense emotions and sustain day-to-day social competence in the world of work and community. Duke reported drinking heavily every other day, using marijuana almost daily, using cocaine "ten to twenty times," and experimenting with other drugs, all in early adolescence. When it came to the night in 2005 when he killed Roberta Teebee while robbing Teebee's house, Duke was drunk and in no condition to be making critical decisions.

A 2009 review of the effects of heavy drinking in adolescence conducted by L. M. Squeglia and colleagues documents numerous cognitive effects. Most relevant here is the finding that "Deficits in executive functioning, specifically in future planning, abstract reasoning strategies, and generation of new solutions to problems, have also been found." Brains adapt, for better or for worse. In the case of youths who drink heavily and chronically, the adaptation is mostly for the worse. It certainly was for Duke.

CAN A KILLER LIKE DUKE BE HEALED?

Duke made a colossally bad decision when caught in the act by Teebee, and in his drunken state, the rage that infected him because of his life experiences boiled over. Teebee died as a result. When I met with Duke in prison before his trial, he was sober and lucid. This is what I wrote about him in my report for the court:

> I think that the prognosis for Duke would be very good if he receives competent psychotherapy and matures (he is still a very young person). He is very intelligent (scoring in the "high average range" and "excelled in tasks that required the use of abstract thinking") and quite sensitive. He has a positive relationship with his young son. Although his family and cultural socialization and his self-defensive pattern of dissociation have led him to avoid reflection that brings to consciousness previously suppressed thoughts and issues, he does have the potential for insight and reflection. For example, I believe that the last few minutes of our interview session set him to thinking about things in a somewhat new light. I think he could progress to a point where he is capable of doing very good things with his life, and therefore should be given the opportunity to do so through the court's sentencing decision.

Duke pled guilty to the murder of Roberta Teebee in a state that does not have the death penalty, and the judge sentenced Duke to seventy years in prison. Before being sentenced, Duke read a five-minute statement before the court in which he apologized for what he did and for the hurt he caused, including to his six-year-old daughter. He said, "If I was in a sober state of mind, all of this could have been averted. Nobody chose to drink but me and now I must be held responsible."

BAD CHARACTER?

Drug addicts, alcoholics, and sex addicts often say they feel powerless to resist the temptations that their cravings generate and make bad choice after bad choice as a result. In the abstract, of course, each incident of taking drugs, drinking, or having sex represents a choice, a decision. But those who have not experienced these addictions may underestimate their power and falsely attribute the addicts' bad choices to "moral weakness" or "lack of character." Of course, some addicts end up making good choices and sticking by them, but it usually involves expert guidance and powerful social support (e.g., by training in self-control practices). Even then, backsliding (i.e., a return to the "bad choices") is common.

Similarly, abused children are at risk if they have developed the cognitions embedded in a negative social map. According to research conducted by Kenneth Dodge and his colleagues, these include being oblivious to positive social cues, being hypersensitive to negative social cues, identifying a narrow range of behavioral responses when emotionally aroused, and believing that aggression is a successful social strategy. If their thinking is characterized by these four features, they are eight times more likely than other abused kids to develop a chronic pattern of aggression, bad behavior, acting out, and violating the rights of others (what is officially diagnosed as "conduct disorder"). Kids with conduct disorder generally make a long series of "bad choices" that abused children who do not develop ("choose"?) such negative social maps do not.

All these issues can come into play in understanding violent criminal behavior and the "choices" made by the individuals. When I think about these choices, I am drawn to an appreciation for how the decisions we make reflect not just our character and our brain's executive function. I am drawn to think about the context in which we are asked to make decisions.

MAKING CHOICES UNDER SOCIAL AND
CULTURAL DURESS

In Cambodia in 2010, I visited a World Vision–supported shelter serving girls who were rescued after they'd been subjected to sexual trafficking and forced into prostitution. These girls often choose to return to prostitution unless they receive intensive trauma-informed cognitive behavioral therapy. The "bad choice" to return to the sex trade often occurs because the girls are ashamed and believe that their society considers them "garbage." In fear and unable to trust adults, even those trying to help, they may believe they can never return to positive relationships with the community and their families of origin. They may feel so damaged that they believe their psychological wounds will never heal. What does this tell us about free will?

In 1995, a cancer prevention program informed me that focus groups of inner-city youths who had been traumatized by community violence revealed that these kids often chose to ignore antismoking messages because they didn't expect to live to old age and thus didn't see the need to worry about lung cancer. Their disconnection from the future ("terminal thinking") put them at risk for bad health choices. What does this tell us about free will?

When I testify in murder cases that involve juveniles or young adults, I am always interested in knowing something about where they live. Why? Research reviewed by criminologists Rolf Loeber and David Farrington in their classic book *Serious and Violent Juvenile Offenders* revealed that in "bad" neighborhoods, 60 percent of ten-year-olds with conduct problems "choose" to become violent delinquents. In "good" neighborhoods, only 15 percent "choose" to do so. Where you live (meaning the habits of heart, mind, and behavior of your neighbors and peers) affects the choices you will make if you are a child with a history of aggression, bad behavior, acting out, and violating the rights of others. What does this geographic effect imply about the process of choosing? It makes the odds of good choices by high-risk kids better if they live in good neighborhoods and worse if they live in bad neighborhoods. What does that say about free will?

In 1985, I traveled to Sudan to visit a female child whom my family and I were supporting through an international aid organization (Plan International). There I was confronted with the reality of choices made by Sudanese women for their children. Almost 90 percent of mothers in Sudan chose to have their daughters genitally mutilated because they themselves had gone through it as children, regarded it as normal, and believed that not doing it might ultimately be a bar to marriage for their daughters. The over-arching goal of this practice is to deprive females of sexual gratification. Given the primitive state of medical care among poor Sudanese, the mutila-tion often causes infections that can lead to sterility or death. If those women had grown up in the United States, they would never have made the decision to have the clitoris and labia of their daughters cut off. An American mother who approved the genital mutilation of her daughter would be a criminal. Are Sudanese women who subscribe to this practice making criminally "bad choices"? It is, after all, illegal in Sudan, despite its extraordinary prevalence. Are Sudanese mothers exercising free will?

My point here is that the degree to which individuals make choices reflects the social and cultural environment in which they live. And it reflects their personal psychology, not just their "character."

CHOOSING TO CONFESS

The U.S. Constitution offers protection from self-incrimination under the Fifth Amendment. In 1966, in the case of *Miranda v. Arizona,* the U.S. Supreme Court defined this right in practical terms. Police are required to inform everyone they arrest of their right to consult with an attorney before and during questioning and their right to not make self-incriminating state-ments. The court further stipulated that the person being arrested must understand these rights and must waive them only voluntarily. The court ruled that incriminating statements can be admitted into evidence in a trial only if they were made within these parameters. This being the case, one is left to wonder why anyone confesses to a crime. Yet many people do. Why do they make that choice?

Among the reasons why guilty people confess are feelings of guilt over the crime they have committed, the expectation that they will be treated more leniently in the criminal justice system if they confess, their desire to protect someone else from prosecution, interrogation techniques that lead them along a path of gradual disclosure, and fear of the interrogating officers. I have watched the videotapes of several murder confessions and seen all of these at work.

But consider the fact that significant numbers of individuals "choose" to confess to crimes they did not commit. FalseConfessions.org is "a public advocacy organization committed to raising awareness of the incidence of false confessions in criminal prosecutions leading to wrongful convictions." Their analysis of the data concludes that false confessions are particularly likely to occur in homicide cases and are particularly likely to be made by young men. The rise of DNA evidence analysis has brought this to light: more than two-thirds of the DNA-cleared homicide cases documented by Northwestern University's Innocence Project involved false confessions that led to wrongful convictions. Some individuals make false confessions out of a demented desire for attention or in a state of delusion in which they really believe they are guilty, but most do so in response to pressure and manipulation generated by police interrogation techniques. As Douglas Starr found when he looked into this matter, common police interrogation techniques inadvertently convince investigating detectives that the interviewee is guilty, and this leads to escalating pressure to confess. After hours of interrogation, afraid and confused detainees often confess out of desperation and exhaustion, usually with the "guidance" of police and the promise of being released.

As I was writing these words, the press was reporting on the 1992 case of two men, Antonio Yarbough (eighteen at the time of the crime) and Sharrif Wilson (fifteen), who had been released after serving twenty-one years for a triple murder they did not commit (when DNA evidence cleared them). The CNN account lays out the bare bones of what happened in 1992:

> [Yarbough] opened the door to find his mother, sister and a close family friend lying stabbed and strangled to death. The two girls were partially undressed.
> Police came.
> "I was asked to come down to the precinct," he said. Officers said they wanted him to tell them who might have killed his family, he said.
> "Before you know it, I had this photograph shoved in my face, and I was being threatened and slapped around, and they wanted me to sign a false confession. And I wouldn't," Yarbough said.
> Police also took in Wilson and questioned him separately from Yarbough. But he got similar treatment, he said.
> "I was scared, afraid; I was lied to, manipulated into believing that I was going to go home, if I do tell . . . what they said happened," Wilson said.
> Faced with a life behind bars, the young boy cooperated for the promise of lighter treatment.

Sometimes individuals confess because unscrupulous police interrogators have threatened or assaulted them physically, sexually, and/or psychologically. I was involved in the case of twenty-year-old Robby Trainor*, who confessed to killing an acquaintance after being beaten with a flashlight for two hours by detectives acting on the orders of their precinct captain (who subsequently was prosecuted for a pattern of abuse and intimidation). Like a lot of "crazy" things people do out of fear, confessing may well seem like the "right choice" at the time and in the situation.

Many years ago, I tutored New York State Police investigators in "applied psychology." At the end of one ten-week course, my two best students (who had the highest confession rate of any team in the state police) invited me to visit them at their station and go through a mock interrogation. They hooked me up to a polygraph and proved to me that they could detect any lies I told. It worked. And then they began to use the classic "good cop/bad cop" approach, at which they excelled.

The "bad cop" was a tall, imposing figure with cold gray eyes and an intimidating manner. The "good cop" was short, with twinkling blue eyes and black curly hair. It was all in fun, but I quickly realized how powerful the pressure to cooperate with them would be if it were happening "for real." Indeed, they told me that after a little time with the "bad cop," most people were eager to confess to the "good cop."

Add a little physical intimidation to the emotional pressure, and making the "choice" to confess falsely is not out of the question by any means, particularly for the young, the poor, the poorly educated, and the ethnic minorities who have the most experience with police power and discriminatory treatment. While research by Saul Kassin and his colleagues shows that most jurors find it hard to believe that anyone would confess falsely to a crime, I don't find it hard to believe at all. After the flood of exonerations due to DNA evidence and for other reasons, no one else should either.

Despite the Constitutional protection offered in the 1966 *Miranda* decision against involuntary self-incrimination, decisions to confess are often made in situations in which the foundation for "free choice" is compromised or lacking completely. Decades of research and the work of ethicists have shown that you can't really make a "free" choice unless you are in a position to give informed consent.

INFORMED CONSENT REQUIRES FREE WILL

As a general rule, informed consent requires that an individual is both free from coercion and able and motivated to appreciate the consequences of an action. Unless these conditions are met, a person cannot give valid consent, even if he or she chooses to do so. Thus, for example, children are presumed by law to be unable to give valid consent to sexual activity with adults, even if a particular child seems to do so voluntarily. Once my colleague David Finkelhor explained this, public and professional understanding of child sexual abuse improved greatly. Focusing on the impossibility of informed consent shifted the focus away from assessing the harmful effects on children of having sexual experiences with adults (which are sometimes hard to prove and may even be absent). It shifted the whole process toward the principle that *regardless of consequences,* children cannot, by definition, make good choices when faced with adult sexual overtures. The same is true of prisoners being asked to participate in medical experiments: there is always the specter of coercion, and they have difficulty appreciating the risks, given their life experience and lack of future options.

The larger point is that choices are always made in a context. Violent youths have typically grown up in contexts where trauma—untreated trauma—is typically the rule rather than the exception. This untreated trauma often makes them "dangerous" in the sense that they are driven by unconscious motivations that predispose them to bad choices. From their perspective, the range of options realistically available is often so narrow that there is no "good choice," at least in the way mainstream society would classify it. The options appear to be especially narrow for males who carry a profound sadness—and accompanying rage—in a culture that teaches boys that "it is better to be mad than to be sad." Sometimes this leads to horrific choices.

THE MARVIN TOLMAN CASE

Californian Marvin Tolman* killed his whole family—his wife and his three stepchildren. It was horrible. He annihilated them with a semiautomatic weapon and then waited for the SWAT team to come and dislodge him from their home as their shattered bodies lay around him. The forensic evidence was clear. He did it. But Marvin does not remember doing it. I have sat with defendants who denied they were guilty, but this was different. He was not lying. Mental health professionals who assessed Marvin concluded that he really did not remember. It would appear that Marvin experienced dissociative amnesia, an inability to remember brought on by the trauma of the violent acts he committed. These acts were so at variance with his intense emotional bonds with his wife and stepchildren that killing them was more than his fragile psyche could bear. Such traumatic events are known to produce dissociative amnesia, and Marvin appeared to be an example of this phenomenon, which occurs in highly stressful situations like war and natural disaster.

But why did he murder his family? It appeared that his lifelong, intense emotional neediness was triggered by his wife's expressed intention to leave him. Studies by Jacqueline Campbell have documented that the most dangerous point for a woman in a relationship prone to domestic violence is the three-month period after she communicates to her husband that she intends to leave him (or after the situation in the home is altered significantly in some other way, like a pregnancy or job change). In Marvin's case, this was coupled with his two stepsons making contact with their biological father and his stepdaughter (whom he had raised from infancy) also showing signs of rejecting him. It's not unusual for men with extreme "rejection sensitivity" (an extreme form of normal "separation anxiety" that we will explore in chapter 4) to react with violence when it is triggered, as it was for Marvin. All of this was true, yet the jury voted to sentence him to death for the "choice" that he had made—but, at the time of his conviction, didn't know or believe that he had made.

THE MELVIN GRANDJEAN CASE

Many who live in the worlds from which most killers come are faced with making choices that few of us mainstream adults will ever have to face (and probably could not handle if we were to do so). That was the case with Melvin Grandjean*, who "chose" to shoot, and killed Tyrone Banks in 1999, in St. Louis, Missouri. Understanding how he came to make that choice illuminates the dilemmas he faced. Evidence of the social toxicity of the neighborhoods in which Melvin lived is available from published sources. For example, crime data for 1999 indicate that among the city's neighborhoods, Greenbelt, Westside, Downtown, and Mt. Pleasant are above average in the rate of community violence (as defined by the incidents of "crimes against persons" and "crimes against society" according to data compiled by the police department). The reported rates are 0.0213 for Greenbelt, 0.0295 for Westside, 0.0265 for Downtown, and 0.0190 for Mt. Pleasant, versus rates for low-crime areas like 0.0021 for Country Town, 0.0049 for North Park, and

0.0058 for Eastland. The highest rates reported in 1999 were 0.0374 (for Johnson, immediately adjacent to the location of the crime for which Melvin was being tried) and 0.0572 (for Streetsville). Thus, Melvin lived his life in neighborhoods in which the crime rate was four to ten times higher than in some low-crime areas of the city. This documents the relevance of the "war zone" analysis to understanding Melvin's behavior. This analysis was confirmed by the head of the police department's gang unit, who described these areas as being consistently "among the highly active" areas for gang activity. The war zone nature of his home area is important in understanding the choices Melvin made. Reports in the city's newspapers testify to the dynamics of this war zone. One article that appeared just after the murder that Marvin committed was titled "Gang-related deaths increase dramatically." The killing of Tyrone Banks by Melvin Grandjean was mentioned in that article. An article published a year later reported that "Gang-related homicide rate more than doubles this year." The incident in which Tyrone was killed appeared to be part of this escalation—perhaps even playing a direct role in the escalation reported for 2000.

The police department's gang expert confirmed this analysis with respect to the city's gangs, namely that it is realistic to fear assault as the result of escalating conflict initiated by acts of disrespect and that youths carry guns for protection in this environment (as well as because they have the intent to commit a crime and/or are holding the gun for someone else). The gang expert also confirmed that among gang members in the city, issues of honor and respect are salient. He affirmed that any incident of disrespect involving gang members has the potential to escalate into a homicide. Even among adolescents, acts of disrespect can and do lead to immediate acts of violence, as with the mobilizing of gang allies to offer an aggressive response, including homicide. The critical incident that precipitated the shooting of Tyrone Banks conforms to this pattern.

On their way to a prearranged "girl fight" in "The Ropes" (the Deuce Two gang's home base), Melvin and his cousin, Chantel Wilkins (with her two young children in the car), encountered John Robbins (with whom Melvin had been in conflict for several years, beginning with an incident when Melvin "disrespected" him and thus initiated an ongoing "beef"). Hostile words were exchanged (Chantel reported that Melvin "called him out" and said, "Fuck the Deuce Twos," and that John responded, "Get them down"), and an altercation ensued. This conflict with John involved escalating insults and fighting, in which Chantel intervened (saying, "Please don't do anything here 'cause the kids are in the car"). John reported that Melvin said, "Fuck you, I will catch you next time and I know where your baby's mama stays."

Immediately thereafter, Melvin and Chantel drove into an area in which twenty to fifty people were present. Many in the crowd were rival gang members who were called to the scene to participate in the "defensive" confrontation (i.e., to repel the invaders and restore the honor lost by the mishandling of John Robbins at the hands of Melvin Grandjean). John reported shouting to his comrades, "There are those bitches—drop on 'em" (i.e., shoot them). Chantel reported that she heard Tyrone and others in the group say, "Flip them" (shoot them). The police department's gang expert confirmed that it is common for gang members to use "callouts" (verbal signals) to get the attention and support of their gang allies to provide backup in conflict situations. A witness on the scene reported that he saw Tyrone "reaching in a jacket" (at which point Chantel—who had been fired upon previously in a gang-related incident—said she saw a gun), and then Melvin shot once, striking (and ultimately killing) him. The police department's gang expert confirmed that "reaching for something" is commonly interpreted as a threatening action in such a context (not just by gang members, but by police officers who observe such actions in an area with high gang activity or by an individual who arouses an officer's suspicion that he is a gang member). After Melvin saw Tyrone reach into his jacket and Melvin shot Tyrone, John distilled the situation in the typical language of the street: "Melvin did what he had to do." He added that "Melvin acted in self-defense." From the perspective of the war zone mentality that all the persons involved in this incident shared, he did. Chantel said that "if Melvin wouldn't have shot Tyrone, Tyrone would have shot him." One of the police reports in the case quotes a middle school student saying he heard other kids talking about the shooting committed by Melvin: "a Deuce Two was shot and killed by a Northside boy."

What are we to make of the choice Melvin made that night? The court seemed to have little trouble in making its decision. The jury convicted Melvin of "Extreme Indifference Murder One," and he was sentenced to life in prison without the possibility of parole. But I think that given his life experience and what Elijah Anderson has called the "code" of the urban war zone, it was "reasonable" for him to interpret Tyrone's action of reaching into his jacket as the beginning of a potentially lethal assault against Melvin, his cousin Chantel, and the children in the car with them. That being the case, he chose to fire his weapon first (exactly the kind of "preemptive assault" affirmed by the war zone mentality). The chain reaction of attacks and counterattacks often escalates to shooting, and some of these shootings produce fatalities.

Tyrone's "best friend" Malcolm was shot and killed a month before Tyrone himself was killed. Melvin's brother had been shot and killed a year earlier. Melvin's family home had been fired upon in a gang-related drive-by shooting earlier in 1999. A year after the killing of Tyrone, while Melvin was in custody and awaiting trial, in the early hours of the morning when Melvin's mother, sisters, and other children were sleeping in the house, a car pulled up and opened fire, hitting the house with 25 bullets.

Since Melvin's trial, Tyrone's older brother, Johnny Banks, has been arrested for assaulting Melvin's younger brother, Montrel. Montrel was in an intensive care unit for several days because of his wounds. He recovered, but his future is unclear. There were Facebook postings from Johnny in which he expressed pride in his assault on Montrel.

There's one more chapter in this story. The lawyers who defended Melvin at his trial had enlisted Ronald Bobbs as a consultant. Bobbs is a former gang member who had turned over a new leaf and was working to reduce gang violence. A month after the jury pronounced its verdict in Melvin's case, Bobbs himself was arrested for shooting another gang member "in self-defense."

. . .

When you live in a war zone, making "good choices" is not easy despite your good intentions, even when you are trying to become a noncombatant. It is extremely difficult to meet the standards of mainstream society when you don't really live in mainstream society, but rather in a parallel social universe where different rules apply. Recently I was talking with a young man about his experience with community violence. He told me that he witnessed his first shooting when he was six, and his second when he was eight. I asked him this question: "If we asked one hundred eight-year-old children around the country if they had witnessed a shooting, how many do you think would answer 'yes'?" He thought a moment and then replied, "about fifty." When I told him the number nationwide was about six, he looked stunned. When you live in a war zone, your normal decision making can be distorted by the abnormal "facts on the ground" where you live.

MAKING LUCID CHOICES IS DIFFICULT

Beyond the life-and-death choices many killers have to make, there are the economic choices that confront them because of their position at the bottom of the economic ladder in America. How many of us would choose to forgo making $250 a day by selling drugs when the alternative appeared to be $8 an hour at McDonald's, if our families were poor and we had never known anyone who held a "real" job? How many of us would choose to risk being beaten up or even killed if we decided not to join the powerful gang that runs our neighborhood, if there were no one in our life powerful enough to protect us? How many of us would choose to work hard to stay in school if we didn't know anyone who had graduated, if we had lost hope for a positive future in the mainstream of American life? Honestly.

Starting from the position of being radically "pro-life," a lucid person sees that killing is wrong. A killer is, in this sense, deluded. I am using the term *lucidity* here as a spiritual teacher might, to mean seeing to the heart of the matter without the delusions of ego and bias. Spend forty days and forty nights in meditative reflection and prayer, and self-interested ego and dehumanizing bias are revealed for what they are, delusions. Listen to French Buddhist monk and scientist Matthieu Ricard's teachings on "Happiness" (and read his bestselling book of the same title), and these delusions are crystal clear. Then we see the path to lucidity right before us, through the insight gained by daily meditative practice. In this sense, moral decision making hinges on the ability to perceive the world in a lucid rather than delusional way. That kind of lucidity leads to compassion.

At the very least, we should have compassion for the difficulties that these youths and adults come face-to-face with when challenged with making "good choices," and avoid the temptation to choose to judge them from our lofty, privileged vantage point. The saying is that "people who live in glass houses shouldn't throw stones." But people who live in fragile glass houses have a harder time making good choices about throwing rocks than people who live in houses with safety glass, or homes where there aren't even any rocks around to throw.

The Dalai Lama teaches that compassion requires concern for the well-being of the "other" despite what the other does. In fact, he teaches that we cannot really learn compassion unless we are confronted with enemies who require us to do the psychological and spiritual hard work necessary to care about the enemy as a person while still opposing his behavior. I think that Pope Francis, a Jesuit, understands this as well.

Of course, even in difficult environments, some kids make good choices. But in very difficult environments, it is not simply a matter of making good choices. In a sense, it is about making *all* the right choices, because in such environments, often *all it takes is one bad choice* to start you down the road that leads to the dark path of delinquency and social "failure." For many kids, once they start down that path they don't get much opportunity to engage in what my colleague Fred Bryant calls "the psychology of second chances." You can hear all that looming in the account of one of my best students as he reflects on the choices he made that led him from one of Chicago's "worst" neighborhoods to my graduate course on "Risk and Opportunity in Childhood and Adolescence." He writes:

Two children were born in Chicago to two sisters in the early 1980s. The sisters were both Jamaican immigrants. They came to America with hopes of achieving a better life, a piece of the meritocratic dream that eluded them in their native country, plagued by years of political unrest and poverty. Each sister gave birth to a son during this time. For the eldest sister, her newborn son was the second and last child she would bear; for the younger sister her newborn son was the first of three sons she would bring into this world.

Both children were born into lower-middle-class, Catholic, two-parent families, each having more life goals than financial resources to reach those goals. Moreover, both sisters biologically contributed (or passed down) their intelligence to these boys, these cousins. This was evident in the exceptional marks each boy received on his report cards during the early phase of their academic careers.

Despite the similarities in genetic makeup and environment, the lives of these two baby boys would take markedly different trajectories. The elder of the two cousins began to display troubling signs during elementary school. First, he began "hanging with the wrong crowd." This peer group introduced him to a few influences that some might call vices: hardcore hip hop, pornography, and marijuana. Soon his grades were slipping. Furthermore, his father—who took a rather permissive parenting approach to all of their children, allowing them to make their own decisions about many things once the children became teens but then punishing them harshly if they made mistakes—responded to his son's adolescent mischief with physical violence. It wasn't unusual for him to beat his son, punching him and hitting him with whatever blunt object he could find. By the time he was well into the teen years, the elder cousin lacked direction and focus with regard to his academics. He finished high school, but took only a few college courses before leaving school. He currently dabbles with fixing computers as a "side gig" and is looking for full-time employment. He has a 4-year-old daughter out of wedlock. Often feeling misunderstood, he has had a history of confiding in his younger cousin.

The younger cousin's story is a bit more uplifting. Following in the footsteps of his older brother, this young man excelled academically throughout his educational career. He developed well psychologically. He finished at the top of his class in elementary school and went on to graduate as salutatorian of his high school class. Afterward, he went on to a highly ranked university where he earned both a bachelor's and a master's degree. Currently, he is furthering his education by pursuing a doctorate. Psychosocially, the younger cousin has a best friend that he has known for over 20 years. In addition, he married a college graduate after earning his master's degree and has two intelligent, well-adjusted children by his wife (whom he met during his undergraduate training). Finally, this young man has forged a stronger relationship with God. Though he has experienced some trying times—such as being unemployed for stretches—this spiritual component has served as an anchor. The elder cousin is my cousin John. The younger cousin is me.

Making good choices is a matter of life and death when you grow up in environments predisposed to violence, crime, and social failure, environments loaded with risk factors and often barren of developmental resources, where what you and your parents bring to the equation is crucial in an unforgiving way.

As we will see in more detail in the next chapter, the difficult choice the rest of us face is deciding how to approach those who fail the challenge of negative social environments. Can we choose to approach them with compassion? Chapter 2 explores the critical importance of empathy in generating and sustaining the compassion necessary for understanding killing and killers, as well as the society that gives rise to them and must decide what to do with them.

2

Keeping Killers inside Our Circle
of Caring

June 30, 2010, Snake River Correctional Institution, Alabama: I have come
to the prison to interview Danny Samson* in his death penalty murder case,
but driving from Mobile with his lawyer, I remembered that I had interviewed
another inmate at the same prison eight years earlier. Thinking he might still be
there, I asked the lawyer to call ahead and see if I might talk with him again. She
made the call. Billy Bob Wilson* is indeed there (still in the appeals process for
his death sentence), and I can see him. That pleases me. I have thought of Billy
Bob many times since I first met with him, and I feel that I have unfinished business in understanding him.

On the night of May 9, 1993, Billy Bob Wilson and his girlfriend, Jean
Lamont, kidnapped Connie Kerry and robbed the diner where she worked.
In the early hours of May 10, they murdered her. The circumstances were
terrible: Billy Bob killed her with a hunting knife. According to court documents, "Kerry suffered massive blows from a long-bladed knife before finally
bleeding to death. In addition to the pathologist's testimony, a State Police
agent testified that the blood stain patterns indicated Kerry had fallen in one
spot and then crawled to her final resting place several feet away. The agent
opined, 'that Kerry had tried to crawl away after the initial blow.' Moreover,
photographs presented by the prosecution indicated Kerry had suffered a
defensive-type laceration on her right ring finger. Therefore, we conclude that
the evidence warranted the submission to the jury of the aggravating circum-
stance of physical torture." I can only imagine the horror, hurt, sadness, and
rage of her loved ones reading this. My compassion for killers does not dimin-
ish my sympathy for victims and their families and friends.

Jean Lamont made a deal with the prosecution. She pled guilty and, in
return for testifying against Billy Bob, received a twenty-year sentence. Billy

45

Bob received a death sentence. He was forty-two years old when I interviewed him as part of his appeal for a new trial in 2004. Like many of the killers I have listened to, Billy Bob had a devastating history of trauma, abandonment, and deprivation.

Billy Bob was born into a severely dysfunctional family full of abuse and neglect. He was beaten and starved to the point that he was removed from the home by the state's child protection agency. He was then placed in a series of state residential facilities. To compound the experience of child maltreatment in his family, he was placed in residential programs in which numerous forms of abuse occurred, including sexual, physical, and psychological maltreatment. This pattern of being victimized continued into adolescence; it was not until he was fourteen that he left the "care" of the state. Even before he was removed from his family, Billy Bob—at seven years old—witnessed a murder (he was walking in the woods and stumbled upon a killing in progress). Even decades later, when I interviewed him, he retained a clear visual memory of this experience, but he wasn't aware of any emotional or psychological consequences of it. This lack of emotional memory is common among childhood trauma victims. When asked about the trauma, abuse, and neglect that characterized his childhood, all Billy Bob could say was, "it was just a normal part of growing up." That someone could describe such things as a normal part of growing up is profoundly sad and disturbing, and part of the problem (as we will see in chapter 4).

In many ways, Billy Bob was frozen in time. When asked to name the "worst thing that happened to you as a child," he cited "being sent away from home." When asked about the "worst thing you ever saw as a child," he reported witnessing the deadly shooting when he was a seven-year-old, with the same matter-of-fact resignation that he conveyed when he spoke of the abuse and neglect he experienced at home at the hands of his parents and in the state institution at the hands of some staff members.

Billy Bob's history of chronic trauma and emotional deprivation played an important role in shaping his behavior and was pivotal in his incarceration at seventeen (after just four years out of institutional "care" by the state), his difficulties in prison as a young man, his drifting on the edges of life after he was released from prison, and ultimately the murder for which he received the death sentence. The person before me in 2004 was a tough forty-two-year-old man, but inside he carried with him many psychological scars from the untreated trauma he experienced as a young child. In a sense, there was a traumatized child inside the man, and that child's unmet needs had played a powerful role in shaping the experience and behavior of the man.

The conditions in which I conduct prison interviews vary dramatically, from place to place, but also as a function of the inmate's history and status. Defendants with a history of violent behavior in the jail or prison are sometimes shackled—even to the table, chair, or floor. In the case of Billy Bob, however, there were no shackles. In most cases the interviews take place in a small room, with a thick glass partition through which a guard observes us (for my security as well as to prevent the transfer of contraband). When I interviewed Billy Bob in 2004, we were not in a small interview room, but rather in a classroom of the prison's education wing. What is more, there was no guard present, just me and Billy Bob sitting at desks. The interview went well, and a couple of hours later we were done. But we were alone—no guard outside, no one visible at all, and no phone to call someone to come get us. So we waited.

After a few minutes of waiting in our seats, we moved to the doorway of the classroom, me in my usual khakis and blue shirt, and Billy Bob in his bright orange prison jumpsuit. We waited for someone to come get us, to bring him back to his cell block and guide me to the reception area to make my way back to the airport. We waited. And we waited.

Twenty minutes later, there were people in the hallway: a group of "civilians" touring the prison. The visitors all had stickers on their chests with their names on them. To call it surreal is an understatement. But there was a taste of reality as the tour came down the hallway, because as they approached one-by-one, they could see me first—and most smiled—but then as they got closer they could see Billy Bob in his orange jumpsuit that blared "Criminal! Danger!"—and one-by-one their expressions changed from casual friendliness to fear and alarm. After they had passed by us, Billy Bob turned to me, smiled, and said, "Man, if I could get me one of those badges I could walk out of this place!" Sad, wishful thinking. Even he knew that.

I knew all about Billy Bob's horrible crime in 2004, when I wrote my report. What I couldn't explain to myself then was why this man who had committed such a brutal murder, and who had spent so many years in one form of prison or another, touched me so. His humor tickled me, to be sure, but there was something more. One reason I wanted to see him again when the opportunity presented itself was to make another attempt at figuring it out.

After I had finished with Danny Samson on that day in 2010, they brought Billy Bob into the interview room. He vaguely remembered me, but I knew him in an instant. We spent the first few minutes reacquainting. He talked about how half his family (siblings and their children) had disowned him, while the other half still came to visit him, and said he understood the former and appreciated the latter. Toward the end of the conversation, he told me about his deteriorating health, a liver condition that was not responding well to treatment. At that point, he opened his shirt to show me the shunt that the prison doctor had put in so that Billy Bob could get the medication he needed to treat his condition.

Billy Bob, like many inmates, had arms that were covered with prison tattoos—skulls, crosses, women, lightning bolts. But when he opened his shirt, I saw for the first time what might be called his "private collection," tattoos I had not seen six years earlier, tattoos that are not so often seen in public, sometimes to protect tender feelings in an otherwise brutal world. Among them, in the middle of his chest, was the clue I had been looking for without knowing it, a tattoo of the Pink Panther, his stuffed animal from childhood. For me, this image represented the mostly invisible connection between Billy Bob the killer who sat on death row and Billy Bob the abused and neglected child who had suffered so much. It all fit: there really was an untreated traumatized child living within this man who had brutally murdered Connie Kerry. It didn't excuse what he did, but it helped to validate why compassion for this killer was not a ridiculous bit of softhearted, wishful thinking on my part, but rather a "scientific" perspective on him and his life, a recognition that within the scary adult was a child, a scared child whose trauma had never been addressed and had never healed.

EMPATHY, NOT DISSOCIATION

What does it take to really listen to killers? I believe it all starts with a fundamental refusal to dissociate and disconnect from their humanity. It starts with a profound empathy for their human condition. For most people in many situations (psychopaths aren't most people, of course, as I pointed out earlier), empathy comes "naturally." This statement flows from the finding that the brain contains what neuroscientist V. S. Ramachandran terms "mirror neurons." These neurons replicate the emotions observed in others. For example, the same pain neurons fire when we see others in pain that fire when we directly experience pain ourselves. Psychologist C. Daniel Batson offered the "empathy–altruism hypothesis" as a way of organizing research findings showing that if you feel connected to someone else, you tend to respond to that person with caring, even if you have nothing specific to gain from helping them. Experimental studies confirm this.

For example, social psychologist David DeSteno and his colleagues were able to induce compassion in their lab. They found that when participants knew that a fellow participant ("Dan") had cheated in a word game (that resulted in cash prizes), they were less likely to punish him (via pouring extra hot sauce into a cup that he would have to drink) if another participant had elicited their compassion by crying and movingly telling that her brother had just received a terminal diagnosis.

In this condition of evoked compassion, participants in the experiment poured no more or less hot sauce in Dan's cup than they did when Dan had not cheated on the task (versus three times as much when he had cheated and their compassion had not been evoked). When the participants filled out a questionnaire that, in part, measured their feelings of compassion, the researchers found that the degree of compassion the participants felt predicted the amount of the reduction in hot sauce to punish Dan.

In another study in the same lab, the researchers found that if they created even a small sense of solidarity between participants (by synchronizing their hand tapping to a tone they heard), it increased their compassion. When they were given a chance to help their "partners" (who were strangers) in the tapping task, the likelihood that they would help the others increased by 31 percent, and the time they spent helping increased from one minute to more than seven. These small measures of compassion in the lab parallel our experience in the "real world."

As Paul Bloom notes in his review of research on this topic, some observers credit empathy with being the "the main driver of human progress." Of course, it's not that simple. Few things are. For one thing, conventional research doesn't deal with issues like feelings of empathy and compassion for killers, but rather with empathy in morally simpler and emotionally easier situations (like helping a fellow student who has been in a car accident or showing generosity of spirit toward a student who has cheated, after being exposed to another student crying). But the complications don't stop there. Bloom wrote an insightful essay on these complications, published in *The New Yorker* magazine in 2013, titled "The Case Against Empathy."

Researchers such as psychologist Paul Slovic and his colleagues Deborah Small and George Samsontien have been studying the limits of empathy. They have found that when it acts alone, it can divert us from the truth, and even produce a mistaken allocation of resources (e.g., in 2005, the mass media focused on the disappearance of one American girl in Aruba, to the relative exclusion of news about the genocide occurring at that time in Darfur). This is because empathy can forge an emotional reaction that one is tempted to generalize in ways that don't hold up empirically. I am very aware of this danger for myself, of course, as I enter the world of killers. I guard against it, but I know it is a threat to objectivity that always lurks in my work as an expert psychological witness, in which empathy is a crucial element in understanding.

Some studies even suggest that empathy can operate in ways that can work against some fundamental matters of ethics and justice. One aspect of this is called the "identifiable victim effect." Economist Thomas Schelling offered a classic example decades ago. He pointed out that the story of one sick child who needs a lifesaving operation will elicit a flood of donations, while the story of how declining tax revenues will lead to a deterioration of health care that will result in multiple preventable deaths gets little or no attention beyond the advocates, activists, health-care professionals, and politicians directly involved.

Psychologists Tehila Kogut and Llana Ritov explored this phenomenon in their lab. They found that when they showed a group of research participants the picture, name, and age of a specific girl who needed expensive life-saving medical treatment, total donations were much greater than when they asked the participants to donate to eight nameless, faceless children (or even one nameless, faceless child) whose "objective" need was as great as that of the personalized girl.

Many public and private programs have achieved public-relations success or failure because of one notable individual example who gave a face to the program, for better or worse. National efforts to educate children with mental disabilities increased when President Kennedy's sister became the poster child for this cause in the 1960s. Prison furlough programs in Massachusetts that reduced criminal recidivism were discontinued in the 1980s, after the highly publicized failure of one individual, whose very name (Willie Horton) became a rallying point for political opponents of the governor. As the Willie

Horton case demonstrates, empathy for a murder victim can stimulate panic and a lust for revenge, not just on the part of a victim's family members and friends, but even on the part of strangers. The result can be unwise and self-defeating policies, as we will see.

I know that empathy is not enough. I recognize that there are limits to empathy. But this is not, I suggest, because empathy is misplaced. Rather, empathy is only the *starting point* and cannot be a substitute for the systematic evidence that comes from counting things. This is one reason why I believe it is unethical to stop at the telling of compelling "stories" like those of Danny Samson and Billy Bob Wilson. *I believe that it is only when these stories work in concert with systematic research that important truths emerge to serve as a basis for social policy and professional practice to guide mental health services, education, criminology, and prison administration.*

And courtroom decisions. Attorney Mark Olive has captured the idea that the key to defending a killer is to tell his (or her) story in a way that elicits comprehension and compassion, despite the terrible crime committed. His analysis of the success of effective narratives as the organizing framework for mitigation at sentencing—and equally if not more important, in postconviction appeals—resonates with what I have learned over my twenty years as a psychological expert witness in murder cases.

Olive's analysis of successful postconviction appeals demonstrates the power of these narratives, particularly when they are able to change the story told by the prosecution in a way consistent with the mitigating facts. He captures this finding in the very title of his 2009 report "Narrative Works." This follows up on the 2008 report he coauthored with fellow attorney Russell Stetler, which included this conceptualization of the mission: "One of the most important tasks for the capital post-conviction defense team is to learn all there is to know about their client's singular frailties and strengths, but also about his or her utter normalcy, and then starkly to convey to decision-makers the unique constellation of conditions and events that unjustly dispatched him or her to death row."

I agree. Conveying the human story behind the inhumane act is the goal, and doing it in a way that flows from what research has taught us about the processes and outcomes of human development is thus both responsible and effective. But it does start with empathy, with the human connection and the adamant refusal to dissociate from the killer. That's not easy in many cases, of course. After all, these men (and in some cases, women) have done terrible things—ripped loved ones from their families and friends and torn apart the social fabric of their communities. But unless we can see the humanity in their often inhumane actions, we will never understand them, and understanding them is the key to begin making a safer, less violent society.

EMPATHY IN THE FACE OF DISGUST AND HORROR

Seeking understanding requires empathy for killers as individuals, when our "natural" reaction may be disgust and horror. But it also requires that we reach across the social barriers that divide us as a nation—class, race, gender, family background, and culture. Let me speak first of what it takes to have empathy at the individual level. It's sometimes very hard, even for me, to find some point of human contact, some shared bit of connection. Bruce Walters and Marvin Tolman provide examples of this challenge.

The Bruce Walters Case

February 24, 2012: I am in Missouri to interview Bruce Walters.* He went to prison for rape when he was eighteen and served eighteen years. Only months after being released, he attacked the parents of a man he believed was involved with a woman he himself was dating. He killed Katherine Roberts, the man's mother, and tried to kill his stepfather, Terry Roberts. Now he is facing a possible death sentence.

It was very difficult to engage Bruce Walters in anything involved in his case, particularly matters concerning his childhood and adolescence (which the records show were filled with abuse and psychological deprivation). Without much direct help from him, I was led to a conclusion that echoed those of other professionals who had assessed him over the years: he indeed was so harmed as a child that by the time he entered adolescence he was seriously damaged psychologically, and his eighteen-year incarceration exacerbated that damage and contributed to the murders for which he was now facing trial. It was tough to find some connection with Bruce, troubled and disconnected as he was.

Eventually I found a way to connect with him, based not on his criminal history or sad life but on his self-proclaimed spiritual status. After offering several topics for discussion that dealt with his incarceration experience— and getting no helpful response or indication of interest in pursuing the topic—I asked about his application for a name change in 1989, to a "Buddhist name"—which translated from Sanskrit means "Amazing Warrior." This topic evoked a smile, and he began to talk fluently. Since I have some familiarity with Buddhism, I engaged him in a discussion of Buddhist concepts. This led eventually to a discussion of how Buddhism and Christianity were part of his larger spiritual path. It was a truly bizarre couple of hours I spent with Bruce, listening to him. Ultimately he explained to me how he sees himself as a profoundly spiritual person, a leader and a teacher, on a par with Christ, and perhaps the reincarnation of Buddha—all this despite his dismal record of violence and antisocial behavior over the years of his incarceration (let alone the crime for which he was being tried).

I left understanding that there were three options to describe his current state: (1) He is delusional about who he is. (2) He is lying intentionally and consciously to misrepresent himself. (3) He is indeed who he says he is, a spiritual leader in the Buddhist and/or Christian tradition whose day-to-day behavior is disconnected from his spiritual merit. The first two possibilities seem most likely. I doubt the third.

Listening to Bruce Walters portray himself as a mix of Jesus and Buddha, I was reminded of the poem "Jabberwocky" that Lewis Carroll wrote for *Through the Looking-Glass, and What Alice Found There* (1871):

> Twas brillig, and the slithy toves
> Did gyre and gimble in the wabe;
> All mimsy were the borogoves,
> And the mome raths outgrabe.

And so on and so on, for another twenty lines. It *sounds* like it should make sense, but upon reflection you realize that it really doesn't. Bruce went on for two hours. Like Carroll's poem, it sounded like it should make sense, but really it didn't. But by the end, I did know him. I didn't like him. I didn't trust him. But I did know him.

The Marvin Tolman Case

Recall the case of Marvin Tolman from chapter 1 (the man who killed his whole family). Because of the dissociative amnesia he experienced about the crime he committed, Marvin didn't know that he had obliterated the family that he had clung to for emotional meaning in his troubled life (as a psychologically neglected and abused child). He honestly thought it was impossible that a jury would convict him, because he believed that someone else had committed the heinous crime of killing his family (perhaps an intruder who had rendered him unconscious and then went about the business of killing the rest of the family). When I walked into the room to meet and interview Marvin, I was searching for a way to connect with him, to validate his humanity. What I said was this: "Marvin, I just want to say how sorry I am for your loss." His eyes teared up, and he responded, "Thanks, man. You're the first person who ever said that to me. I appreciate it." And then we talked for two hours. By the end of our time together, I thought I understood something about how he came to annihilate his beloved family.

This kind of radical empathy is crucial. When I listen to a killer, we are two human beings sitting together in a room. I think I have come to this "kinship" because when I sit with killers, I really do appreciate the fact that "there but for the grace of God go I." The objective work of forensic developmental psychology comes after that, after the connection is established, the affirmation of shared humanity made and recognized.

A PERSONAL STARTING POINT FOR EMPATHIZING WITH KILLERS

For me, the process of getting to the point were I can find some spark of common humanity with killers started on a dark night in 1966. Let me say at the outset that my direct experience with guns is very limited. I didn't hunt as a child, but I was an avid toy-gun enthusiast—playing army, cops and robbers, and cowboys and Indians was a staple of my 1950s childhood in a lower-middle-class suburb of New York City. The only real guns I ever fired were part of the undergraduate ROTC program in college (not including a couple of county-fair shooting galleries, where the goal was to win a teddy bear). Mostly it was the required target practice with my rifle, but one night in 1966, it became much more.

For extra credit, my fellow sophomores and I could volunteer to be the "enemy" in night maneuvers in which the upperclassmen practiced their leadership skills. This was 1966, and many of those upperclassmen were going to Vietnam as officers when they graduated, so this was important stuff. Before we left to set up our ambush in the woods that night, the regular Army officer in charge warned us: "Although you have blanks in your rifle, that doesn't mean it's not dangerous."

To illustrate his point, he put an empty tin can over the end of a rifle, chambered a blank round, and fired. The resulting force blew a hole right through the tin can. "If you shoot a blank at someone at close range you can blind them," he told us. "So do not under any circumstances fire your rifle at anyone at close range!" And he meant it. I got it. We all got it. No problem.

But all that reasoned caution did not last long. It was dark in the woods that night when the upperclassmen started their attack. They shot off flares, started firing at us, and came up the hill we were defending. That's when it got real in a way that is hard to understand unless you have been there, there being "in combat," even simulated combat.

The student next to me yelled that his rifle had jammed, and he started screaming, "They're gonna kill us!" I remember my own rifle jamming and being infected with the same terror that was flooding my fellow student-soldiers. I too felt they were going to kill us. So much for rationality under fire.

Finally, as we were able to clear our rifles, the upperclassmen charged up the hill in front of us. We rose to our feet and fired, aiming at the only thing we could see in the darkness, their faces illuminated by the flares, literally "the whites of their eyes." In that moment, we would have killed the students in front of us if we could have. Had we shot them in the face as we were trying to do, we might well have blinded them. It was over in moments, but the reverberations of those few moments have lasted a lifetime for me. I felt them that day with Marvin Tolman. And with all the others.

I learned, on that night in 1966, that for regular people like me, strong emotions—like terror, rage, and hate—can be deadly. I know there is more to the story than our shared humanity, but it does start with that fact. Only then does the analysis of the destructive psychological histories begin. *Then* we can talk about the fundamental truth that many, perhaps most, killers are "untreated traumatized children inhabiting the bodies of scary men (and in some cases, women)."

In 2014, a movie version of the life of rhythm and blues legend James Brown was released with the title "Get On Up." It chronicles the traumatic early life of the singer in the South of the 1930s and 1940s, complete with abuse, abandonment, poverty, exposure to community violence, and being the target of racism as a child. At one point in the film, the adult Brown responds to feeling disrespected by threatening a group of people with a shotgun, and then he takes off in a pickup truck when the police are summoned to the scene. After a high-speed chase, Brown's truck is surrounded in a field by police officers with guns drawn. In what is certainly one of the most powerful images of the consequences of childhood trauma I have ever seen, when the truck door opens it is not the adult James Brown who emerges, but the eight-year-old child James Brown. Inside the scary man is an untreated traumatized child. This understanding of killers resonates with those who know these wounded souls best.

UNTREATED TRAUMATIZED CHILDREN
AND SCARY MEN

Kerry Max Cook spent twenty-two years in prison, awaiting execution for a crime he did not commit. Finally exonerated and released, he chronicled the ordeal in his book *Chasing Justice*. I met him in 2010 in Florida, at a meeting of public defenders, mitigation specialists, and others involved in the defense of killers and other violent offenders. I was presenting the keynote address on the theme "Untreated Traumatized Children and the Scary Men They Become." After my speech, Kerry approached me, obviously moved by what he had heard. "Man, I spent twenty years with these guys and what you said is exactly what I observed." It helps to have that kind of validation from someone who has lived in that world that I only visit, a world full of abused children in men's bodies.

Testifying in murder cases offers an internship in the destructive consequences of child maltreatment, particularly when coupled with other forms of trauma and deprivation. In case after case, I read the records and conduct the interviews that give rise to this conclusion, and in doing so I come face to face with the tales of trauma—physical, psychological, and sexual abuse; street violence witnessed, suffered from, and inflicted; gangs, drug dealing, oppression, and racism. It is an awful opportunity to witness what "the accumulation of risk factors" really means to a human life.

Many of the cases I work on were initially decided years earlier but have been sent back for retrial by an appeals court—sometimes by the U.S. Supreme Court. Therefore, some of the defendants I interview have already been convicted and sentenced to death and thus already sit on death row. Because death row prisons are often located in small rural communities (where they are sometimes the biggest employer), I usually drive out into the countryside to some rural site where the prison is located. At the gate, I surrender ID, cell phone, and anything that might constitute or hide contraband. Security is usually intense—for example, having a guard watching every moment, either from inside the room, or just outside, perhaps looking through a thick glass observation window. Sometimes the condemned is shackled in front of me in the interview room—hands and feet chained to a post. It's grim.

DEAD MAN TALKING

But the logistics are not what's so hard. What's hard is knowing that I am looking at a dead man (the term *dead man walking* refers to death row inmates as they are moved about the prison)—unless I and the others involved in the case succeed in court. What's hard is knowing that I will walk out the door into the fresh air in a short time, but the man in front of me most likely will *never* go through that door alive—for most, the best outcome in the sentencing hearings and retrials in which I am involved is life in prison. When he does leave, it will be as a corpse on its way to a grave.

Even harder is hearing the stories of human lives brought so low. The litany of suffering, experienced and inflicted, is emotionally and spiritually grueling. Some have given in to the temptation to live as savage barbarians in prison. But some of these men have forged a monk-like spirituality out of the crucible of their suffering. Jarvis Masters is one, as he tells in his book *Finding Freedom: Writings from Death Row.*

Jarvis was sentenced to life in prison at age nineteen. A few years later, he was sentenced to death on charges that he was involved in a prison killing. He eventually found a spiritual path that led him to be ordained as a Tibetan Buddhist monk in prison (the first ever) and to create an exemplary life that has been an inspiration to many others, inside and outside the prison walls. I was pleased—honored, in fact—to write a book-jacket endorsement for *That Bird Has My Wings,* his second book. "All across America, boys are lost to trauma and deprivation. Few of them have given voice to their experience and the redemptive power of spirituality as has Jarvis Jay Masters." That is what I wrote, and I meant it.

Jarvis exemplifies the positive possibilities. Many others—most, probably—are demoralized and bitter about the lives they lead in prison. When I asked one man on death row what he had learned from 30 years of life on planet Earth, he simply said, "Life sucks." I usually swallow and digest this suffering. But not always. One summer, in 1998, when three of my cases were coming to fruition at the same time, I traveled to a death row in rural southern Illinois three times in less than five weeks (this being before the death penalty was ended in Illinois, in 2011). After the third visit, I spent the drive back to the airport sobbing. The weight of the suffering was crushing—and I was "just visiting."

Over the years, I have heard many stories with the same themes. Only the particulars change. What differs is who abused the child, what kind of abuse it was, what the child's injuries were, how soon the child began to come unraveled, what form the breakdown took, how deeply violence was integrated into the child's strategies for dealing with the world that had dealt him a raw deal. But always, I feel that I am sitting with an untreated abused child inhabiting the body of an adult man (and in a couple of cases, a young woman).

These cases often float through my consciousness like ghosts. The obligation to reach out with empathic humanity is an individual challenge. But there is another challenge, and that is to reach out across the social barriers of race, class, gender, ethnicity, and culture to "the other" who is doubly other to me as a White, highly educated male approaching the age of 70.

THE MALCOLM JONES CASE

Malcolm Jones* shot and killed Dolores Jones on July 2, 1996, in the course of robbing her. This young man had taken a human life, and that fact would determine the rest of his own life. But before he was a killer, Malcolm was the childhood victim of severe, pervasive, and prolonged child maltreatment, including physical abuse, sexual abuse, psychological maltreatment, and neglect. He was beaten and burned with cigarettes. He was repeatedly raped. He was starved of food and affection. He was treated like a piece of garbage. Literally no one was "there for him" in any way, shape, or form. In my forty years as a professional working in the field of child abuse and neglect, I have rarely encountered a case equal to this one in the severity and pervasiveness of the abuse. And there is no evidence that Malcolm received any psychotherapeutic intervention to ameliorate his victimization. In addition, at age six, he witnessed a murder in his home, committed by the most significant adult male in his young life—his de facto stepfather. Given the larger negative picture of his life, the trauma associated with this experience is itself a significant risk factor predisposing him to troubled development, socially and psychologically. Once again, there is no evidence that Malcolm received any psychological intervention in response to this horrifying experience. What is more, his mother refused to talk with him about this experience throughout Malcolm's childhood. This denied him perhaps the most important therapeutic resource naturally occurring for children (i.e., emotionally available parents to help children process traumatic experiences). He was left to his own inadequate devices.

Is it any wonder that Malcolm haunts me? He should haunt us all. Our society failed to protect him as a child and now there is hell to pay.

THE JANE MONTERO CASE

In the early morning hours of March 17, 1993, when she was twenty-one years old, Jane Montero* was part of an infamous double homicide in Los Angeles. She and two other female members of the Latin Avengers—Audrey Carranza and Mandy Topas, both sixteen—set out to avenge the fatal shooting of Melvin Flores, a fellow member of their gang, by members of the rival Emperors gang. The three met up with Emperors Johnny Caputo and Manuel Copacino late at night and lured them into L.A.'s Centennial Park, with the prospect of sex. After kissing him, Montero shot Copacino in the back of the head in a park bathroom, then handed the gun to Carranza, who shot Caputo in the head.

When I sat with Jane, we spoke about her troubled life and how her family was immersed in L.A. gang culture—her parents and all her brothers were members of the gang. I knew from talking with her lawyer that Jane had been sexually abused by her maternal uncle over a long period, but that Jane did not want it to come out in open court because her mother would be there. "I have put her through so much already," she told me. "I can't go in there and tell her that her brother sexually abused me. I just can't." I felt compelled to lean on Jane on this point, because her lawyer thought that revealing the fact of her abuse to the jury was perhaps her best chance for avoiding the death penalty, and I agreed. I knew that Jane had a child. While it may seem unfair to use this as a bargaining tool, I went ahead and suggested that she owed it to her daughter to do what she could to stay alive, and not leave her motherless. Ultimately she agreed, and I focused on the psychological implications of being a victim of sexual abuse in my testimony on her behalf.

While I spoke, I watched the jury. As I chronicled what had happened to the teenage Jane Montero and what it meant for her development, I could see a glimmer of compassionate recognition on the faces of the several women in the jury. In the end, the jury voted to reject the state's demand for the death penalty and sentence Jane to a life in prison instead.

Jane's life was saved by her last-minute agreement to expose in public the fact that she had been sexually abused. I am haunted by how Jane's hope to shield her mother from the ugly fact that her brother had raped her daughter was only displaced by her love for her own daughter. As a result, she is alive today.

THE NATHANIEL BRAZILL CASE

Nathaniel Brazill was thirteen years old when he shot and killed his teacher, Barry Grunow, at Lake Worth Middle School in Florida, on the last day of school in 2000, because he had been suspended and thus would not have a chance to say goodbye to a girl in his class with whom he was infatuated. There was no doubt of his guilt—the shooting was captured on the school's video security cameras. It seemed to be a classic case of a troubled teenager reacting with violent emotion in response to melodramatic romantic frustration.

After I testified about the accumulation of risk factors in the boy's life and offered my assessment of how his life situation had affected his state of mind on the day he killed his favorite teacher, and after I withstood the prosecutor's onslaught of cross-examination, the judge did something extraordinary. He asked me what I thought should happen to the boy. Given this opportunity, I told him two things. First, it was appalling and inappropriate that Nathaniel had been tried as an adult rather than the immature teenager he was. Second, what Nathaniel needed was a period of assessment and protection—a time and place where he would be safe, and the community would be safe, so that mental health professionals could find out just how troubled he was and get a better idea of what it would take to rehabilitate him. "How long would this take?" he asked. I said that I supposed that by the time Nathaniel was eighteen or twenty-one, the answer might be clear. The judge listened, but he replied that the law gave him no sentencing option less than twenty-five years. It was a victory of sorts when the judge opted not to impose the maximum sentence of life in prison without possibility of parole, but instead decided on twenty-seven years followed by seven years of probation. This meant that Nathaniel went into prison a fourteen-year-old child, and if he survives, he will leave a forty-something-year-old man.

I am haunted by the fact that the teenage Nathaniel disappeared into the penal system and that if he survives, a man will reappear in the community in his place more than two decades from now. Who will that man be?

THE UGLY FACTS ABOUT RACE AND ETHNICITY

It's not merely incidental that Malcolm and Nathaniel are Black and that Jane is Latina. According to data compiled by the U.S. Justice Department, rates of homicide by young Black males are, on average, about eight times those of Whites, and Hispanic rates are about four times higher than White rates. Overall incarceration rates mirror these differences. Writing for The Sentencing Project (a private research and advocacy group), Mark Mauer reported that incarceration rates of Blacks are eight times those of Whites and almost three times higher than those of Latinos (who are incarcerated at a rate almost three times the rate of Whites). Race and ethnicity constitute the ugly fog that hangs over everything in the criminal justice system— indeed everything in American history.

This discussion of race in the criminal justice system is difficult for several reasons. First, *any* discussion of race is painful and difficult, given the complex history of racism in America. Second, I believe that race is an intellectually difficult issue to understand without bias creeping in and intense emotions flooding the process of clear thinking. Third, when it comes down to it, race is, in many ways, only one risk factor, and in the larger scheme of things, one risk factor generally weighs no more or less than other risk factors in the cumulative risk equation for any individual when trying to understand why killers kill (although when it comes to violence, race tends to have a special status as a risk factor for historical reasons, as we will see in chapter 4).

Let me turn to the issue of bias. Research by Amnesty International and Human Rights Watch reveals that even though Blacks and Whites are murder victims in nearly equal numbers of crimes, 80 percent of people executed since the death penalty was reinstated in the United States (by the Supreme Court in 1976) have been executed for murders involving White victims. More than 20 percent of Black defendants who have been executed were convicted by all-White juries. Given the legacy and present realities of racism in America, this is a disturbing red flag when it comes to justice.

But this racial disparity is lodged within a much bigger problem, namely the centrality of racism in the overall criminal justice system that leads to the massive incarceration of people of color. Some have captured this insidious issue with the concept of "the school-to-prison pipeline" to reflect the many ways in which far too many children of color move seamlessly from educational institutions to penal institutions. Among other research and advocacy groups, the American Civil Liberties Union has laid out how the failure of the schools to educate and socialize minority youths leads to punitive disciplinary practices that, in turn, set in motion alienation and rage, opening the door to the criminal justice system as surely as if an actual pipeline linked schools and prisons.

In her 2012 book, *The New Jim Crow,* law professor Michelle Alexander makes a compelling case for this understanding of why such racial disparities in incarceration occur and persist. She starts from the fact that in the past 30 years, the U.S. penal population has grown from three hundred thousand to more than two million. The United States has the highest rate of incarceration in the world (higher even than Russia's) and the highest proportion of racial minorities in prison. As Alexander writes, "The United States imprisons a larger proportion of the Black population than South Africa did at the height of apartheid" (p. 6).

This is mostly the result of the War on Drugs, but not for the reasons that most of us assume (i.e., that Blacks and Hispanics are more involved in drugs). The dramatic increase in the incarceration of Black and Brown people caught up in the War on Drugs is the result of racism. Despite the fact that minorities use and sell drugs at rates no different from those of Whites, law enforcement efforts have targeted minority communities and individuals. It does no good to say that in principle the law applies to everyone equally if the prohibited behavior is widespread in the whole society and most of the effort to enforce that law is directed at minorities. If the laws against jaywalking provided felony charges but were enforced vigorously only in minority communities, only minority jaywalkers would be in prison (even if jaywalking were as common in other communities as in minority communities).

The legacy of racism is strong in the United States. This means that it is easy to rationalize the differential incarceration of Black and Brown people because so many Americans think it "makes sense," given the dark suspicion that Black and Brown people really are more antisocial, immoral, incompetent, and less responsible than Whites. One need only look at the sizable number of Americans who didn't grant Barack Obama legitimacy as president because of his race (as evident in the slogan "Give us back our country"). As my mother said of her reason for not voting for him in 2008, "There's just something about the way he looks." Really? And what might that be?

It's not just a matter of a few nasty bigots (or even "nice" bigots, like my dear mother). Even Americans with open hearts and goodwill struggle with the psychological and cultural impact of racism, with the way it distorts our thoughts and feelings. I know I am part of that struggle, remaining vigilant so that the racism that seeps into me as an American does not shape and control my thoughts and reactions to people and events.

The effect of racism on interpreting information is a manifestation of the problem of "confirmatory bias" that I spoke of in chapter 1: when you "know" something is true, you only attend to, acknowledge, and incorporate information that conforms to that preexisting belief. Confirmatory bias ensures that counterevidence is ignored or dismissed (as the "exception that proves the rule"). My mother is that kind of racist. When we lived in public housing in New York City in the early 1950s, her best friend was a Black woman down the hall—an "exception."

But there is more to consider than just the racist origins of the massive incarceration of people of color. There are social, economic, and psychological consequences of that massive incarceration that set in motion toxic effects that can develop a life of their own. I see and hear that in the lives of killers.

The consequences of being arrested, convicted, and incarcerated at the entry level in the Drug War include disenfranchisement (felons can't vote), vocational discrimination (it's mostly legal to discriminate against felons in employment decisions), brutalization (being likely to learn bad habits and to be traumatized in prison), and disrupted family relationships (which put the next generation of kids at risk for adverse development). I think this means that what begins as "simple" racism becomes more complex racism over time as Black (and Brown) men (and women) are denied the vote, denied mainstream employment, and denied an opportunity to be good parents.

The result is the downward cycle that tends to push many products of this system toward violent crime, which, unlike drug offenses, does happen more often among minority populations (for multiple reasons that we will explore in later chapters). I am reminded of what Anatole France wrote in 1894: "The law, in its majestic equality, forbids the rich as well as the poor to sleep under the bridges, to beg in the streets and to steal bread."

If the racist law enforcement that Michelle Alexander (and others) have documented pushes Black and Brown people into prison and thus into homelessness, poverty, and hunger, it does little good to say that the law is "colorblind" in its prohibition of sleeping under bridges, begging in the streets, and stealing bread. That's the full social reality of the racism that drives the criminal justice system, a system that imagines racial disparities in moral character and competence and then takes actions to create those disparities and ensure they continue to exist among the most vulnerable. The result is a disproportionate murder rate among those victimized by that system (and their children and grandchildren).

The shooting of eighteen-year-old Michael Brown in August of 2014; the subsequent mix of fear, confusion, suspicion, outrage, and violence that enveloped the community of Ferguson, Missouri; and the responses by the police force provided a social laboratory for many of these issues. Whatever the specifics of Brown's case (for example, his actions in stealing from a convenience store minutes before he was confronted by a police officer and the ensuing struggle), the legacy of American racism and the history of racist law enforcement in that community (and around the country) provided fertile soil for the community's interpretation of the events in which White officer Darren Wilson shot and killed Black teenager Michael Brown. Anyone who does not acknowledge the possibility, even likelihood, of contemporary and historical racism infusing those events is blind to what race has meant and means today in America. Beyond that blindness is research that documents the cognitive and emotional impact of race in individual decision making about crime and public response to crime.

Research on Racial Bias in Jury Decision-Making

The available research suggests that racial bias operates in the microprocesses of the criminal justice system as it implements the law in the courtroom. For example, a study conducted by Mona Lynch and Craig Haney and published in 2010 used simulated trials in which they could randomly vary the race of defendants and victims and see how it affected the judgments and decisions of participants who were playing the role of jurors.

Lynch and Haney found that participants who viewed videos of a trial with a Black defendant were more likely to sentence the defendant to death than if the defendant were White, particularly when the victim was White. Naturally, I thought of this study when George Zimmerman was found not guilty of murder for killing Trayvon Martin in Florida (in 2013), and some commentators asked whether the jury would have been so forgiving if the Black youth (Martin) had shot the White man (Zimmerman) in similar circumstances. These doubts lingered in 2014, when a jury in Jacksonville, Florida, could not at first convict Michael Dunn (a White man) of murder after he shot into an SUV full of Black kids and killed one of them—seventeen-year-old Jordan Davis. The fact that the jury did eventually convict Dunn of first-degree murder for the shooting seems to be evidence that race does not have the power to create legal impunity that it once did in America, but it still leaves the basic issues of racism to linger (and, in some cases, fester). After all, Jordan Davis died; Dunn's attempt was successful—all because of a car full of Black teenagers playing loud music.

Questionnaires in the Lynch and Haney study cited above showed that the jurors gave more weight to mitigating evidence when the defendant was White than when he was Black. What is more, and particularly worrisome, participants were significantly more likely to improperly use what was offered by the defense as mitigating evidence *in favor* of a death sentence when the defendant was Black.

I have heard defense attorneys worry about this phenomenon in real-life cases. The fear is that if the defense demonstrates a history of traumatic child abuse, the jury may respond, not with sympathy for the abused child inside the adult killer, but rather with even more fear, and thus believe he should be executed. All this is magnified when the defendant is Black or Hispanic, because the fear that the child has been damaged by abuse and trauma compounds rather than reduces the underlying, racially based fear of Black and Hispanic criminals.

In summarizing their results, Lynch and Haney noted, "We surmised that the racial disparities that we found in sentencing outcomes were likely the result of the jurors' inability or unwillingness to empathize with a defendant of a different race—that is, White jurors who simply could not or would not cross the 'empathic divide' to fully appreciate the life struggles of a Black capital defendant and take those struggles into account in deciding on his sentence." The jury in the Dunn case consisted of four White women, two Black women, four White men, an Asian woman, and a Hispanic man. That it was so hard to get a first-degree murder conviction (the jury was initially hung) speaks to these issues.

Law professor Dorothy Roberts has summarized the type of research conducted by Lynch and Haney and others in her book *Fatal Intervention: How*

Science, Politics, and Big Business Re-create Race in the Twenty-First Century.
She cites, for example, the results obtained by psychologists Aneeta Rattan,
Cynthia Levine, Carol Dweck, and Jennifer L. Eberhardt. The results of their
study demonstrated that White respondents exhibited bias when asked about
sentencing decisions involving juveniles of different races. The participants
were read accounts of a fourteen-year-old boy with a long history of juvenile
convictions who raped an elderly woman and were asked how the criminal
justice system should handle him. Half of the respondents were told the
offender was White, while the other half were told he was Black. Participants
were more likely to support sentencing juveniles convicted of violent crimes
to life in prison without parole if they had in mind a Black rather than a
White offender.

The differences reported were small but statistically reliable and significant (4.4 versus 4.2, on a scale on which 1 means "not at all likely" and 6
means "extremely likely"). In line with this finding, respondents indicated
they thought that juveniles were more similar to adults in their culpability
for such a crime if they had in mind a Black rather than a White perpetrator
(at about the same levels as the measure of support for life in prison). As
Dorothy Roberts points out, this is just one illustrative study among many
demonstrating the reality of racial bias in the way people process decisions in
the criminal justice system.

Although the racial-bias effects observed in such social psychology experiments are small in absolute terms, they represent significant departures from
the principle enshrined in American constitutional law. The Fourteenth
Amendment to the Constitution mandates: "nor shall any state deprive any
person of life, liberty, or property, without due process of law; nor deny to any
person within its jurisdiction the equal protection of the laws." And interna-
tionally, Article 7 of the Universal Declaration of Human Rights states that
"All are equal before the law and are entitled without any discrimination to
equal protection of the law." Race matters. It makes a difference in both
expectations and outcomes, and Black kids are aware of this.

WHAT DIFFERENCE DO THESE DIFFERENCES MAKE?

Some years ago, I was chairing a panel of teenagers in Albany, New York,
when a member of the audience asked, "Can you talk to us about your relationships with the police?" In reply, Robert, a seventeen-year-old African

American boy on the panel said this: "First, let me tell you that I am president of the Honor Society at my high school, and I have been admitted to an Ivy League university for next year. But since I turned fifteen, I have been stopped and searched on the street by the police five times." He paused for dramatic effect and then continued, "I don't think it's because I am president of the Honor Society!" After the audience laughed, he continued, "You know, you all are lucky I am a good person."

It was an eloquent expression of where and how race fits into the lives of kids in America. When the boy said that "you all are lucky I am a good person," he was suggesting that with all the positives in his life—academic success, family support, a bright future, peer acceptance—he could and would tolerate the racism that targeted him for "special treatment" by the police. But the reverse implication was clear too: if he were dealing with the poverty, abuse, school failure, and trauma that so many Black kids face, he would be the proverbial camel, and racism the straw that would break his back.

Research conducted in New York City on the effects of the massive "stop and frisk" program of that city's police force shows that Robert's experience is hardly unique. Researcher Jeff Fagan and his colleagues Andrew Gelman and Alex Kiss have found a direct relationship between the number of times a person is stopped and searched and the degree to which they have negative attitudes about the police and society: the more they are stopped, the more they develop a negative view. This same research confirmed that Black and Hispanic young men were being stopped disproportionately, and by a wide margin. Robert's story finds validation in this research.

I repeated his story at a conference in Ohio once, and the African American mayor of the city in which I was speaking took me aside afterward to validate the story. He told me, "You know, I have three sons. When they go out driving in this city I tell them, 'if you are stopped by one of my police officers, you keep your hands on the steering wheel, smile politely and say "yes sir" and "no sir" to whatever the officer asks you.'" The mayor knew that simply by being young Black males, even his sons were an object of suspicion, even in "his" city.

THE TANGLED WEB OF RACE, CLASS, AND CULTURE

It's difficult, perhaps impossible, to untangle all the intertwined elements that make race a predictor of outcomes in the American criminal justice system. The links between race and class strengthen the connection, as I mentioned in reviewing the work of Michelle Alexander earlier in this chapter. According to the U.S. Census Bureau, in 2011, the average (median) income of White households was about $55,000, while for Blacks it was about $32,000 and for Hispanics it was close to $39,000. But these averages are not the main story, and increasingly so because of rising economic inequality in America. Being poor is related to criminal behavior, and Blacks and Hispanics are more likely to be poor than Whites, at a time when being poor increasingly means living in a world radically different from that of the affluent. In 2011, 21 percent of White households had incomes less than $25,000 per year, while for Blacks the figure was 40 percent and for Hispanics it was 31 percent.

Also relevant are the links between growing up without a father and the kind of juvenile delinquency that leads to jail. Black kids are three times more likely to live in a single-parent home than White kids (66 versus 24 percent), and Latino kids are almost twice as likely as White kids to do so (41 versus 24 percent). These effects combine psychology (the parent–child dynamics of single-parent households—which in about 90 percent of the cases means a mother-only family) and economics (the odds that a single-parent household is poor are more than four times greater than if the household contains a married couple). Nearly 40 percent of single-family households in which the single parent is female (and 24 percent in which the single parent is male) are poor, compared with about 8 percent of married households.

What is more, Sarah Garland has explored the fact that in the past half century, while racial differences in educational success have remained the same (with Whites doing much better than Blacks and Hispanics), social-class differences in educational success have increased markedly. While Blacks still lag behind Whites by about a year and a half on academic achievement scores, the gap between the poor and the rich (which used to be about one year) is now four years.

We can add to all these factors the historical roots of the Black population in the American South, with all that implies for the "culture of honor" that I will examine in chapter 4. As always, however, it is the *accumulation* of risk factors that does kids in, that puts them on the track that leads to violent crime. Add to this the psychological effects of rejection linked to racism as kids come to suspect that they really are inferior and adapt to that fear (one consequence being the elevated levels of narcissism I noted earlier). Add to these "real" effects the biased judgments in the criminal justice system that flow from racism, and it is little wonder that Blacks and Latinos are disproportionately represented in the killers I have listened to for the past twenty years.

Race and racism, poverty and the violent gang culture, rejection and abandonment—all these potentially toxic influences on human development fall on fertile ground when and where there is the trauma of child abuse and neglect. In so many ways, the bloated criminal justice system and the killers who inhabit it are the bitter fruit of a society failing to protect children from abuse—failing to protect the most basic human right of all, the right to be safe from physical, sexual, and psychological assault. There literally is hell to pay. One form that hell takes is the convoluted and contradictory emotional life of many killers.

THE JUNIOR MERCEDEZ CASE

Twenty-four-year-old Junior Mercedez* lives in Texas. In 2011, he beat the two-year-old son of his girlfriend to death. But at the same time, he was a doting father to his own four-year-old son. The mix of rage and aggression with tenderness and love is a big part of his story, as it is in the stories of other killers, like Billy Bob Wilson, a violent adult within whom a needy child lives.

How does this split develop? There's no easy answer, of course, but the key seems to lie in the process by which children disconnect or "dissociate" to protect themselves in the short run, ironically putting themselves in greater danger in the long run (a topic I will examine in detail in chapter 4). Junior Mercedez exemplifies this splitting and the compartmentalizing of feelings that results, often with terrible, even fatal consequences.

Given the highly traumatic nature of the household in which he grew up, it is not surprising that self-comforting was an important aspect of Junior's life, from a very early age. When I spoke with his mother, she remembered that, like many children, Junior relied on a pacifier until he was nearly three years old. He then was switched to a soft, fuzzy white blanket (which she still has). At age five, this was replaced by a soft, fuzzy stuffed animal. At age nine, Junior turned to sports for emotional support and gratification. For children who grow up in a nonviolent, nontraumatic family, these "normal" forms of self-soothing and emotional gratification are enough, but for Junior, they were not.

Junior told me that as he made the transition to adolescence, his own power began to replace his fear by an understanding that "a punch only hurts for a second." He conquered his fear through his own aggressive behavior and assertion of power. When asked what words he would use to describe himself, he offered a clue to just how split he was as a person when he said, "Pride, drive, and empathy. Overall I'm an alright person . . . on the surface." *"On the surface" is a big part of the story.*

Like many kids facing the kind of negative home life he experienced, Junior engaged in chronic alcohol use from an early age—as a kind of self-medication (as is common among traumatized youths dealing with anxiety). By age thirteen, he had added marijuana to his alcohol use. Junior's use of alcohol and marijuana to cope with his internal distress and his family life experience did not dissipate his feelings, but he told me that "being a drunk helped me cope."

A fractured sense of self is a common side effect of using dissociation and disconnection in the struggle to deal with the fact that the people you love are also the people who terrify and abuse you. Junior acknowledged in our interview that "I am like a chameleon, I can fit in anywhere with anyone." Junior engages in a great deal of compartmentalizing, walling off disturbing thoughts and feelings behind what appears to be a "cool" front. But it is a front that can come crashing down when he faces events or persons who force him to connect to the dark emotions below the surface, like the frustrating, crying child he killed in 2011.

In searching through Junior's records, I found this; in a 2002 interview with Junior as part of juvenile detention programming, a prison psychologist described him as "smug and indifferent throughout the interview. He was not at all concerned and he showed little emotionality. He denied all psychological problems and most types of misconduct. . . . He did seem likely to be very defiant, but he was passively cooperative with this evaluation." When I asked him about this (ten years later), Junior replied that "you keep yourself to yourself."

Five years after that psychological evaluation (in 2006), a social worker evaluating Junior offered the following assessment: "Counselor sees no signs which cause him to doubt client's assertion that he is not a violent person. Client has good coping and good support and good motivation and prognosis is positive." This is ironic, given that during this period Junior was involved in a wide range of violent behavior, was struggling with domestic disruptions, and was seriously abusing alcohol.

I believe that Junior's tendency to minimize his internal struggles and to present himself as "alright" is a long-standing issue that goes well beyond any short-term, self-interested attempt to avoid the legal and social consequences of his behavior. It is also a result of his overall, lifelong strategy for coping with the enormous pain and fear that he experienced in childhood, living in a family characterized by domestic violence while attempting to maintain attachment to his emotionally and physically abusive father.

His mother told me that Junior would "go through phases of not talking. He would be angry and scared, but then if his father asked him to go out with him he would enthusiastically agree to go with him." However, Junior told me, "it always ended badly." To this very day (in our interview) Junior says that his father has "charisma." Fractured as he is, I believe that Junior and many others like him could recover if given a chance (a topic to be explored in chapter 6).

WHAT TO DO WITH DAMAGED KILLERS?

For offenders who are the product of chronic trauma (particularly young offenders), to be locked away in adult prisons for the rest of their lives seems to me a crime in its own right. Most of the rest of the civilized world considers this barbaric. The idea that at twenty years of age you can take an action so decisive that it irrevocably determines the rest of your life, with no possibility of redemption, is one that troubles me greatly.

I recognize that there are individuals so damaged that we (and they) cannot be safe with them outside prison and unsupervised (and in some cases, even in prison where they are highly supervised). As I mentioned in chapter 1, I testified in the death penalty trial of serial killer Jorge Susindo, and it is clear that he is one of those people. Jorge started his life as a child growing up in the war zone of Guatemala during the period of violent political repression that dominated life there in the 1970s, with a father who was in prison for murder and a mother who "abandoned" him to seek work in the United States. After his grandfather was murdered in front of him in 1981, his mother returned to get him and bring him to Los Angeles, where he moved into the dark world of the street gangs—and the rest of his story is a history of brutality, murder, and sexual assault that resulted in him receiving a death sentence in three different states.

Was Jorge born to be a killer? Was he doomed from birth? Some children are so lacking in the basic requirements to become a decent person and live harmoniously in society that they seem almost destined to be killers. Perhaps Jorge was one of these kids. But listening to relatives and friends of the family in Guatemala describe him as a child, it seems unlikely. He was probably a sensitive child sent down the dark path by his early life as an untreated traumatized child in a morally fractured world.

Some children may be born so damaged that they are on a fast track to violent delinquency. Some are so brutalized and psychologically maltreated in childhood that they join the congenitally damaged on that fast track. But these individuals are not the main story, and indeed, some if not many of these people become *irretrievably* damaged only after they go to jail or prison the first time. What they fear most, and what we who care about the future quality of life in our society should join them in fearing most, is that they will experience sexual assaults that will distort their minds and hearts in ways that lead to terrible acts of violence, against others and against themselves.

The Damage Done by Early and Long Incarceration

How criminals are treated in prison can cast a long shadow on the lives they lead after release, and indeed can affect the quality of life of everyone they encounter after release. This is the conclusion of psychologist Craig Haney, who for many years has studied this process. Writing in 2001, one of his conclusions was that "as a result of several trends in American corrections, the personal challenges posed and psychological harms inflicted in the course of incarceration have grown over the last several decades in the United States."

Responding to crime with the fear- and revenge-based punitiveness of long prison sentences is a losing strategy in the long run for everyone, not just the criminals themselves. It joins with the widely recognized de-emphasis on rehabilitation as the goal of incarceration in worsening the effects of going to prison, particularly the damage done to vulnerable young criminals. It comes back to haunt our society when they are released.

The insanity of our emphasis on punishment over rehabilitation was illuminated in 2014, when a man serving a ninety-eight-year sentence who had been released through a clerical error in 2008 (after serving just eight years) was discovered. During that six-year mistake, Rene Lima-Marin had lived an exemplary life, starting a family, working, and generally being a responsible member of the community. In 2014, the error was detected and Lima-Marin returned to prison. As his wife, Jasmine, said, "He was given an opportunity to live again and it was taken away from him." If the goal is rehabilitation, would not the lucid action on the part of the state be to pardon him and celebrate his "accidental" success? If the system is punishment driven, the statement of the prosecutor makes sense: "He should go back because the law requires the sentence he received."

Of course, there have been cases of inmates mistakenly released who committed additional crimes—most notably the Colorado case in which a man released mistakenly four years early killed the state's chief of corrections. But clearly, too many men and women are serving excessive sentences, from the perspective of rehabilitation. Rene Lima-Marin's case illustrates that much. To quote Craig Haney again, "As a result, the ordinary adaptive process of institutionalization or 'prisonization' has become extraordinarily prolonged and intense. Among other things, these recent changes in prison life mean that prisoners in general (and some prisoners in particular) face more difficult and problematic transitions as they return to the free world." As his research reveals, the category of "some prisoners in particular" includes young prisoners especially.

Although more and more offenders have been receiving long sentences, even life sentences, in recent decades, only about 10 percent of all inmates in American prisons are serving life sentences, according to a report prepared by Solomon Moore. Thus, most of those who are incarcerated will be released at some point. It should not come as a surprise that most killers have been incarcerated before, given that for most of them, the murders they commit arise out of a long-standing problem of antisocial and delinquent behavior that, in many cases, started in childhood or early adolescence. (The major exceptions are youths who commit mass school shootings, those who kill an intimate as a "crime of passion," and those who kill as a result of a crisis linked to the onset or worsening of severe mental disorders.) But it is also clear that the initial incarceration experiences of those who later become killers shape their development, for better or for worse. Usually for worse.

Don't Give Up

I believe that we should not give up on killers of any age. Some will not undergo transformation and recovery until middle age, perhaps as a process of psychological maturation, perhaps as a process of spiritual discovery that brings them out of their darkness and into the light. Others will quickly find their way out of their personal darkness if given a positive place to stand in the universe and appropriate therapeutic support. (We will explore these issues in detail in chapter 6.) I think that legal policy should reflect these facts, and not make the definitive decisions inherent in a sentence without possibility of parole at the time of the crime, not just for juvenile offenders but for most offenders, and not just for life sentences but for all long sentences.

Watching the Swedish detective series *Wallander,* I am struck by the relative brevity of prison sentences in Sweden (and other Nordic countries), in contrast to those in America. It's not just on TV. A systematic analysis comparing Nordic prisons and prison policy with those in the United States, conducted by Katie Ward and her colleagues in 2013, found that American prisons are generally less effective than Nordic prisons in preventing future criminal behavior (recidivism rates are much lower in the Nordic system) and in keeping individuals out of prison in the first place. The U.S. incarceration rate is eight times higher than rates in the Nordic countries—indeed, than in most of the rest of the world: there are more than seven hundred inmates per hundred thousand citizens in the United States, and less than one hundred inmates per hundred thousand in most affluent and modernized societies.

The key is that the Nordic system focuses on rehabilitation with dignity, through treatment and education (including substance abuse treatment) coupled with efforts to return individuals to the community safely (with electronic monitoring in many cases). The United States, by contrast, focuses on punishment and the use of long sentences as a kind of preventive detention. It's difficult to look at the American approach without thinking about revenge, whereas in the Nordic system one sees an affirmation of humanity. Historical wisdom concurs with the statistical analyses of Katie Ward and others—to wit, the adage attributed to the Chinese sage Confucius: "When you begin a journey of revenge, start by digging two graves, one for your enemy and one for yourself."

Consider, for example, Duke Jimenez*. He was twenty years old when he killed seventy-year-old Roberta Teebee and was sentenced to seventy years. Is it possible to see the terrible crime he committed and yet still be open to the possibility of rehabilitation, transformation, and redemption, instead of focusing on revenge? I think so. My interview with him and our subsequent communication reinforce that belief, as I will show in chapter 6. Yet many states require forty, fifty, or more years in prison before parole is even possible, no matter how dramatic the incarcerated individual's rehabilitation, transformation, and redemption may be.

Death in Prison

The death penalty claims the lives of about fifty inmates each year, according to an analysis by Brian Palmer. Suicide and homicide by other inmates claim about ten times as many lives each year, even though the numbers of suicides and homicides in jails and prisons have declined dramatically since 1980—by 90 percent for homicides and 50 percent for suicides. This seems to be attributable, in large part, to better management of jails and prisons, including segregation of violent from nonviolent prisoners. But I suspect there is more to this story, and that the decline in prison deaths is also a result of improved medical trauma technology saving lives that would otherwise have been lost to acts of violence (a topic I will address fully in chapter 7). We do know, from an FBI report, that if medical trauma technology today were at the same level as in the 1930s, the national homicide rate would be eight times higher than it is. This is all the more reason to include a focus on the problem of "nonlethal assaults"—which, by most accounts, have increased in recent decades.

As I write in 2014, thirty-two states (along with the federal government) still impose the death penalty. Unless legal and political conditions change in these states (changes that speed up the process and shorten the time from conviction to execution), it seems likely that most of the "non-natural causes" of deaths in prisons will continue to be suicides or homicides by other inmates, rather than actions of the state. Of course, some states are not content with this. In 2013, Florida passed legislation designed to expedite the processing of appeals in death penalty cases so as to hasten the date of execution: once an inmate has exhausted his legally mandated appeals, the governor must sign a death warrant within thirty days and the execution must occur within sixty days after that. But even in states where the process takes so long that a death sentence becomes a de facto "life in prison/eventual death in prison" sentence, we still face the moral issues inherent in capital punishment.

I don't think that the slowness of the process absolves us of the moral issue of state-sanctioned killing. As I said in chapter 1, the ethic of "not killing" is, in one sense, a matter of simple lucidity. I say this as someone who listens to killers: it is a measure of our moral and scientific failure that we continue to execute these damaged individuals. As Billy Bob Wilson said to me years ago as he sat on death row, "Execution is a shameful way to die." And so it is. Shame on us.

In my visits to the "land of the lost"—as twenty-two-year-old John Christianson*, who had been in prison since he was fourteen, so eloquently called it in a letter to me from prison on Father's Day in 2001—I have learned to see the child inside the man (and sometimes the girl inside the woman). I have learned about the terrible and durable psychological toxicity of untreated trauma. I have learned about how the dark side takes a toll on human development. But I have also learned about the capacity of the human spirit to find a toehold of goodness, even in the bleak world of our prisons. I receive letters from such men from time to time—mostly because they have found my book *Lost Boys* in their prison libraries, and discovered within it a resonance with the suffering they endured as children, and sometimes with the transformation and insight they have experienced as adults. I will return to these issues in chapter 6.

The challenge we face is to avoid our own collective and individual process of "dissociation" from the killers among us, to find the foundation of lucidity in public policy and in our answers to public opinion surveys. This mandates that we commit to compassion in an ever-larger circle of caring. The Dalai Lama teaches that compassion is more than a feeling dependent on the sympathetic nature of the "other." Pope Francis agrees: solidarity with the poor and the maligned "other" lies at the core of the Christian mission.

Compassion is the ability to remain fixed on caring for the other person, regardless of what that person does—not just out of sympathy for the other person, but from the recognition that it is best for ourselves to live in a state of compassion rather than hatred. One of the Dalai Lama's most important lessons is that true compassion is not just an emotional response, but a firm commitment founded on reason. It is easy to feel hatred for our enemies and sympathy for the victims of violence—human decency seems to demand it. But getting close to killers means something more. It does not mean ignoring evil and violence. It means that even in the face of human behavior that is evil, violent, and in violation of basic human rights (what those of us who approach these issues from a religious perspective would call "sin"), we still care for the offender, even as we seek to control that person's dangerous behavior and protect ourselves and the community. Indeed, the crucial concept for those who seek to live by compassion, not just sentimentality, is "the circle of caring" I spoke of in chapter 1 with regard to the small circle that killers often have. Here the issue is how big a circle of caring the rest of us have.

In the 1997 film *Seven Years in Tibet,* Heinrich Harrer, a European friend of the young Dalai Lama, begins work on a building—a movie theater to satisfy the Dalai Lama's interest in films. He arranges for workmen to dig a trench as the start of building a foundation. As they begin work, one of the laborers approaches Harrer and asks him to stop the digging because they are killing worms that live in the soil. As a monk explains when Harrer calls him over in frustration, for Tibetan Buddhists, the circle of caring includes even the lowly worm. None of God's creatures is excluded, and each creature deserves care and concern.

Every culture struggles with this issue of who is "in" and who is "out" of the circle of caring, particularly when it comes to violence. Some of the fiercest warriors in armies throughout history have matched their bloodthirsty ruthlessness on the field of battle with a soft caring for friends and family. Some of our warriors today do this in their own lives, as news footage of veterans returning home from Iraq and Afghanistan to children, spouses, and dogs so vividly illustrates.

Even some of the world's most monstrous killers may have a small circle of beings for whom they care in a morally elevated fashion. Hitler had his well-cared-for dog, and Nazi Germany had some of the most humane animal protection laws in Europe in the 1930s. This is the conclusion of sociologists Arnold Arluke and Clinton Sanders in their 1996 book *Regarding Animals,* which explores the paradoxical and contradictory views and values of human treatment of animals. In *Lost Boys,* I reported on the fact that one very violent adolescent I got to know (Malcolm) made money in dog fighting but kept his "pet" dog out of the ring. Out of the ring and inside his circle of caring.

Conversely, even some of the kindest, most law-abiding citizens have holes in their circle of caring. A friend in Germany told me of her loving father, who for decades sensitively ministered to the needs of his patients but, to his dying day, maintained that if Hitler had succeeded in killing all the Jews, the world would be a better place.

The renowned seventeenth-century French philosopher René Descartes is famous for his rationalist concept of human existence, captured in the statement "I think, therefore I am." But he thought that animals were "automatons," not sentient beings. To "prove" this, he nailed a dog to a door and eviscerated him, all the while claiming that the screams that emanated from the tortured creature were not sounds of pain but, rather, similar to the sound of grinding gears that a machine might make. Human experience is complex and rarely one-dimensional, and the list of beings we include in the circle of caring speaks to that complexity. I struggle to keep René Descartes in my circle of caring even as I find his treatment of dogs reprehensible, evidence of the kind of moral and emotional damage I find in killers.

As I see it, the circle of caring must be as big as we can tolerate—and then bigger still. After the 9/11 attacks, I, among other Americans, wrote that even as we seek to stop terrorism by neutralizing those who would commit it, we must not allow ourselves to dehumanize our enemies. Rather, we must have compassion for them and seek to heal the wounds that spawn terrorism where we can. Our spiritual teachers tell us we must love the killer: "Love the enemy." This is the path that leads to joy, contentment, and peace in our hearts and minds. Thus, compassion is not just a "value" in the ethical sense; it is a valuable component in the psychological foundations of inner harmony and well-being, and ultimately of resilience.

RELIGIOUS JUSTIFICATION FOR PUNITIVE EXCLUSION

The impulse to demonize and dehumanize the killer is understandable. However, it does not come without unfortunate side effects in the long run. It deprives us of the moral comfort afforded by the world's great spiritual teachings, which at their core offer the wisdom of believing in compassion, universal dignity, and reconciliation, regardless of whether someone is friend or foe.

Of course, religious traditions are not so simply described in these terms. Karen Armstrong's writings demonstrate that once the silent profundity of spiritual awareness is translated into specific theological and cultural terms, it can be transformed into something nasty. The initial purity of transcendent insight can result in something as imperfect as any human enterprise, compromised by unconscious dark forces and ego-driven behavior. Pope Francis understands. He chose as his papal namesake Saint Francis, who declared, "Preach the Gospel, and if necessary use words."

An excellent illustration of the dark dangers of theological words above compassionate action is to be found in Scott Gibbs's analysis of the dark side of the three Abrahamic religions (Islam, Christianity, and Judaism). Each has a strain that justifies violence and exclusion of the "other." But, as William Cavanaugh's wide-ranging historical analysis reveals, it is idolatry, not religion per se, that gives rise to the dehumanization of the other that is at the root of societal violence. And idolatry can be religious or secular. For example, as Cavanaugh documents, idolatrous fanaticism in the Communist Soviet Union, China, and Cambodia resulted in vast numbers of tortured and dead victims—far in excess of what "religious" violence has caused.

Compassion is our principal resource in the struggle to maintain our spiritual integrity in the face of worldly and internal temptations to hate and dehumanize our enemies. Killers are typically caught up in their own scenarios of revenge and retaliation. Often they have experienced personal suffering or family loss, or historical victimization, and are seeking a way to give meaning to that suffering through acts of violent revenge.

Tempting as it is to put killers outside the human circle of caring, where our best moral principles don't apply, we must resist this temptation. Instead, we should embrace what spiritual counselor Dave Richo calls "utter reconcilability"—an absolute unwillingness to dehumanize the other, no matter what the crime. Regardless of their legal status, killers are often excommunicated from the human community. But connection can be transformative.

THE TRANSFORMATIVE POWER
OF HUMAN CONNECTION

In 1997, while waiting to testify in a resentencing hearing for a man who had been on death row in Illinois, I struck up a conversation with a corrections officer—I will call him "Ted"—who had worked on death row for ten years. He told me with a smile that when he started as a guard he was "a typical southern Illinois redneck cracker," and his basic approach to the death penalty had been "Fry the bastards." But now, after coming to know the inmates, his views were changing. Case in point: he had taken his day off to drive the three hours from his home in southern Illinois to testify on behalf of saving the life of the inmate whose hearing was going on in the courtroom thirty feet away. "You know," he said, "when you get to know some of these guys you come to realize that what they have been through in their lives made them the way they were when they committed their crimes."

Ted's report of growing compassion was extremely moving. He is not alone in this effort—many similar testimonials exist. As noted earlier, experimental lab studies have measured compassion in ways that are replicated in the "real world." They validate the kind of programming promoted by organizations such as the Center for Compassion and Altruism Research and Education at Stanford University, and by peace advocates around the world. At the heart of these efforts is often the practice of meditation, mindfulness, and empathy building.

Jesuit priests Michael Kennedy and Gregory Boyle offer an alternative to the punitive and aggressive approach embodied in the classic "Scared Straight" program that tries to intimidate delinquent kids as a way of diverting them from the path that leads to violent crime. Their alternative approach is a program of humane education and spiritual development they call "Cared Straight" (we will look at other such programs in chapters 6 and 8). Father Boyle's book *Tattoos on the Heart* is must reading for anyone who wants to grow compassion for these young people.

Few of us are willing to meet the challenge of finding a path to compassion for America's killers, whether they are on death row or not. But some of us *are*. And when we *are*, it can be transformative for everyone willing to listen.

REACHING ACROSS THE DIVIDE TO THE LAND
OF THE LOST: MARY'S LESSON

After I published *Lost Boys* in 1999, I regularly received letters and phone calls from people who were emotionally involved in a killing. Once such call came in 2001. Mary wanted to talk to me "in secret," she said on the phone. Wondering what the mystery was, I agreed to meet with her at a restaurant downtown. The forty-five-year-old who greeted me looked tired and drawn; she was clearly apprehensive, looking around the restaurant to be sure there was no one there who knew her. We sat down and she explained the reason for the secrecy.

"My niece—my sister's daughter—was murdered eighteen months ago by her boyfriend. No one saw it coming," she said, as tears welled up in her brown eyes. Smiling weakly, she continued. "I had met this boy! I had him in my home. And now my niece is dead at his hands. There's no doubt he killed her, but I couldn't sleep at night wondering why he did it. So I went to see him at the jail. At first he was afraid to talk to me, but eventually he did. I asked him to explain and he tried to tell me about the emotional struggles he had been going through in the months before he killed Anna—that's my niece. When I left, he asked if he could write to me and if I would visit him again. It was a real dilemma for me because I knew the rest of my family wouldn't approve. But I did it anyway. I have been writing to him and visiting him secretly for the past year—even after he was tried and sent to prison. My family would disown me if they knew what I was doing. They just hate him so much. But I felt like I had to understand him, and then I felt like I had to try to be a friend to him. Everyone else has abandoned him—even his parents, who were not really there for him before he killed my niece."

"Why did you call me?" I asked.

"Because I saw your book *Lost Boys*," she replied. "There's no one else I can talk to about this, and I thought maybe I could talk with you, that you might understand. Do you think it's crazy that I have a relationship with this boy?" We talked for an hour and then she left, reassured that it was not "crazy" to be compassionate in the face of such a profound loss and such anger in her closest relatives.

. . .

Mary's approach is wise. Each of us could learn from her. It may seem a counterintuitive discovery, but in the long run, holding on to our anger and hurt imprisons us, just as seeking compassion and caring liberates us. This is why we must go beyond our horror and rage to a place of compassion and caring, even for the killers, so that we may foster these qualities in ourselves, as people and as part of an American society in which these qualities are often in short supply.

Compassion is not only a positive emotional response, but also an intellectual commitment to care for the well-being of the other, no matter what. And the intellectual commitment requires an informed understanding. To that end, the next two chapters will try to understand the fundamental human realities of killers, namely the emotional and moral damage that accumulates in their lives.

3

Moral Damage

GROWING UP WITH A WAR ZONE MENTALITY

October 5, 2009: I am sitting in an interview room at the Portland, Oregon, jail with twenty-year-old Robert Tallman.* He is facing possible execution for killing two teenagers in his neighborhood thirteen months ago. There is little doubt of his guilt—the forensic and eyewitness evidence in this case is compelling. As I listen to him, he describes numerous occasions when he was involved in a cycle of assault and revenge: he estimates that he has been in sixty one-on-one street fights. He reports that he won't let anyone take advantage of him. The incident for which he is currently in jail awaiting trial appears to be but one example. He and his brother had been involved in conflicts with other male youths in the neighborhood that led to an escalating pattern of assault prior to the lethal violence of June 20, 2006. There had been fistfights before, but that day, Robert's brother Marcus was stabbed by a youth in the community. Later that evening, Robert confronted some of the youths he believed had been involved in the assault on Marcus. He shot fifteen-year-old Christopher Clemons and fourteen-year-old Lasalle Bronson. Fists gave way to knives, knives gave way to guns, and people died. Clemons survived, but Bronson died.

It is as if I am hearing a modern version of the Capulets and Montagues in Shakespeare's *Romeo and Juliet.* Robert says his mother taught him that honor and respect were the most important things in life. He reports that when he was in third grade and was in a fight with a boy, he was punched and he started to cry. The boy said, "You a bitch." His mother heard this, and told him he had to fight the boy, saying "Robert—you soft." Robert says his father taught him that whenever he faced conflicts he should handle them on his own: "Never tell the police. Don't snitch. Take care of it." "My father taught me how to fight with knives and my fists," he tells me. "Why did you shoot those boys?" I ask. "You just do what you gotta do," he replies.

Three weeks after we met, Robert Tallman pled guilty to the murders and received a life sentence, in exchange for the prosecution taking the death penalty off the table.

Many individuals who have grown up in communities with high levels of violence develop this sense that violence is a moral imperative when one is threatened, challenged, or disrespected—and that death is morally preferable to dishonor. This is particularly true when their families—like Robert's mother and father—reinforce this moral damage through the messages they send their children about honor, conflict resolution, and the legitimacy of violence as a tool in interpersonal relations. Like Robert, they come to adapt their system of moral reasoning and behavior to include justification for aggression as a legitimate response to conflict, and as an appropriate form of social influence. When this belief system comes with a heightened sense of being at risk from assault by others, it becomes the war zone mentality.

WHEN VIOLENCE IS NORMAL

I should be clear that in most cases, the adaptations we are talking about are psychologically "normal," in the sense that they are not based in diagnosable psychopathology (although, of course, in some cases these adaptations *accompany* profound mental health problems related to emotional damage—as we will see in the next chapter—and that is a particularly terrible outcome). When I asked Robert why he shot those two boys and he told me, "You just do what you gotta do," he was expressing a widespread pattern of morality among those who have grown up in similar circumstances. They have a sense of violence being a fact of community life so extreme that it steers them to a point beyond conventional moral considerations.

As I mentioned in chapter 1, when people learn that I talk with killers they often ask me, "Don't they know the difference between right and wrong?" I respond that it's not so much that they don't recognize any difference between right and wrong. Indeed, many have very strong ideas of right and wrong. It's just that they live by what sociologist Elijah Anderson has called "the code of the street"—a code that is rooted in some conclusions about survival that they form from their experience, and in what they are taught explicitly or implicitly by parents and other adults (e.g., older gang members), peers, and siblings.

Robert Tallman is a case in point, but hardly unique. When he moved from one neighborhood to another, it was like exchanging the frying pan for the fire, so consistent was his experience of community violence. For example, he reported that when he was thirteen, he and his brother were "jumped" by five boys who "saw we were the new kids on the block and wanted to show off by attacking us." As he grew up, Robert's experiences at school fed the escalating pattern of aggressive antisocial behavior in his community. At school he responded to bullying with preemptive assaults to protect himself and establish an identity as a powerful figure in his peer group. In doing so, he became a target for others who were trying to establish their own power. It was an arms race of sorts, one that started with fists and ended with guns.

This same approach to preemptive assault worked on the streets, where he sought to gain power by carrying a gun, engaging in reckless behavior, gang-related violence, and drug dealing. And it worked when he was sent to juvenile detention facilities and, ultimately, jail. Of his time being locked up, he said, "I smile at them. But I've been through too much to let anybody take advantage of me. I don't mind getting beat up if that's what it takes."

Surrounded by Enemies

Like Robert, John Mendoza* learned early to see himself as a kind of urban soldier, surrounded by enemies, and to see aggression as the measure of a man. And as a result, like Robert, he was facing possible execution for murder when I met with him in March, 2012, in Dallas, Texas. When John was a child, his father would drive around with him in the car and stop when he saw a group of kids, often kids older and bigger than John. He would order John to fight these other kids, and threaten to beat him if he failed to win. John's father was physically abusive to John's mother, and his home was itself a kind of war zone of domestic violence.

Like a soldier learning the ropes on the battlefield, John conquered his fear through his own aggressive behavior and assertion of power, and by putting together a worldview in his head that rationalized it. He told me, "Whatever don't kill you makes you stronger" and "I am ruthless when it comes to fighting. If you don't strike first, you show weakness, and that is the worst thing there is." For kids like John Mendoza, the war zone on the streets is amplified and reinforced by the war zone at home, and results from brain research validate that this has neurological effects. My friend and colleague, psychiatrist Bruce Perry, was a pioneer in understanding this process by which young brains are "incubated in terror."

The frequent finding that violent populations have different patterns of neurobiology is often taken as evidence of congenital, genetic differences between these groups. This misunderstanding flows from the (faulty) assumption that the brain a person has is the brain that person was destined to have genetically. It's not unlike the common misunderstanding that group differences in IQ result simply from genetic factors, when the truth is that these differences are principally the result of environmental factors interacting with genetic factors in a variety of ways. As researchers Michael Rutter, Terrie Moffitt, and Avshalom Caspi have demonstrated in their work, although differences among individuals within the same environment may be related to genetic factors, differences between groups are mostly the result of experience, not genetic destiny.

Bruce Perry pioneered efforts to bring this kind of understanding to the dynamic relationships between early experience with violence and brain development. While a common, simplistic model suggests that correlations between brain function and violence reflect a one-way causal relationship—brains cause violence and brain development results from genetic factors—Perry counters that "nothing could be further from the truth." Rather, brains develop and reconfigure in response to experience, and perhaps only then produce effects that manifest as violence. As Perry puts it, "Experience, not genetics, results in the critical neurobiological factors associated with violence."

Many of the most important brain issues affecting killers with a war zone mentality are related to their thinking processes—most notably, the issues with "executive function" I discussed in chapter 1 when trying to understand the choices killers make. Living in a war zone distorts brain development because chronic fear and deprivation lead to an overdevelopment of the more primitive parts of the brain and underdevelopment of the most sophisticated part of the brain—the cortex, involved in complex cognitive functions and reasoning. In chapter 4, I will attend to the issues of emotional damage, which, like all human functions, take place in the brain. As we will see, these issues are dangerously important in the emotional ("affective") lives of killers. Here, the point is that living in a war zone redirects brain development for the particular survival and status issues demonstrated in that environment. Operating within such a framework, the youth views and responds to the world much as a young soldier in a combat zone would, but without the support of the prosocial adult leadership, chain of command, and ethic of responsibility that soldiers have (at least most of the time). Indeed, recent research reveals that the brains of children exposed to violence react much the same way as soldiers' in combat.

Eamon McCrory and his colleagues conducted their research on war zone brains in London. The goal was to compare the brain function of soldiers exposed to violent combat with that of children exposed to domestic violence (admittedly, not exactly the community violence in which we are most interested, but close enough for our purposes here, as Perry and others have noted). In this research, the participants were asked to look at pictures of faces. Importantly, both groups were *not* asked to identify the emotion present in the face, but only whether the face was masculine or feminine. Thus, any "emotional" reaction would be a result of viewing the faces without guidance or suggestion from the researchers.

Using a "functional MRI brain scan (fMRI)," the researchers found that when both groups (combat veterans and children who lived with domestic violence) viewed pictures of angry faces, there was increased brain activity (compared with the brains of children from nonviolent homes and soldiers without combat experience) in two specific brain areas: the anterior insula and the amygdala. These areas are associated with "threat detection" (and anxiety as well) according to neuroscientists, and, as the study's authors point out, appear to be the result of living in a state of hypervigilance. This is important, because one of the key elements of the war zone mentality is extreme sensitivity to threat (hypervigilance—being highly attuned to verbal and physical threats). If just seeing angry faces sets off the threat response in a person, then that individual is already halfway there when it comes to the war zone mentality. Couple that with a belief system that validates aggression, and you have a high probability of responding to a perceived threat with aggression (including preemptive assault—"get them before they get you"). These two factors often provide the basis for rapid escalation of conflicts in a kind of vicious spiral of aggression, as seen in Robert Tallman's case.

GROWING UP IN A WAR ZONE

Stephen Buka, Felton Earls, and their colleagues with the Harvard University Project on Human Development have reviewed the available evidence and report that in some communities, only 1 percent of the residents will witness a murder over the course of their lifetime. In other communities, the figure is 43 percent. The figures for witnessing a stabbing range from 9 to 55 percent, and for witnessing a shooting from 4 to 70 percent. Not surprisingly, homicide is the leading cause of death of adolescents in the communities with the highest overall levels of violence. What is more, Mark Rosenberg, former head of the Centers for Disease Control's National Center for Injury Prevention and Control, and his colleagues have estimated that for every one fatal assault, there may be one hundred nonfatal assaults (a ratio that has increased as modern medical trauma technology saves more and more people whose injuries could be life threatening). It is little wonder that brains develop capacities for "overdeveloped threat detection" when threat is such an important part of the fabric of life.

In communities like those in which Robert Tallman and many other individuals I have interviewed grew up, most (perhaps two-thirds) report having witnessed a shooting by the time they are in elementary school. In these areas, by the time they reach high school, a third have witnessed a murder. The numbers only go up after that, to the forty-three percent (or higher) noted above. This high level of violence constitutes a kind of war zone. To many who are unfamiliar with the psychological and social realities of growing up in a community war zone, the adaptations that kids exhibit often seem pathological. But in fact, in most cases, they are normal adaptations to an abnormal social environment. It's the environments that are "crazy," not the kids—*at least initially*. Of course, the pressures of this life can and do drive some people crazy.

The war zone manifests in many ways in the lives of children. When I first lived and worked in Chicago (from 1985 to 1994), my colleagues and I wrote a book titled *Children in Danger: Coping with the Consequences of Community Violence*. Preparing for that book, we heard reports of young children who lived in some of the city's most violent communities playing a game they called "funeral" in the blocks corner in their kindergarten and preschool classrooms. After building a coffin out of the wooden blocks, each child would take on a familiar role—dead kid, grieving parents, pastor, and mourners.

We heard Head Start staff talk about their classroom management techniques for "when the shooting starts," and 69 percent of them reported that they themselves had unresolved issues of trauma related to community violence. In 1992, the *Chicago Tribune* committed itself to do an in-depth story about every kid under the age of fourteen killed in the city during a twelve-month period. The number killed was fifty-seven.

Now, twenty years later, again living and working in Chicago, I hear the current versions of these same stories. On September 19, 2013, the *Tribune* published a special report on each of the children twelve years of age and younger who were shot and killed in Chicago over a two-year period. The number was seven. Twelve and younger. Shot and killed. Over a two-year period. It's better than it was twenty years ago, but little kids are still playing funeral.

These kids were then, and are now, simply doing what children everywhere do, namely using play as a way to make sense of what they have experienced and observed. But they live in communities where attending the funeral of a child or teen killed on the streets is not that unusual. Once again, it is not evidence of psychological pathology in the children, but a normal response to an abnormal social environment. Among teenagers, this striving to deal with abnormal social reality often manifests as self-medication with drugs and alcohol. It manifests as a profound fatalism about their prospects of living to and through adulthood. It also manifests as a reckless and aggressive bravado, and as participation in gangs as social vehicles for protection, access to resources, and identity.

You can see and hear the war zone mentality in some of the videos these young people make and post on YouTube (in a practice called "internet banging"). In one such video that I viewed (on YouTube) in 2013 as part of a murder case, allies of a murdered gang member in Los Angeles used a rap-music format to commemorate his death and spell out, in chilling detail, their plans for violent revenge. And in a bracing demonstration of just how much like real war zones the lives of such inner-city youths are, some military veterans from Iraq and Afghanistan have posted their own commemorative videos in which they, too, rap about their plans for revenge.

Once immersed in this war zone mentality, youths act tough to ward off attacks from others (and to enhance their status with peers). The adolescent toward whom such gestures are directed is already hypervigilant, perceives even more threat than may be intended by the first youth, and thus responds aggressively (often with the hope of causing the other adolescent to back down). The first youth perceives the threat and responds with increased aggression. The cycle continues, and the war zone mentality flourishes.

ADOLESCENT BRAINS FEED THE ESCALATION OF VIOLENCE

The upward spiral of aggression can be particularly strong in youths, whose very adolescence puts them at special risk. Adolescents are prone to make errors in social perception linked to both their limited life experience and the relative immaturity of their brains, in precisely the areas that are involved in perceiving the emotions of others and making informed and reasonable judgments in response. Psychologists Laurence Steinberg and Elizabeth Scott reviewed this evidence and came to the conclusion that as a result of these limitations, adolescents should be treated legally as "less guilty by reason of adolescence." I will return to these issues in more detail in chapter 5, when I address the special issues faced by adolescents in the criminal justice system.

All of this brain-related misprocessing by adolescents occurs in a cultural context, of course. The more the culture surrounding violent communities—and embedded in the consciousness of the parents and kids who live there—validates elements of the war zone mentality, the more likely it is to produce the moral damage that I hear in so many killers. One such cultural element is the "culture of honor." For our purposes, perhaps the most studied and relevant example of this in the United States has its origins in the Old South (the eleven states that formed the Confederate States of America during the Civil War in the mid-1860s).

THE SOUTHERN CULTURE OF HONOR

It has long been known that murder is more common in the southern part of the United States than in other parts of the country. Over the ten years from 2001 to 2011, for example, the average rate of murder in southern states was 6.5 per 100,000 people, while for the rest of the country it was 4.6 per 100,000. During that same ten-year period, none of the southern states was among the twelve states with the lowest murder rates. Virginia was the only southern state that came close, presumably because among the southern states, Virginia has been most influenced by an influx of northerners (and the northern part of Virginia, where most of those northern immigrants live, has become very distinct from the southern half, politically and culturally). Again looking at the same ten-year period, the South contributed half of the twelve states with the highest murder rates. Looking back in history to the early twentieth century (before World War I precipitated migration into the South from the North and from the South to the North, thus diluting the effect), southern murder rates were at least double those in the North.

In his classic exploration of homicide in America, *All God's Children*, Fox Butterfield laid out the origins and consequences of this cultural phenomenon in our country. Simply put, individuals who are immersed in the culture of honor and have it embedded in their consciousness are hypersensitive to disrespect, social status, and reputation. Historically, these individuals disproportionately grew up in the South. Historians have traced this southern culture of honor to its disproportionate settlement by immigrants from Scotland, who brought it with them from their homeland. Although it stretches historical accuracy quite a bit, it is still useful to recall the Scottish thirteenth-century national folk hero William Wallace, as portrayed in the 1995 film *Braveheart*. Wallace sought to protect and avenge the honor of his family and countrymen during the English invasion, and in so doing provided a vivid sense of the role of honor in traditional Scottish culture.

I should mention that when I lectured in Scotland in 2000 and touched on the link between Scots immigrants to the American South and the problem of violence, this was reported in some local newspapers under the headline "American Blames Scotland for America's Violence Problem." Then the emails started coming in from Scots, the general theme of which was "It's England's fault for invading us!"

The Southern Culture of Honor and Black America

The southern culture of honor is particularly relevant for understanding the demography of killing in the United States today, because this creation of White southerners who had their roots in Scotland was absorbed by the African American population in the South during and after slavery. Fox Butterfield's analysis makes this clear. When coupled with the corrosive social and emotional effects of racism, it has played a significant role in the highly disproportionate rate of homicides committed by African Americans today. As I noted earlier, this rate is some eight times higher than for White Americans (a difference that is reduced somewhat, but not eliminated, when the effects of income and education are taken out of the equation) and is mostly "Black on Black" crime—accounting for more than 90 percent of the homicides committed by African Americans. How does the culture of honor translate into murder?

Using data from major national surveys, Richard Nisbett and Dov Cohen have shown that people in the South did not support violence generically more than people from other regions of the country (for example, in their response to statements like "People only learn through violence"). The difference was limited to "violence used for self-protection, to respond to an insult, or to socialize children." This included agreeing with statements like "A man has the right to kill to defend his house." They were more likely to approve of a man punching a stranger who "was drunk and bumped into the man and his wife on the street." It's easy to see how this resonates with the war zone mentality as it exists in so many of the killers I have listened to. But it goes further, as it does with the killers. These same individuals (southern White males) also stigmatized men who did *not* respond with violence in such situations. They said that nonviolence in such a situation means they "are not much of a man" if they fail to fight or shoot the person who has challenged or affronted them.

Most of the African American population in the United States has its origins in the South. According to the U.S. Census Bureau, 90 percent of the African American population lived in the South in 1910, prior to the great migration stimulated by the need for workers in northern factories during World War I (by 2010, only 55 percent of the African American population lived in the South). They brought with them southern (originally *White* southern) attitudes about honor. What is more, these attitudes continued to hold sway even generations later, passed along from parents and other adults to children who may never have even visited the South.

The Culture of Honor Takes Root

You can hear these beliefs echoed in many of the African American killers to whom I have listened over the years, most of whom had their family origins in the South. Psychologists have demonstrated that behaviors that were once originally under the control of specific reinforcements can, over time, develop a kind of self-sustaining psychological momentum and thus no longer need those original reinforcements to continue. In this way, they develop what is called "functional autonomy." I believe this has happened in many African American communities with respect to the southern culture of honor: they are no longer located in the region that gave rise to this culture and reinforced it, but they continue to promote it in the behaviors and beliefs they model and teach their children.

The Daniel Wellington Case

Thirty-year-old Daniel Wellington* was southern in background, though he grew up in the north, in Detroit. He avoided the death penalty by pleading guilty to murdering James and Jennifer Fortune, an elderly couple in their seventies who surprised him while he was robbing their house while visiting relatives in Omaha, Nebraska, in 2001. As he walked by their house, he thought it looked nice enough to contain valuables and that no one was home; he needed some money and decided to rob the house. When the Fortunes interrupted his robbery attempt, he beat them to death with a stick he found in the garage and made off with money and items to sell.

In return for his guilty plea, he received a 110-year sentence on February 10, 2004. When I interviewed him on November 5, 2003, I heard a lot about his war zone mentality and how it grew in his mind and heart. Like so many who share his experiences of the community war zone, he conveyed a fatalistic acceptance of his world, telling me, "that's just the way it is; there's nothing you can do about it." Even when he was very young, he understood that he was bound by the "common law" (as he called it) of the dog-eat-dog world of threat and counterthreat, assault and retaliation, that he lived in: "You had a gun or belonged to a gang to survive."

He told me, "In my world I knew that if you were timid you got walked over. I got my first gun for $125 with money I got from selling drugs. I did not have to be timid once I got a gun. . . . At school I figured out that once somebody learns they can get over on you, they are going to keep doing it, so you hit first to protect yourself. . . . I don't like to overpower people, but if you aren't going to help yourself I'm not going to help you." War zones often provoke a ruthless ethic of self-preservation. When the Fortunes surprised him while he was robbing their house and tried to call the police, he felt threatened and responded "accordingly," although to someone without his life experience and cultural framework his actions seem crazy and callous.

But crazy and callous is where the culture of honor leads. John C. Calhoun, senator and seventh vice president of the United States, came from a Scots-Irish family, and it is reported that as part of his socialization as a southern male, his mother taught him that when insulted or disrespected by someone in the community, he must either kill that person or die trying and be brought home dead—otherwise she would disown him. Calhoun was born in 1782. Born two centuries later, Robert Tallman said that his mother taught him that honor and respect were the most important things in life, and that she would disown him if he failed to meet the test of honor. As a result of that teaching, he will spend the rest of his life in prison.

The war zone mentality and the culture of honor that is often midwife to its birth are not just words and ideas. Research by Dov Cohen and his colleagues shows that a whole system of behavior and beliefs becomes wired into the brains of those who are immersed in this culture. Their 1996 study titled "Insult, Aggression, and the Southern Culture of Honor: An 'Experimental Ethnography'" helps to show how this happens. In this study, the responses of northern and southern young males were compared when "A confederate of the experimenter bumps into the unsuspecting participant as he walks down a hallway and calls the participant an 'asshole.'" For a start, the results showed that the southerners were mostly angry after the bump in the hallway, whereas the northerners were mostly amused. This study included only White males, by the way, which highlights the fact that the South's culture of honor is first and foremost a cultural, not racial, phenomenon.

In the first experiment, the researchers asked the young men to complete various fill-in-the-blank tasks. These included completing a story that starts at a party when another man makes a pass at the respondent's date. The purpose was to see if the anger they felt over the confrontation in the hallway would carry over to later expressions of feelings. It did. The researchers reported that "If southerners were insulted, they were much more likely to end the scenario with violence, whereas northerners were unaffected by the insult. Seventy-five percent of insulted southerners completed this scenario with events in which the man injured or threatened to injure his challenger, whereas only 20% of control southerners (who were not disrespected in the earlier hallway encounter) did so. . . ." Northerners were unaffected by the manipulation, being somewhat less likely to conclude this scenario with violence if they had been insulted (41 percent versus 55 percent). These results speak to the fact that the problem is not that southerners are more disposed to violence in general, but only in response to the provocation of insult and disrespect. Their baseline aggression was *lower* than that of the northerners (20 percent versus 55 percent).

In the second experiment (using the same provocation, being bumped into and verbally insulted), the researchers measured the level of physiological arousal by assessing cortisol (a hormone connected with high levels of stress, anxiety, and arousal) and testosterone (a hormone associated with aggression and dominance behavior). The insulted southerners showed higher levels of physiological arousal in response to the provocation: cortisol levels rose 79 percent in insulted southerners and 33 percent in insulted northerners; testosterone levels rose 12 percent in insulted southerners and 6 percent in insulted northerners.

The third experiment employed a variety of measures to assess the effect of the bump and insult on how aggressive, dominant, and "macho" the men were. Overall, the study found that "southerners who were insulted in front of others saw themselves as diminished in masculine reputation and status. Perhaps partly as a result, the insult produced more aggressive or domineering behavior. Although un-insulted southerners were, if anything, more polite than northerners, insulted southerners were much more aggressive than any other group."

Dangerous Social Maps That Result

All told, the three experiments described above point provocatively to why the war zone mentality is so dangerous and why it is so common among killers. The belief system (culture of honor) becomes embedded in the psychology of those who learn it from parents, peers, siblings, and community opinion leaders. The psychology (perception of insult and threat to self-esteem) translates into different arousal patterns (higher cortisol and testosterone levels), which lead to more dominance, aggression, and macho posturing. This kind of brain effect is why, according to science writer Virginia Hughes, neuropsychologists like Stephen Morse and Rubin Gur say that "People don't kill people; brains kill people." I would break it down this way: "Brains develop social maps in response to human experience; social maps guide the way to action." It's less elegant, but probably more true.

The dangers presented by the war zone mentality are compounded by the fact that young adolescents have difficulty interpreting the emotions of others accurately as a result of their immature brains (as demonstrated by the research that Steinberg and Scott reviewed in their important 2003 article "Less Guilty by Reason of Adolescence," to which I referred earlier). Add fists, knives, and guns to the equation, and the result can be lethal aggression, sometimes arising from what, to an outsider, would appear to be "small" provocations.

As I will show in chapter 7, it matters what types of weapons are available. Although the southern culture of honor has its origins in Scotland, the relative absence of guns in Scottish conflicts means that the youth homicide rate there is lower than it would be if the gun situation there were more like it is

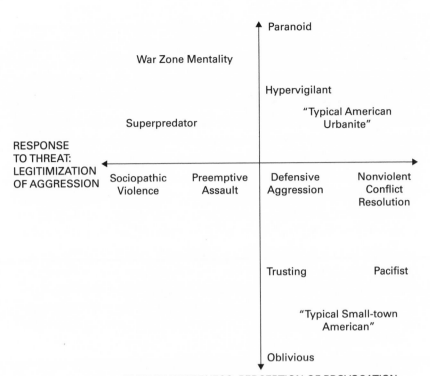

here. As it is, Glasgow is the most violent city in the United Kingdom and is known as "the knifing capital of Europe." As a colleague in Scotland once told me, "If our kids carried guns at the rate your kids do, we'd be number one in youth homicide." Things have shifted a bit over the past decade and a half, but in 1990, among countries not at war or engaged in social breakdown, Scotland was number two in youth homicide rates, the United States being number one. New Zealand was number three, and when I visited I was not surprised to find a culture that seemed cloned from Scotland.

I have attempted to represent the social maps that flow from the war zone mentality in the above figure. Note that there are two dimensions at work here. The horizontal dimension is the "legitimization of aggression." At one end is the pure pacifist, who will not justify violence for any reason. At the other is the psychopath, who justifies violence under any and all circumstances that meet his needs or fulfill his goals. Most of us are somewhere in between. Of course, given the exigencies of conflict and the frequent neurological problems killers have that manifest as difficulties with "executive functioning," in any specific incident a killer may not (in fact probably doesn't) engage in a prolonged, rational decision-making process. But the legitimization of violence is operating, even at an implicit level.

The vertical dimension is the "perception of provocation." Once again, while some individuals are at the extreme ends of this continuum, most of us are somewhere in between—neither "paranoid," in the sense of perceiving threat when it is not there, nor "oblivious" by virtue of failing to see threat when it is present. These different social maps are evident when most killers have time to reflect and articulate the rationale for what they did (as in the case of being interviewed by me months or years after the crime).

My point is that growing up in a war zone community tends to move kids toward the upper left-hand corner of figure 1, toward preemptive assault (the higher end of the legitimization-of-aggression continuum) *and* toward hypervigilance (the higher end of the perception-of-provocation continuum). You can hear this when you listen to killers explain their social maps, their understanding of the social environment.

THE INHIBITION AGAINST KILLING AND
THE WAR ZONE MENTALITY

It is worth noting that the war zone mentality has consequences for the inhibitions that restrain most of us from acting on our aggressive impulses. As military psychologist Dave Grossman reports in his book *On Killing,* most human beings—perhaps 85 percent of men—come complete with a natural inhibition against killing others that, in World War II, translated into only 15 percent of soldiers in their first combat engagement firing their weapons at an enemy they could see in front of them. This inhibition works against the violent behavioral implications of the war zone mentality, of course. But it is not fixed and immutable. It can be neutralized.

Grossman reports that after World War II, research revealed that simply learning to shoot at bull's-eye targets (as was the norm until then in military training) left the inhibition against killing intact and thus incapacitated soldiers when they faced combat. Military psychologists eventually determined that the inhibition could be broken down through training, so that most soldiers could fire their weapons at the enemy soldiers in their line of sight. They found that modern point-and-shoot video games were the most effective methodology for accomplishing this.

However, surviving combat experience could accomplish the same result. What I hear when I listen to murderers is that kids who grow up in a community war zone have their own "combat experience" (to complement whatever "training" they get from playing violent video games). And this combat experience provides a parallel "desensitization" process that prepares them to kill when their war zone mentality tells them it would be "doing what you gotta do." Robert Tallman, Junior Mercedez, and many others have lived out this scenario. James Jackson is another example.

The James Jackson Case

Eighteen-year-old James Jackson* grew up in a social environment in Chicago in which he was exposed to a high level of violence, both inside his family and in the larger community. In his family, he experienced abuse and neglect. His mother beat him with a belt about twice a month, and when he was sixteen she hit him on the side of the head with a vase and he was taken to a hospital. His family was involved in chronic antisocial and violent behavior. For example, there was an incident in which his favorite uncle, Bobby, came home bleeding with a cut on his forehead from an attack or fight, and the family response was to stand guard in front of the house with a pistol and an Uzi. In the period between his ninth and twelfth birthdays, James witnessed two shootings firsthand.

When James was ten, two teenagers came to his neighborhood and a fight began. One of the teens was dragged out of a car and beaten. When the second boy got out with a gun, he was attacked (after shooting someone in the hip). Both boys were beaten unconscious and went to the hospital in an ambulance. When James was twelve, a boy he was with was shot while they were hanging out together at a local basketball court. These and other experiences confirmed in James an appreciation for the nature of living in a war zone. He learned that when people were shooting, "you just found you somewhere to get and find a hiding spot a bullet ain't going to penetrate. Gunshots could happen any time, you could just be chillin' and hear gun shots." James knew several individuals who were killed by gunfire: fifteen-year-old Charlie, twenty-one-year-old "Spud," fourteen-year-old KG (whose brother had been shot when James was eight or nine), seventeen-year-old "Deerboy" (who was killed in retaliation for KG's death), and sixteen-year-old "BoyBoy."

James experienced all this without the benefit of a strong and loving father to guide him: his father was incarcerated from the time James was seven (for cocaine dealing). What is more, his mother herself had a long criminal history and neglected James. This lack of positive strong parental role models in his life left him feeling particularly vulnerable, and (not surprisingly) seeking alternatives to his parents. He found one alternative to his cold and rejecting home in peers, most of whom were in gangs. He found another in his athletic coaches, who recognized his talent as a basketball player and helped him gain admission to a prestigious magnet school far from his home neighborhood, where he was enrolled in the college prep curriculum. He grew up in the war zone, immersed in the culture of honor, which was embedded in his consciousness. As a result, he became hypersensitive to disrespect, social status, and reputation, even though he was attending a magnet school that put him in touch with the larger society outside the war zone in which he lived.

At a party one night after a basketball game, James's seventeen-year-old friend D'Angelo was threatened by two older boys from a rival neighborhood. James stepped up to defend him and the honor of his neighborhood. Given his childhood and adolescent experiences, it appears that joining in the fight was a kind of "solidarity" gesture on James's part, in recognition that as a "prep school kid," he was now distancing himself from his home community and peer group and needed to assert his loyalty to them. He and his friend D'Angelo fought well: they beat the rival teenagers to death.

A recent ethnographic study of inner-city African American male youths who move beyond the educational and vocational prospects of their peers by attending an elite charter school supports this interpretation. In that study, Desmond Patton found that such youths must engage in a complex negotiation between the two worlds they inhabit, and cultivate protective relationships in the old to permit their safe participation in the new. For example, he reports that "While the presence of gangs was mentioned by participants as a factor of an unsafe area, participants have figured out that having relationships with gang members is an important aspect of navigating a violent neighborhood. These relationships are complicated for some African American males who are motivated and engaged in school but fully understand the value and benefit of being connected to the neighborhood."

In the present case, James felt the need to reassure people that his new identity (as an upwardly mobile prep-school student) would not constitute betrayal of his old friends and old identity (as a "homie"). Patton's research speaks to this point: "Most participants in this study expressed a need for two identities: one that can easily navigate a chronically violent neighborhood and one that is productive within a peaceful school environment."

Given that James had a history of aggressive behavior linked to his old identity (his records indicate numerous fights, most of them tied to his social network and identity in his neighborhood), the present case can be viewed as a kind of "backsliding" on his part. In the presence of his old friends and their shared life in the war zone, he "reverted" to his old identity and pattern of behavior. It seems clear that he did this, at least in part, to prove to his old friends that he was still one of them, that he could still be counted on to be "honorable" in the war zone.

The community experiences of kids like James growing up in the war zone stimulate and reinforce the mentality that comes with the additional burden of being immersed in the culture of honor. But we must remember that many boys and young men "graduate" from the war zone neighborhood to the war zone prison as part of their development. One in ten youths of color enters the juvenile detention system. One in three Black men will be imprisoned at some point in his life. Whether it happens in adolescence or in early adulthood, it means that a very large number of individuals who come from the urban war zone will face the threat of homosexual rape, an experience of dishonor that can propel them along the path to becoming a killer.

DYING FOR HONOR RATHER THAN BEING RAPED

For adolescent boys and young men, homosexual rape is a matter of existential honor, regardless of their geographic heritage, but particularly if they come to the experience with the ethos of the war zone and the culture of honor. Many say they would rather die than be dishonored in this way, as it represents a devastating attack on their very manhood. Rape is pervasive in the jails and prisons that are so often part of the socialization experience of killers, and thus it contributes to developing the war zone mentality that leads to murder.

A 2001 Human Rights Watch report estimated that at least one hundred and forty thousand inmates had been raped while incarcerated in the preceding year. Of course, it's hard to know how much to trust this or any other estimate, because "official" reports are few and far between (numbering in the hundreds each year, while the estimates of actual occurrences number in the tens of thousands). Most studies have concluded that the risks are greater in jails and detention centers than in prisons. This contributes to the concern that young offenders are most at risk (and thus vulnerable to early assault that puts them on a negative developmental pathway). When the Human Rights Watch report offered a list of risk factors for becoming a rape victim, "youth" was the first factor listed.

In a survey of 1,788 male inmates in midwestern prisons reported by Cindy and David Struckman-Johnson in *The Prison Journal,* about 21 percent claimed they had been coerced or pressured into sexual activity of some sort during their incarceration, and 7 percent claimed that they had been raped in their current facility. With almost two and a half million men in prison in the United States each year, that works out to about one hundred and seventy thousand rape victims in prison. It's hard to know which numbers to trust.

I can testify personally to the fact that prison sex is the most difficult issue to raise with incarcerated men. Rarely has a man admitted it to me directly (even when there were prison records confirming that he had been sexually assaulted). Some men choose to fight, even to death, to avoid such a sexual assault (with its concomitant humiliation), and thus risk injury, disfigurement, and even death to resist submission. For example, in the course of our interview prior to his murder trial, Robert Tallman said this of sexual assault in prison: "I can't understand how anybody can let that happen. I would fight to the death to prevent that." Some male prisoners choose what they believe to be the lesser of two evils and agree to be the sexual partners of more powerful inmates to avoid being raped—or beaten up or killed if they resist. This is a choice between two clear evils that few non-incarcerated men will ever have to make, no matter their views on honor.

I have interviewed young men who have made both choices. It's easy to make hypothetical choices about what one would or would not do if faced with this dilemma. I wonder if I would have the strength to make the "right" choice if I were incarcerated. I wonder, even, if there is any sense to the idea that there are "right" and "wrong" choices in such a situation, where either option is terrible. But when you are immersed in the culture of honor, the stakes are even higher than they would be otherwise, because when you are infused with the culture of honor, disrespect threatens you with psychic annihilation. From that perspective, injury, even death, is preferable to the psychological pain that comes with humiliation. Not surprisingly, being a young first-time offender who is victimized increases the odds that the same individual will become a perpetrator somewhere down the line.

Having been sexually assaulted as a juvenile while incarcerated, Danny Samson* developed such a traumatic aversion to the possibility of further victimization that he would preemptively attack anyone in prison who he thought was even contemplating assaulting him. His record was littered with such assaults. Each was a choice, a choice to avoid the humiliation of unwanted sex at any cost. And this choice is but one of many linked to honor that determine the quality of life for inmates and their prospects for the future.

Indeed, this is the key to psychiatrist James Gilligan's analysis of prison violence: incarcerated men have little to live for but their honor, and thus shame means nonexistence. Therefore, protecting your honor is literally a matter of life and death. You will kill for it. If you fail to protect your honor and don't die trying, you are at risk for taking your life, because without your honor, life is not worth living. But if you survive being raped and survive the loss of your honor, there will be hell to pay when you reenter the world outside the prison (as most incarcerated men do at some point).

WHEN THE WAR ZONE MENTALITY BECOMES A WAY OF LIFE

When moral damage leads to a chronic pattern of aggression, criminal behavior against society, and a general unwillingness or inability to respect the rights of others, it may be "diagnosed" by mental health professionals as "antisocial personality disorder." By some estimates, 25 percent of the inmates in prison qualify for this label. Some of the killers I have listened to fit this description (and certainly have this diagnosis in their records). However, most of these individuals are not "crazy" in the legal sense that they have lost touch with reality completely. It's just that they have some very bad habits of thinking and behavior when it comes to their conception of and commitment to standards of right and wrong.

In some extreme cases, however, the moral damage is so profound that it crosses the line from psychologically "normal" to become "abnormal." I identified this in figure 1 as "sociopathic." Sociopaths are completely beyond the normal moral world of human beings, in the sense that they don't see any point to moral limits. Thus, they are truly "amoral" (meaning without morals). As I see it, a subset of these individuals are more properly understood as "psychopaths," meaning that they don't have the normal emotional reactions common to human life. Whether this arises from particularly brutal and dehumanizing experiences in the community war zone or from horrific abusive treatment in their families, it reflects underlying problems with empathy, the ability to feel what others feel. This, in turn, can have both social and psychological origins and can be related to underlying genetic defects, to brains that are not like normal brains in their ability to "get" ordinary human connections and relationships.

British psychiatrist John Bowlby recounted the story of seeing a little boy in his home office who demonstrated this inability to "get it." Called out of the room to take a phone call, Bowlby left the little boy alone in the room, with a fire blazing in the fireplace. When Bowlby returned he discovered that the little boy had been conducting a science experiment to answer the question "What burns?" In his efforts to answer this question, the boy had thrown some paper in the fire. Paper burns. He had then thrown a piece of wood on the fire. Wood burns. He had then thrown Bowlby's cat on the fire. Cats burn. The point is that the boy didn't "get" the difference between objects and sentient beings. I think this is key to understanding psychopaths.

Sociopaths have developed some terrible "moral habits," but most are not truly psychopaths (in that they have the mental capacity to learn to be more normally moral). Some researchers (like neuroscientist Joseph Newman) have argued that a better way to categorize these issues is to contrast psychopathy with "externalizing." The difference is that while an antisocial lifestyle and impulsivity are common to both, the "callous, unemotional" traits of psychopaths differentiate them from the externalizing disorders characteristic of sociopaths (i.e., antisocial personality disorder, substance abuse/dependence) and externalizing personality traits (e.g., little self-restraint).

This broader pattern of negativity is much more common than psychopathy (in the sense of utter lack of empathy and genuine human connection). I believe it also provides the basis for recognizing the existence of what might be called "prosocial psychopaths"—individuals who put their particular unempathic nature in the service of society, as that special brand of cops, soldiers, lawyers, politicians, and business people (and, yes, psychologists and psychiatrists), who can do society's most horrible business without moral and emotional qualms. This differentiates them from sociopaths, who are, by definition, engaged in chronic antisocial behavior (and who may well merit the "antisocial personality disorder" diagnosis they characteristically receive).

The vagaries of definition, assessment, and sampling make it all but impossible to be sure of any estimate of the prevalence of psychopathy and sociopathy. But experts like Christopher Patrick (editor of the *Handbook of Psychopathy*) argue that some 20 percent of the prison population are identified as sociopaths (recognizing that the common use of "psychopath" and "sociopath" interchangeably makes it hard to know just how frequently the narrower definition of "psychopath" is met by prisoners).

Living outside the Normal Limits of Morality

Whatever its origins in a particular case, this particular form of moral damage is scary to be with when it reveals itself. When I interviewed Tim Bankovic* in 2005, he was awaiting a retrial for the 1997 murder that had landed him on death row in Pennsylvania. I listened as the twenty-four-year-old told me, "Any man who shoots at me, I'm not crying at his funeral." Tim was so morally damaged that he lured two sandwich deliverymen—Ricky Pisano and Flavio Gargoni—to an abandoned house by calling in a fake order, and then shot them to death when they arrived.

A press report on the 2005 trial offered this assessment of how the jury weighed the evidence, including my testimony concerning Tim's childhood: "In all, the jury rejected ten of the mitigating factors and approved seven. Most of the ones it approved dealt with Mr. Bankovic's sense of neglect and rejection because his parents abandoned him before his twelfth birthday, leaving him with a grandfather whose life included gambling, crime, suicide attempts, infidelity and drug abuse."

Why did he do it? During Tim's first trial, there was testimony that he had planned the murders, in part, to establish the basis for becoming a hired killer and maybe even earn membership in the Mafia—good indicators of sociopathy. But truth be told, he shot those men to death so that he could experience the thrill of killing someone. When I interviewed him, Tim said, "I wanted to see how it felt to kill someone." Indeed. I felt I was in the presence of an antisocial psychopath. It was sad and scary.

Tim's history included the kind of experiences with the community war zone that often generate the war zone mentality, to be sure. But it went beyond that issue to include profound emotional damage as well (perhaps coupled, in his case, with some underlying biological problems with empathy). I think Tim meets the criteria for being called a "sociopath" and even a "psychopath" in the way I have differentially defined those terms. Underlying his chronic lack of moral lucidity is his emotional disconnection—the result, I believe, of the interaction of his temperament and the maltreatment he experienced as a child.

When Emotional Damage Joins Moral Damage

The moral damage that comes with the war zone mentality is a major risk factor for the developmental pathway that leads to murder, but it is not the only factor. It is all the more deadly when combined with emotional damage from the unresolved chronic trauma, parental rejection, and family disruption that are so characteristic of the lives of many, if not most, killers to whom I listen. For them, the moral damage cannot be contained as an intellectual problem—that is, having socially deviant moral reasoning that justifies hypervigilance and preemptive assault. Instead, it can interact with the rage and emotional instability that are often the products of the sad, tormented lives they have led in childhood and adolescence. Next we turn to that emotional damage—how it happens and how it propels killers into violence.

4

Emotional Damage

THE CONSEQUENCES OF UNRESOLVED TRAUMA

February 1, 2009: It's a sad young man who sits before me. At the request of the North Carolina Public Defender's Office, I have come to interview twenty-four-year-old Duke Jimenez* because he is charged with murder in the 2005 death of seventy-year-old Roberta Teebee and is facing a possible death penalty conviction. The grotesque savagery of the attack is a mystery. I have seen the autopsy report, and it indicates a total of twenty stab wounds. This has all the makings of a "rage" or "frenzy" killing, but such murders typically involve some intense passion arising from the relationship of killer to victim (at least in the killer's mind) or from psychotic delusion. In Jimenez's case, the puzzle is why his rage was turned on this victim—a very old woman in the neighborhood who surprised Duke while he was attempting to rob her house (in part to get money to meet child-support obligations to his son).

Duke had little history with his victim, beyond a mild confrontation about him urinating behind the woman's garden shed when he was drunk and taking a shortcut to get across town. Maybe that's where it started. What may seem like small acts of disrespect in the mainstream world often seem like profound insults in the mind of the war zone. The raw violence of the crime doesn't make sense—partly because, although this young man has a record of violent delinquency, he does not come across as hard and aggressive, like many of the men I have interviewed. Rather, he seems quiet and unassuming; if anything, he seems soft and passive. The combination of his intelligence and sensitivity, on the one hand, and his violent attack on Mrs. Teebee, on the other, seems a mystery. When asked, "What would be the most surprising thing people would learn about you if they knew you?" he responds that he is "a soft-hearted person" and says, "I'm not a tough guy. Mostly I'm a family guy." And yet the record shows that he has been involved in seriously violent behavior, culminating in the terrible homicide for which he is being sentenced.

It doesn't surprise me that in the records there is a note from a psychological evaluation conducted when he was fourteen that calls Duke "an enigma." But as the facts of Duke's young life emerge, the mystery becomes less opaque:

the rage evident in his "senseless" crime grows out of the emotional damage he sustained as a child and adolescent. His biological father abandoned him in infancy. The resentment he feels is intense and is evident in the fact that he prefers to be called by his middle name (Duke) rather than his first name (Juan) because it is his father's name. His mother was physically present in his life, but psychologically unavailable, and plagued by psychological difficulties of her own. She was hardly a consistent positive influence on his development. He tells me that he slept in his mother's bed until he was almost ten years old but was frequently displaced to the couch when she had men over for sex, often while she was drunk. Sometimes she received money from these men in exchange for that sex. It is naturally hard for him to recall and admit this, and he tries to minimize it—"it was just normal in our house," he says. After his older sister was murdered when Duke was seven years old, his mother told him not to talk about it: "We don't talk about those kind of things," she said. He reports that only recently did he learn from his mother that she had been raped by her half brother when she was a child. "She said that's the reason she drank. It helped her bottle things up, to avoid problems."

When "deep" issues are raised, Duke is sad and silent. When I ask if he thinks about suicide, he responds, "No," but then goes on to describe instances when he "wanted to get away from it all, to put an end to it. I wanted to but didn't." His sister did attempt suicide. Says Duke of this, "She cut and burned herself. There was blood everywhere." Duke tells me that he engaged in chronic marijuana and alcohol use from a relatively early age—apparently in part as a kind of self-medication to deal with his tormented feelings—and was high the night he killed Mrs. Teebee. He recalls being called "overly sensitive" as a child by family members. He says, "I was a shy kid." One of his earliest memories as a child is an incident in which he was alone in the house and a huge moth found its way into the living room. He reports, "It scared the life out of me so I ran out of the house and made my way to the bar where my Mom was drinking." This incident is emblematic of the psychological difficulty Duke faced: he was completely dependent on his mother psychologically, and yet he was simultaneously on his own emotionally (and physically) much of the time. This double bind of attachment difficulties—I am desperately attached to Mom, but Mom is behaviorally unreliable and often psychologically unavailable—is a breeding ground for difficulties with emotional regulation. Duke has these issues, and they produced the dangerous mix of blandness above the surface and rage beneath that was evident in his life before and during the crime for which he was being tried when I met him.

Duke reports of his childhood: "I blocked out many things. When my sister died it didn't really register. I didn't cry." There is evidence of his splitting off the bad stuff from the good stuff in his life. He says, "In school I was a kid loving life. At home all that stuff was going on and I thought it was normal." And "It's like there were two different things going on." Duke himself recognizes the "senselessness" of the crime, saying, "There was really no reason for it.

It doesn't make sense. I am pretty smart. I have common sense. Why would I do this?"

I leave the interview with the recognition that Duke has absorbed two decades of emotional damage that have trained him to be an enigma—not just to me, who wants to help him and to the world that can't understand his terrible, "senseless" crime, but to himself—perhaps most importantly and dangerously to himself.

Duke is emotionally damaged. One aspect of that damage is that he has trouble regulating his emotions. This derives in part from the fact that he is not consciously aware of the strong negative feelings that lie beneath the surface, under the façade he offers to the world. These feelings have broken through at times of stress, particularly when alcohol or drugs have impaired his mechanisms of self-control. He is a mystery to himself, and this is part of what makes him dangerous to others. He is not alone in this. Many killers suffer from problems with emotional regulation.

Psychologists James Gross and Ross Thompson define emotional regulation as "goal directed processes functioning to influence the intensity, duration, and type of emotion experienced. . . . Emotion regulation permits flexibility in emotional responding in accord with one's momentary as well as one's longer term goals in any given situation" (p. 401). Thus, emotional regulation is about how people manage their feelings, in both conscious and unconscious ways, in service of both moment-to-moment function and long-term life success. As modern methods have allowed investigators to observe brain functions much more directly than was possible in the past, the role of "implicit" (unconscious) emotional regulation has come to the fore, in tandem with the more obvious "explicit" regulation strategies and tactics that are employed consciously.

Of course, these issues have a long history in modern psychology, as Gross and Thompson acknowledge. For example, more than a hundred years ago, Sigmund Freud made emotional regulation (particularly regulation of anxiety) the cornerstone of his psychodynamic model of human behavior and development. But the limitations of psychoanalysis as a "research tool" marginalized efforts to move beyond Freud's hypotheses scientifically. Research-oriented psychologists abandoned these hypotheses to study more directly observable phenomena, using methods that lent themselves to increasingly sophisticated statistical analysis as the basis for verification (modern neuroscience's imaging studies being the most recent development). Psychoanalysts around the world kept at it, however, often with great energy and intelligence.

But their fundamental problems with verification cut them off from mainstream psychology.

My mentor, Urie Bronfenbrenner, was fond of saying of psychoanalysis, "Never has so much energy and intelligence been devoted to studying things which have never been proved to exist." In the interest of full disclosure, I should add that as a Catholic, I realize that something very similar could be said of Christianity. However, both psychoanalysis and spirituality have seen a resurgence of scientific status with innovations in the study of neuroscience. Two books exemplify this: Norman Doidge's *The Brain That Changes Itself* (in the case of psychoanalysis) and Mario Beauregard's *The Spiritual Brain* (in the case of spirituality).

In the twentieth century, psychologists tended to see the implicit elements of emotional regulation as a kind of opaque black box—they knew something important was happening there but were not well equipped to look inside that box. But twenty-first-century developments in neuroscience are changing that. As my colleague, psychologist Rebecca Silton, puts it,

> There is a very fine line between Freud's notion of the unconscious and behavioral/cognitive approaches to learning and memory. Behavioralism involves theories about implicit learning, and how this learning shapes behavior is not always accessible at a conscious level. Similarly, cognitive approaches involve theories that draw heavily on implicit learning. For example, Beck has theorized that attention, memory, and interpretation biases are guided by cognitive schema (shaped by environmental experiences) that are not readily accessible to conscious awareness. These cognitive biases often occur implicitly (i.e., often within 500 milliseconds of stimuli presentation in laboratory studies). After these biases are observed in an individual, they can be adjusted through therapy. It is still not evident whether therapeutic approaches need to be administered explicitly, and retraining of implicit attentional biases is currently being rigorously studied as a new method to treat depression.

As Gross and Thompson see it, after reviewing the available relevant neuroscience research, "It is now firmly established that willfully and consciously employed emotional regulatory strategies can reliably alter the course of emotional responding, but it is also apparent that people do not and will not pursue conscious regulatory goals unless they have the motivation and the ability to do so" (p. 408).

Where do these problems come from? We know from Norman Doidge's review of the evidence from modern neuroscience that human brains develop in a dynamic relationship with experience. Human brains are malleable across the life span, not just in childhood and adolescence: this is called "neuroplasticity." Thus, the brains of the killers I listen to reflect both what they started with (genetic factors) and what they experienced (environmental factors).

Adrian Raine and his colleagues conducted a study comparing emotional regulation in three groups: "affective" murderers (those who kill in a state of heightened emotion), "predatory" murderers (who kill to achieve some egocentric goal), and a control group of nonmurderers. They found that the affective murderers demonstrated several significant problems with emotional regulation, whereas the predatory murderers were more like the "normal" in their capacity to regulate emotions but still manifested significant problems in the way their brains processed emotionally important information.

Their conclusion: "Results support the hypothesis that emotional, unplanned impulsive murderers are less able to regulate and control aggressive impulses generated from subcortical structures due to deficient prefrontal regulation. It is hypothesized that excessive subcortical activity predisposes to aggressive behaviour, but that while predatory murderers have sufficiently good prefrontal functioning to regulate these aggressive impulses, the affective murderers lack such prefrontal control over emotion regulation." Thus, we might say that the affective murderers (like Duke Jimenez) are acting primarily from a place of emotional damage, whereas predatory murderers (like Robert Tallman) are acting primarily from a place of moral damage as I outlined that concept in chapter 3.

Further evidence for this view comes from a review of the evidence by neuroscientist Richard Davidson and his colleagues. They concluded that "There are both genetic and environmental contributions to the structure and function of this circuitry. We posit that impulsive aggression and violence arise as a consequence of faulty emotional regulation. Indeed, the prefrontal cortex receives a major serotonergic projection, which is dysfunctional in individuals who show impulsive violence. Individuals vulnerable to faulty regulation of negative emotion are at risk for violence and aggression." A "serotonergic projection" refers to the direct links between the production of a chemical in the brain (in this case serotonin, which is associated with feelings of well-being and happiness) and a particular part of the brain. In a sense, it means that the vulnerable individuals get a rush of serotonin in their brains when it comes to aggression; they *feel* good about their impulsive and emotionally disregulated feelings.

Nature and nurture always shape each other, as the classic review by Michael Rutter and his colleagues demonstrated in an article cleverly titled "Gene–environment interplay and psychopathology: multiple varieties but real effects." The dynamics of the connection between nature and nurture vary across social contexts, biological dimensions, and the degree to which an individual's experience contains risk factors and developmental assets. All this is relevant to understanding killers.

When I think about these issues as they apply to antisocial violence and seek research examples that communicate clearly without requiring sophisticated statistical knowledge on the part of the reader, I always return to the findings presented by Sarnoff Mednick and Elizabeth Kandel on this score some thirty years ago. They reported that if babies were born with minor physical anomalies indicative of minor neurological damage and lived in "normal" (i.e., nurturing and stable) families, they were no more likely to end up being arrested for violent crimes by age twenty-one than if they were born without such neurological damage. However, if such neurologically damaged babies were reared in "dysfunctional" families, they were nearly four times more likely than normal babies to end up being arrested for violent crimes (70 versus 20 percent). Many of the killers I interview come from families so terrible that to call them "dysfunctional" would be a gross understatement.

The kind of "real world" study conducted by Mednick and Kandel resonates with the laboratory research that provides the foundation for the conclusions offered by James Gross, Adrian Raine, Richard Davidson, and other scientists. The real-life experience of many killers indicates that their brains have trouble with emotional regulation (and, as was noted before, with executive function as well). In large part, this is because they have witnessed gross emotional *dis*regulation in their families and communities, which they can then model in their own behavior, and they have been taught ineffective strategies for managing emotions. They may have come into this world with genetic vulnerabilities to brain development issues, vulnerabilities inherited from their biological parents. But because of their early life experiences, they often have so much unprocessed trauma that they have difficulty cutting through the tangle of powerful feelings in which they are caught to think lucidly about their feelings. This difficulty is compounded by whatever "brain problems" they have in addressing and managing those feelings. *It is a circular chain: early vulnerability combines with early social deprivation and* *trauma to produce greater vulnerability, which leads to more social deprivation and trauma, which in turn compounds existing vulnerabilities.*

An extreme lack of self-awareness is common among the men I listen to in murder cases. Often it flows not just from their difficulties with "implicit" emotional regulation of the kind studied by Richard Davidson and others. It also comes from the enormity of the hurt they carry around with them, a hurt so big it cannot be acknowledged, a hurt that blinds them emotionally but often shapes their behavior and contributes to the murders they commit.

EMOTIONAL DAMAGE TOO GREAT TO KNOW

Research by anthropologist Ronald Rohner and his colleagues reveals that parental rejection is a "psychological malignancy," an emotional cancer that devours normal human development. On the basis of more than a hundred studies from around the world, Rohner and his colleagues report that by itself, perceived parental rejection is responsible for about 25 percent of all the major behavioral and psychological problems that children face in becoming competent and caring human beings. That's on average, not taking into account the other socially toxic influences that might be in a child's life and push the figure higher than 25 percent for some groups, groups that include most of the killers I listen to.

It's bad enough when your father rejects you. I hear that in the anger and resentment men like Duke Jimenez express when they talk about their absent fathers. But at least with respect to father abandonment and absence, there is a normalizing cultural framework. After all, according to the U.S. Census Bureau, one in three kids lives without his or her father; it's so common here and around the world that it is almost "normal." But to be abandoned by your mother? How do you ever make sense of that, how do you digest it psychologically?

In 1995, I was interviewing fifteen-year-old Tashan Jones*, who was in a New York State juvenile detention center because of a long series of armed robberies. In our interview he boasted of having committed fifty such crimes. Tashan was a tough kid, not soft like Duke, but when I broached the subject of how his mother had abandoned him, the tough veneer disappeared: he put his thumb in his mouth and began rocking in his chair. This tough guy was an emotionally wounded and needy child who wanted his mother back. It was hard to sit in the room with his pain and yearning.

I thought of Tashan ten years later, in 2005, as I sat in a cell in Kansas with twenty-one-year-old Ron Richardson* while he awaited trial for murdering a police officer (a crime for which he eventually received the death sentence). After crashing a stolen car while being chased by the police, Ron fled the scene on foot, with officer Thomas Wendt in pursuit. When Wendt caught up to him, Ron shot wildly at the officer, hoping to avoid capture, but shots found Wendt and he died.

After he was convicted of killing Wendt, the trial moved to the penalty phase. In support of its application to have Ron sentenced to death, the prosecution offered the following "aggravating factors" (factors that amplified the heinousness of the crime): the fact that the victim was a law enforcement officer and the fact that Ron was on parole for another crime at the time of the murder. In response, the defense offered these "mitigating factors" (factors that might encourage the court to spare his life out of sympathy for the negative effects of the life he lived as a child):

Youth

Unstable family

Diagnosis of intellectual functioning problems

Low IQ

Abused as a child, with resulting head injuries

Mother abused drugs and alcohol during pregnancy

Biological father unknown

Poverty

These bare-bones facts are but the table of contents for understanding the emotionally damaging life Ron experienced as a child and adolescent.

The records showed that Ron's family was characterized by instability and violence. Because his mother had numerous sexual partners at the time Ron was conceived, she didn't know the identity of his biological father. Neurological testing indicated diffuse damage to his brain, in all likelihood because of his mother's drug abuse during pregnancy. Because she engaged in prostitution, his mother exposed Ron to numerous men, some of whom abused him. Because her drug abuse and sex life took precedence over caring for her child, Ron was neglected in the early years of his life. Beyond the implicit abandonment by his biological father is the clear and explicit rejection he experienced from his mother. When he was five years old, she took his younger brother and her drugs and left Ron behind, emotionally devastated. Although to an outsider it might well appear that this was for the best—"having no mother is better than having the mother that Ron had"—for Ron it was emotionally devastating to lose the only semblance of an attachment figure he had in his life, inadequate as she was.

After several informal and completely inappropriate "placements," during which time Ron was exposed to inconsistent, neglectful, and abusive treatment, he was placed with his official adoptive parents, Elizabeth and Stan Richardson, who were plagued by a host of problems, including substance abuse. They seem to have been sexually inappropriate toward Ron (the nature of that behavior is unclear).

As I sat with him, the first thing I noticed about Ron was his superficial cheerfulness. Despite what he faced in court, and despite the terrible facts of his childhood and adolescence, he was so well defended against the enormity of his loss and the corresponding enormity of his rage that he offered up a startling obliviousness to the emotional dynamics driving his life, and instead presented himself with a nonchalant smile. But the emotional damage was there to be heard, once I found a way to listen for it. The records showed that he had been suspended from preschool and kindergarten for assaulting his teachers—all women. In fourth grade, he was again suspended for assaulting his teacher—a woman. In sixth grade, he was suspended for assaulting the driver of the school bus—again a woman.

"Looks like you had some trouble with women in positions of authority," I said. "Yeah," he replied, "I guess so." Then, as gently as I could, I asked this question: "Do you think it had anything to do with your mother leaving you when you were a little kid?" He paused, then replied, "Man, I never thought of that!" And he hadn't.

The enormity of that wound, that hurt, that profound insult, is too much to bear, so kids often "forget" it, dissociate from it, minimize it, push it deep within. But doing so does not defuse the rage they feel. It does not repair the emotional damage. It only buries it beneath the surface, creating the risk that it will burst forth from them in acts of violence against others or themselves.

Dissociation is a major theme in Ron's life. For example, he reports—with a laugh—that as a child he was so afraid of needles that when getting an injection at the doctor's office, "it took eight people to hold me down." Yet his body is covered with prison tattoos (which are created in a particularly painful process). When asked about the pain associated with these tattoos, Ron replies that he is sensitive to pain but can tolerate it. Terrified of needles, he "volunteers" for the tattoo needle. Ron shows the kind of fractured self and dissociation from his feelings common among untreated victims of chronic trauma.

He says that "as a child there was no one I could rely on." From this feeling of insecurity arose his preemptive and defensive aggressive behavior, carrying a knife and eventually a gun for this reason. He reports recurrent dreams of being stabbed. As a child he had a recurrent dream of dying in a car crash.

Like many others with a history of chronic trauma, Ron conveys a fatalistic acceptance of his world. For example, he says of being in prison since he shot Officer Wendt in 2002, "I'm glad I was arrested. I wouldn't have lasted until twenty-one. It's a dangerous occupation being a stickup man." At age eight, he told a school psychologist that he wanted to die. Children who express suicidal thoughts are almost always very, very sad children. Beneath the surface bravado, Ron is such a child, still.

As we sit talking, Ron expresses a strong attachment to his young daughters. Speaking of the first time he saw one of his daughters, he says, "I love babies. They are perfect and ain't all messed up." He also has a strong protective impulse toward extended family and friends, saying, "There's nothing I won't do for family and friends. That's all I got. That's all a man's ever got."

Nice words from someone who called out "Fuck you, bitch!" to the widow of the police officer he shot, when she read her "victim impact statement" in court. Ron is a mixture of nasty aggressiveness and wounded childish emotions, sociopathic violence and sentimental affirmations. In short, he is an emotional mess.

THE MEANING OF TRAUMA

Duke, Tashan, and Ron are emotionally damaged. Most of the killers I listen to are, and it's not because they were born that way (although they may have been born with heightened vulnerability to the kinds of socially toxic environments in which they grew up, as psychiatrist Michael Rutter has demonstrated in his research). Some babies are born with brains that put them on the fast track to emotional damage, but that is not the predominant story of killers. They are the way they are because of what they experienced as children and adolescents. Few of them would have walked the path in life that they have walked if they had been born into and grown up in a stable, positive, loving, functional family. To be sure, as young children some of them exhibited temperamental vulnerabilities that in a child with "normal" experiences would have created adjustment difficulties, perhaps, but would not have led down the path to murder.

Listening to these killers, I hear stories of physical, psychological, and sexual abuse that make a mockery of dismissing the relevance of their experience as "the abuse excuse," as some prosecutors (and others) are prone to do. I hear stories of profound emotional deprivation, devastating rejection, and catastrophic abandonment. I hear stories of trauma, often with lifelong effects. To deny the long-term developmental connections between early devastating trauma and later destructive behavior is intellectually and morally repugnant to me.

I think of the case of Robert Simpson*, whose childhood in Oklahoma was characterized by some of the most pervasive and severe sexual, physical, and psychological maltreatment I have ever encountered. He was psychologically crippled by this fundamental and devastating assault on his very humanity. At age thirty-five, Robert sexually assaulted and murdered an eleven-year-old girl.

When asked to assess the relevance of Robert's childhood as a mitigating factor in deciding between the death penalty or a life sentence, the prosecution's psychologist wrote this: "Did Mr. Simpson's difficult childhood have some bearing on his antisocial behavior as a child and as an adolescent? Perhaps, but that was more than twenty years ago. I find it hard to believe that Mr. Simpson's disadvantaged background had any direct and significant connection to the crimes he committed in 2001."

I find that to be an extraordinary statement (even for a prosecution expert). One definition of trauma is "an event from which you never fully recover," and the minimization of Robert Simpson's incredibly traumatic childhood inherent in this psychologist's assessment is appalling. If he were looking at a thirty-five-year-old man whose leg had been traumatically amputated by a shark attack when he was a child, would he say that the man's inability to walk was unrelated to the fact that he had not received a prosthesis or crutches or physical therapy after he was crippled as a child? This kind of blindness to the long-term effects of early trauma is wrong.

Trauma arises when children cannot manage the arousal they feel and give meaning to frightening experiences. This is contained in the American Psychiatric Association's definition of post-traumatic stress disorder (PTSD), which refers to trauma as a response to an "event such as a natural disaster, a serious accident, a terrorist act, war/combat, or rape or other violent personal assault." This approach replaced the older definition, which focused on threatening experiences outside the realm of normal experience. As I see it, trauma has two principal components: overwhelming negative arousal and overwhelming negative cognition. The former component is especially relevant to young children. Specifically, because the development of the brainstem is not complete until the age of eight years, younger children are not yet fully equipped to effectively modulate arousal. Trauma involves an inability to handle effectively the physiological responses of stress in situations of threat.

The second component of trauma—overwhelming negative cognition—is captured in Judith Herman's formulation that to experience trauma is "to come face to face with human vulnerability in the natural world and with the capacity for evil in human nature." Beyond hurricanes, tornadoes, earthquakes, and accidents, this description illuminates the traumatic nature of living with the kind of abuse, neglect, and deprivation experienced by Ron Richardson and others like him (and the experience of children and youth around the world affected by war and terrorism).

It also highlights the fact that it is dangerously simple to accept the "diagnosis" approach contained in the official definition of PTSD as a psychological "disorder." I say this in agreement with Bonnie Burstow, who wrote: "People who are not traumatized maintain the illusion of safety moment to moment by editing out such facts as the pervasiveness of war, the subjugation of women and children, everyday racist violence, religious intolerance, the frequency and unpredictability of natural disasters, the ever-present threat of sickness and death and so on. People who have been badly traumatized are less likely to edit out these very real dimensions of reality. Once traumatized, they are no longer shielded from reality by a cloak of invulnerability." It is too easy for professionals to "diagnose" traumatized kids (and adolescents and adults, for that matter) and not appreciate that those kids are confronting realities that hardly register in the consciousness of many, if not most, of us who live in "the normal world."

I think of a woman who had been an abused child and years later made the following report as part of a film that Cornell University's Family Life Development Center produced: "One day someone called the police and they came to our house while my mama was out. They asked me if my mama had been beating me, and I said 'no.' When my mama came home she asked me if I had told the police that she beat me and I told her I hadn't. 'Why didn't you tell the police that I beat you?' she asked me. I looked at her and said, 'cause you could kill me mama.'" Whatever "symptoms" she displayed, this child knew something about "reality" that few of us appreciate, that *your mother could beat you to death.*

ACUTE AND CHRONIC TRAUMA

It's important to distinguish between acute and chronic trauma, what psychiatrist Lenore Terr called "Type I" and "Type II" trauma. The term *acute trauma* refers to a single overwhelming event that has not been preceded by other such events. This can be conceived of as "single-blow" trauma. *Chronic trauma* refers to long-standing exposure to persistent overwhelming events, what might be called "existential" trauma.

But I join with Eldra Solomon and Kathleen Heide in arguing that even calling it "chronic" (Type II) trauma does not do justice to the massive developmental challenges some kids face growing up. It's worth quoting their 1999 definition of a third type of trauma: "Type III trauma is more extreme. It results from multiple and pervasive violent events beginning at an early age and continuing for years. Typically, the child was the victim of multiple perpetrators, and one or more close relatives. . . . Generally, force is used and the abuse has a sadistic quality."

When Solomon and Heide took a look at twenty-three possible long-term effects of the three types of trauma, they found that only two were "typically" found with Type I cases ("full detailed memory" and "PTSD symptoms"). For Type II trauma, four additional effects were commonly observed ("poor self-esteem/self-concept," "interpersonal distrust," "feelings of shame," and "dependency"). But for Type III trauma, there were typically all these plus sixteen more (twenty-one in total)! These additional symptoms included *many* of the issues commonly found among the killers I have interviewed over the years (including "emotional numbing," "foreshortened sense of the future," "rage," "affective dysregulation," "narcissism," "impulsivity," and "dissociative symptoms").

Of special note is the fact that about the only long-term effect *not* typically found in Type III that was found with Type I is "full, detailed memory." As Solomon and Heide note, this alone is a major social problem. It means that whereas Type I and Type II trauma cases are likely to be recognized (because the trauma victim can recount the traumatic incident and thus be recognized as a victim), individuals who experience Type III trauma are often not even identified as victims. They are likely to be "misdiagnosed" on the basis of the long-term effects of the experiences they frequently cannot "remember" with a full and detailed account because of dissociation and their habitual coping tactics. Sad but true. Solomon and Heide captured this well when they wrote, "Asking the client how he or she would like his or her life to be different 5 years from now can be an effective diagnostic tool. A Type III survivor typically either looks at the therapist like he or she is crazy or with a sense of bewilderment. The client may say that he or she cannot even think about tomorrow or next week. The concept of having a future in 5 years is almost incomprehensible."

Because chronic trauma, particularly Type III Trauma, is the type that is likely to be experienced by children living in the kind of toxic social environments of kids who grow up to be killers, it is this type of trauma that will be my focus in this chapter. However, before turning to the effects of chronic trauma, let me briefly discuss the effects of acute trauma on children.

An experience that is cognitively overwhelming may stimulate conditions in which the process required to "understand" these experiences has harmful side effects itself. That is, in coping with a traumatic event, the child may be forced into patterns of behavior, thought, and emotion that are themselves "abnormal," compared with patterns prior to the event or patterns characteristic of untraumatized children.

Children—particularly those six to eleven years of age, who may be too old to benefit from the parental buffering that can insulate younger children—are especially vulnerable to trauma caused by threat and fear. For example, results from a study conducted by psychiatrists Jonathan Davidson and Rebecca Smith showed that children exposed to a trauma before age ten were three times more likely to exhibit symptoms of PTSD than those exposed after age twelve (56 versus 18 percent).

While symptoms of PTSD in children may vary according to the age, developmental level, and individual characteristics of the child, sleep disturbances, daydreaming, extreme startle responses, and emotional numbing are common responses. Children may also display a repetitive pattern of play in which they reenact the trauma. As Bruce Perry and his colleagues have demonstrated, they may even experience biochemical changes in their brains that impair social and academic behavior, as well as psychological problems that interfere with learning, behavior, and parent–child relationships.

Children who experience disruptions in their relationships with their parents, along with intense traumatic stress, are especially vulnerable to permanent "psychic scars." These may manifest as excessive sensitivity to stimuli associated with the trauma and diminished expectations for the future.

While some children suffer permanent effects of trauma, others will achieve resolution and return to normal functioning shortly after the experience. Many children will require months to fully process the trauma. The good news is that most kids will recover from a single incident of trauma within a year, as was found by John Saigh and his colleagues in their study of young kids exposed to the 9/11 attacks in New York City in 2001.

COPING WITH CHRONIC TRAUMA

The more common variety of trauma seen in the lives of people like Ron Richardson is not acute trauma, however, but the early chronic danger and repeated, overwhelming violent and abusive experiences characteristic of Types II and III. Chronic traumatic danger imposes a requirement for developmental adjustment, as the long list of effects observed by Solomon and Heide shows.

From the perspective of Jean Piaget's developmental theory, these developmental adjustments result from the inability of the child to assimilate traumatic experiences into existing conceptual frameworks ("schemas," as Piaget called them). Rather, traumatic experiences require the child to alter existing concepts to permit the new experiential information to be known. This involves what Piaget termed "accommodation."

In the case of chronic danger, children must accommodate their psychic realities so that they allow for the processing of life's atrocities. Put simply, children must adopt a negative view of the world. Lev Vygotsky's model of development provides additional dimensions to this analysis. By focusing on the intrinsically social nature of development, this approach highlights the role of adults in mediating the child's experience of trauma.

The key is the concept of the "zone of proximal development," which posits that children are capable of one level of functioning on their own, but a higher level in relationships with the "teacher" (i.e., anyone who guides the child toward enhanced development by offering responses that are emotionally validating and developmentally challenging). This provides a developmental grounding for understanding the "natural" therapeutic efforts of adults (as parents, relatives, and neighbors) and for the "programmatic" efforts of professionals (as teachers and therapists). It is why having even one parent who is psychologically available, stable, and nurturing can go a long way toward helping a child heal from even chronic trauma.

We found this years ago in a study I conducted with Kathleen Kostelny of Palestinian children dealing with the chronic trauma of the uprising against the Israeli military and police forces known as the "Intifada." Children whose mothers were psychologically available to them to engage in the processing of trauma were better off emotionally than kids whose mothers were not available or were unwilling to engage in the process with their children. This is why the emergence of "trauma-focused" child therapy is so important for the well-being of children who experience chronic trauma in their families and communities. Kids like Ron Richardson have grown up with access to neither the "natural" healing of psychologically available parents nor the "professional" healing offered by therapists, and we can see the results in what they do and say and feel as young adults.

How do a child's accommodations to traumatic events manifest? Without effective adult "teaching" (in Vygotsky's sense), they are likely to include persistent PTSD, alterations of personality, and major changes in patterns of behavior and values—all the "symptoms" noted by Solomon and Heide in their analysis of Type II, and particularly Type III, trauma cases. Chronic traumatic danger demands that children redirect their behavior and rewrite their stories—and, in the case of Type III trauma, perhaps "conveniently" forget or distort their narrative accounts entirely.

These accommodations are likely to be especially pronounced when the danger derives from violent overthrow of day-to-day social reality, when communities are substantially altered, when displacement occurs, or when children lose important members of their families and social networks. In the case of children exposed to the chronic horrors of Pol Pot's Khmer Rouge regime in Cambodia in the 1970s, a study by Grant Marshall and his colleagues found that more than 60 percent of the survivors exhibited persistent symptoms of PTSD 20 years after "exposure."

According to psychiatrist Bessel van der Kolk, explosive outbursts of anger, flashbacks, nightmares, hypervigilance, psychic numbing, constriction of affect, impaired social functioning, and the loss of control over one's life are all characteristic of the chronically traumatized child. In the long run, there can be a wide range of effects on prosocial behavior and moral development, including antisocial behavior, using drugs as self-medication, and diminished future-orientation.

Acute trauma is generally amenable to resolution through some combination of what the National Child Traumatic Stress Network calls "psychological first aid," in the form of reassurance, and the passage of time as things return to normal. Chronic trauma is not so amenable to resolution because there is no possibility of a simple therapy of reassurance: a "return to normal" is not a solution because normal *is* the problem.

Research by Bruce Perry and others has demonstrated that chronic exposure to trauma in childhood can have effects on the development of the brain by overstimulating more primitive parts of the brain at the expense of the more sophisticated regions. This can produce overdevelopment of the amygdala (which processes emotions, particularly anger and fear), to the detriment of the more sophisticated parts of the brain (e.g., the prefrontal cortex) that are involved in higher reasoning processes. If all a young child's energy goes into holding on emotionally (amygdala), in many cases there is less energy for reading, writing, and arithmetic (prefrontal cortex). This negative effect is most clear when chronic trauma is experienced in early childhood, but given the malleability of the brain even in adulthood, adolescents who experience chronic trauma can also be affected. I think we can see this effect in the troubled life of Charles Smith.

THE CHARLES SMITH CASE

It's not easy to understand the life that Charles Smith* led up to the point when I met him, particularly because of his difficulties in remembering and reporting his childhood experiences. These difficulties appear to be linked to both the traumatic nature of those experiences and the "family tradition" of secretiveness in which he was raised. This meant that I had to lean heavily on reports made by other family members to augment what I could learn from listening to him. But I did have the advantage of listening to Charles as he was developing an emerging ability and willingness to report his experiences directly.

Charles says his mother was like a "CIA director," keeping the family's life as secret as possible—for example, moving multiple times and never leaving a forwarding address, vigorously enforcing her rules that family matters not be discussed or disclosed outside the family, and denying that experiences had ever happened. Charles's loyalty to his mother (which is only now changing as he gains some perspective on her and his early experience) creates another impediment to accessing information about his development as a child and an adolescent.

Charles was born into a dysfunctional family characterized by highly conflicted and broken relationships, as well as high levels of impairment due to substance abuse. He had no relationship with his biological father. He reports that "you never knew who was going to be around" and that "they had no concept of what a family is." As a result of this pattern, care and responsibility for Charles as a child was fragmented and inadequate, including a severely compromised mother–child relationship. His mother's substance-abuse problems clearly disrupted Charles's relationship with her, as did her extreme treatment of him. These early experiences are readily classified as child abuse and neglect by any standard definition in law and custom.

But child abuse and neglect can become part of the fabric of daily life for kids like Charles, so when asked to describe "the worst thing that happened to you as a child," he doesn't speak of the abuse and neglect. Rather, he reports experiencing a classic traumatic experience—being molested by a drunken adult male "friend of the family." He retains a clear visual memory of this experience but reports no emotional or psychological consequences of it. This is not surprising, given what is known about how children use emotional disconnection to protect themselves when faced with trauma. His inability to recall the incident as he experienced it emotionally indicates, not that there was no effect, but rather that he defended himself as many children do, through dissociation. His family compounded the damage by arranging for this child molester to be killed in retaliation for what he did. Charles reports a vague memory of having been taken to a park to witness this, but he is not sure what it is he is remembering.

Charles says that "every day it was something." He cites incidents such as the one in which his Aunt Gertrude was thrown out of the grandmother's house (for hitting her in the head with a hammer) and then was shot at by her lover. He recalls, at age twelve, being spanked outside his home by his mother—bare-bottomed and in front of a group of girls. But amid this sort of humiliation and trauma, Charles cites as particularly painful his Aunts Valerie and Arlene moving away, because they were the two people in his family in whom he could confide. This made worse the problems Charles faced in dealing with trauma in his family and neighborhood, because it increased the pressure to suppress disclosure and process feelings in favor of "being a man."

In Charles's world, being a man meant steely emotional coldness and disconnection. He had only one birthday celebration during his childhood—a group party with his sisters that wasn't even on or near the date of his birthday. Being a man meant not getting what he needed to contend effectively with the trauma in his life, namely nurturing and psychologically available caregivers who could and would listen to him and help make sense of his stressful and frightening experiences.

These traumatic life experiences would be hard for any child to bear, but they were made worse by the fact that Charles was a temperamentally vulnerable child. He was identified in his family as being "bashful and humble" as a young child. He reports that his mother's homes were always full of unrelated men (usually involved in drugs). He says that "these men with deep voices petrified me." He remembers that as a child he liked to listen to classical music and watch ballet. This sensitivity (and, presumably, his slight stature) led to taunting by family and others that he was "going to become a homosexual." It also led to repeated efforts by his mother and others to "make a man out of him." For example, he told me that when he was eight, his mother observed him being bullied (e.g., being hit in the head with a rock). Rather than comforting him, she told him, "Either you kick that boy's ass or when you come home I am going to kick your ass." Charles says, "I never cried—my mother would not tolerate it." When his mother died (in 1995), he reports that he felt "disappointed," but not angry or sad. He says that "I observed and loved my mother." These words are a testament to how excruciatingly difficult it is for children to give up on their mothers, no matter what.

Charles points to her own difficult childhood and youth (a pattern of abuse and deprivation). He reports that his best memory of his mother is "sitting up at night on the sofa sharing a soda and looking out over the city at the stars, just the two of us." How can a child reconcile these heartbreakingly positive images and his warm feelings of attachment with the anger her treatment of him elicits? It is a tough emotional equation to solve for any child, but for a child surrounded by trauma and threat in the social environment, it is often too hard a task for a child to accomplish.

For such a sensitive child, efforts to "toughen him up" are likely to produce a mixture of rage, self-loathing, and compensatory aggressive behavior.

Charles told me that his mother, grandmother, and uncles (but not the two aunts whose departure from his life he mourned) were "control freaks." He reported that in reaction, "If I feel that I am being controlled I walk out immediately—I rebelled against being controlled by the gangs or others in prison because I won't accept being put in a feminine role." Charles describes himself as being "like a tea kettle ready to explode." He recalls that smoking marijuana had the effect of "making me more aggressive." Charles says, "I have a big grudge against my family." He reports that he was visited by family only once in three years while he was in prison.

When he was a child and showed interest and talent in drawing, his aunt and uncle offered to send him to art lessons, but his mother vetoed it. Charles says of his family, "Every dream I ever had they stamped out." When asked what he would have become if he had lived in a more supportive family and neighborhood, Charles replied, "An artist." He speaks of how he spent as much time as possible during childhood in his room, "reclusive." This is the focus of his current life in the controlled and isolated environment in which he lives as a prisoner: he is an artist. He says, "If I can't paint they may as well strap me on the gurney."

Charles's life is overflowing with emotional damage linked to trauma from his social deprivation, psychological and sexual abuse, and mis-socialization by the important people in his life. He is not alone. Death row is full of such individuals. Marquan Banner is one of them.

THE MARQUAN BANNER CASE

When he was sentenced to death in 2007 for the murder of a casual acquaintance, twenty-three-year-old Mary Valezquez, Marquan Banner* was the youngest inmate on his state's death row (having just turned eighteen when he committed the crime in 2002). This crime (and the other murder for which he is responsible—the killing of Joyce Berns just days before he was arrested in the Valezquez murder in October 2002) testify to what a damaged person he had become.

Evidence introduced during the trial included a letter he had written to another inmate, in which he expressed pride in the brutal nature of the crime and revealed details that contributed to his conviction and the jury's subsequent vote for the death sentence. In that letter, he wrote, "I did a good job on her," commenting on the grisly crime-scene photos that had been shown to the court. According to the jury members, the depravity of this outrage confirmed their inclination to sentence him to death rather than recommend a life sentence. When the death sentence was announced in court, friends and members of the victim's family were present, and many demonstrated their approval by saying "yes."

As a man with a wife, a daughter, a niece, a mother, a sister, and many close female friends, I can appreciate that response. Marquan has inflicted terror, horror, and death upon the world. His rape and murder of Mary Valezquez was monstrous. This is all true. It disturbs me profoundly. Also true, according to the records, is the horrible reality of the path that took him to that depraved end point, and that is what I have to focus on in my efforts to bring a science-based compassion to understanding his life. *I don't excuse or rationalize what he did and what he had become. I try to make human sense of it by documenting the emotional damage he suffered that set him on the path that led to rape and murder.*

It seems clear that Marquan's family was characterized by extraordinary instability and violence. His biological father deserted his mother, and his lack of involvement in Marquan's life constitutes a clear pattern of rejection. The quality of care received by Marquan from his mother during his first five years of life was clearly inadequate. She was addicted to drugs and exposed Marquan to a variety of men—who were mostly very poor role models at best, and abusive at worst. His attendance at school was very poor. There is also evidence in the records indicating that Marquan was the victim of sexual abuse as a young child. The details are sketchy, but it most likely involved one of the men who floated through his mother's drugged life. This compounded the emotional damage he sustained directly at the hands of his neglectful and abusive mother.

After Marquan received the death sentence, his mother offered her apologies to the family of her son's victim, adding, "I'm not a villain. I'm not cruel." If we explored her history, we would probably find evidence of a traumatic upbringing similar to that which she inflicted on her son. Cycles of trauma frequently repeat across the generations, as victim becomes perpetrator and perpetrator begets victim.

When his mother's parental rights were terminated (in 1989, when Marquan was six years old, after she abandoned him), he was in the "care" of his maternal aunt. But her life, too, was characterized by substance abuse, and she too neglected Marquan's basic needs. In 1990, she left his life. The only remaining parental figure for Marquan was his maternal grandmother, who clearly was unable to exert sufficient positive influence to counteract the toxic effects of the neglect and abuse Marquan experienced in a poor neighborhood immersed in violence and crime.

Understanding emotional damage like that experienced by Marquan is a matter of mapping the accumulation of risk factors in counterpoint to the accumulation of developmental assets, the positive factors. But it's hard to find many positives in Marquan's life story. All his traumatic and neglectful family experiences took place in an environment characterized by many kinds of deprivation. He was mired in economic inadequacy (due to the diversion of family resources for substance abuse and his mother's inability as a single parent with little education and skills to maintain adequate employment). He was exposed to a high level of community violence (living in the urban war zone to which his mother's poverty and instability destined him). He was exposed to racism (as an African American child in American society, this is a given in most circumstances). And he lacked support for education in his home and community environment (he was chronically absent from school throughout childhood and adolescence).

Marquan's exposure to trauma included friends who were shot and killed, being injured himself (including a visit to the emergency room in 1997 after "being hit by a bat"), and chronic threats and violence at school and in the neighborhood. Marquan experienced all this without the benefit of strong and loving parents in his life who could help reassure him and process the trauma he experienced. Untreated trauma of the worst kinds warped his life. It warped his sexuality. There is suggestive evidence in the records that he committed multiple sexual assaults prior to his rape and murder of Mary Valezquez; he is known to have raped a young woman immediately before he was arrested for the crime that sent him to death row.

Trauma warped his ability to negotiate normal society. He was expelled from school when he was fifteen for a pattern of negative behavior toward teachers, staff, and other students. Trauma distorted any emotional intelligence that he might have had and led to chronic issues with emotional regulation, most notably his inability to manage his anger (which was considerable, given his life experience). Emotional damage heaped upon emotional damage: anger becomes homicidal rage, sexual victimization gives birth to a rapist. Mary Valezquez died because of it. If the state goes ahead with his sentence, so will Marquan Banner.

THE BIOLOGY AT THE HEART OF EACH
INDIVIDUAL'S LIFE

Rarely, if ever, is a single risk factor decisive in producing emotional damage. For one thing, children differ temperamentally in how and to what degree they will react to traumatic experiences. A passive child might resort to internalized symptoms; a more outwardly oriented child might respond with externalizing symptoms. Children with marginal intellectual competence are at special risk in such situations, because their limited cognitive competence diminishes their ability to think creatively about how to make their way in the world and, thus, their resilience.

Recent improvements in scientific technology have allowed research on these "temperamental" issues to proceed from general statements such as those offered above to more sophisticated explorations of the genetic basis of vulnerability. The field of behavioral genetics explores ways in which genetic makeup interacts with environmental experience to guide, and even direct, behavior. Many view this line of work with suspicion, even outright hostility. History is littered with claims to have discovered the "crime gene," which later turned out to be unfounded, often signaling racial, ethnic, or gender bias. But recent work points to several promising lines of explanation.

Is there a genetic basis for the kind of dangerous thinking and warped feelings that so many killers manifest, beyond the neurological issues identified earlier (i.e., regarding emotional regulation and executive function)? Additional insight has emerged from the work of Avshalom Caspi, Terrie Moffitt, and their colleagues. Their study grew out of research with animals showing that when there was a deficiency of chemicals in the brain that process arousal (neurotransmitters), the affected animals were more aggressive, particularly when put in stressful situations. The chemicals involved affect the brain's response to threat and stress. When there is a deficiency of these chemicals, the brain has trouble processing social information effectively, and these problems lead to more aggressive responses *if that brain is set within an abusive and socially toxic environment.*

Two genes have been the focus of this research: *MAOA,* which affects the level of an enzyme, monoamine oxidase (MAO-A), that works in the brain as it processes emotionally significant information; and *SLC6A4*, which affects the operation of serotonin in the brain and thus affects emotional regulation. *SLC6A4* is related to the likelihood that an individual will manifest depression and suicidal behavior in response to stressful life events. Variants of *MAOA* and *SLC6A4* can turn the important neurotransmitters "off," causing deficiency; or "on," leading to normal levels of these chemicals. Caspi and his colleagues set out to trace the impact of particular forms of these genes on child development.

Worth noting here is that the "off" form of the *MAOA* gene is recessive. This means that it takes two "off" genes to produce the effect in question—diminished capacity to process emotions effectively under conditions of stress—because the presence of one dominant "on" gene will counteract the "off" gene. Recall that women have two X chromosomes, whereas men have one X and one Y chromosome. The *MAOA* gene is found only on the X chromosome (whereas the *SLC6A4* gene is found on chromosome 17). Thus, if *MAOA* is turned "off" on one of a female's X chromosomes, on the other it is likely to be turned "on," and there will be no effect. But for a male, there is only one X chromosome, coupled with his virtually empty Y chromosome (which contains twenty-five genes, in contrast to the X's five thousand). Thus, for the most part, only males are affected by the MAO-A problem: one recessive "off" gene is enough to produce the effect. Indeed, all the participants in the Caspi study of *MAOA*'s effects were male, which, as we will see, is important for understanding some of the persisting gender differences in homicide rates, among other considerations.

To simplify something that is very complex, when *MAOA* (and *SLC6A4* as well) is turned "off," the child does not have the same level of activity in the important neurotransmitters norepinephrine, serotonin, and dopamine as when these genes are "on." The result is that the children *MAOA* and *SLC6A4* turned "off" are less able to deal effectively with stressful information and more prone to overreact to potentially dangerous situations, and to become depressed when faced with stress in their lives. Sound familiar? It does to me—I hear about it and observe it often in the lives of killers.

Caspi, Moffitt, and their colleagues discovered that when children with the *MAOA* gene for low MAO-A activity were abused, they were dramatically more likely to have problems with aggression and misbehavior as children (85 percent, compared with 42 percent of the abused with the gene "on") and to engage in criminal violence as adults (70 percent). If they were not abused, however, the gene became developmentally irrelevant, from the perspective of affecting antisocial outcomes. In those cases, rates of aggression were low and were the same for the kids with the genes turned "on" and "off"—about 10 percent for both groups. The rate for the abused children with the gene "off" was about eight times greater than that for the nonabused children with the same gene "off." The results for the effect of *SLC6A4* on depression and suicidal behavior were similar, but without the gender difference due to chromosome location of the gene, of course.

DOES A GENE CAUSE VIOLENCE?

Does the *MAOA* gene cause violent crime? Is this the fault of the X chromosome? Likewise, can the gene *SLC6A4* be blamed for depression? It depends on whether the *MAOA* or *SLC6A4* problem occurs in a child who is maltreated. And problems with poor conduct, aggression, depression, and suicidal behavior also occur in abused kids who do not have these genetic vulnerabilities, though at lower rates—about half what Caspi and his colleagues found in genetically vulnerable kids.

Psychiatrist William Bernet and his colleagues have brought this research to the courtroom. Reviewing the research by Caspi's team and by others who followed up on that original study, Bernet and colleagues were able to make a compelling argument that the *MAOA* "off" condition among maltreated individuals leads them to be nearly five times more likely to commit a violent offense as adults (and that a similar fivefold risk is present for depression and suicide among maltreated individuals with the *SLC6A4* genetic issue).

Bernet's group took the next step and began testing defendants for purposes of offering expert witness testimony. When I wrote to Bernet in 2012 to ask about the status of his group's work on this issue, this is what he wrote back: "My colleagues and I at Vanderbilt have genotyped about 35 defendants and have testified about 6 or 7 times. In two of those cases, juries decided to NOT give the person the death penalty. I think our testimony was part of the reason. The most dramatic case was *State of Tennessee v. Davis Bradley Waldroup, Jr.,* in 2009. . . . We try hard not to oversell this idea or exaggerate its importance. E.g., the genotyping is only one small part of a large biopsychosocial forensic evaluation."

When you read the press reports of how the jury dealt with Bernet's testimony in the *Waldroup* case, it is clear that for some of them it was an important element in their deliberations. As part of the overall presentation by the defense, it gave jurors a concrete way to conceptualize something that otherwise might seem overwhelmingly complex to a nonscientist. It provided them with a way to deal with the general question "Which is more important, nature or nurture?" by offering a pathway to what is always the best answer to this question—namely, "It depends." For that reason alone, gathering this sort of *MAOA* evidence should be part of the overall assessment of defendants in murder cases.

Bernet concluded his message to me with these words: "Also, one's gene does not force the person to commit a murder; it is only a risk factor that increases a person's chances of being a violent adult." Genetic vulnerability is indeed "only a risk factor." But then, each and every factor is. There is no single "cause" that will "force" someone to commit a murder or even to "choose" to kill. That's the underlying truth in the concept of "risk accumulation" that guides my work in making sense of killers (indeed, in making sense of all human development issues, the most important academic lesson I learned from my mentor, Urie Bronfenbrenner, more than forty years ago).

The underlying truth here is that assessing the impact of *any* particular risk factor depends, to a great extent, on the larger context of an individual's life. If Duke, Tashan, Ron, Charles, and Marquan had experienced just one traumatic event in their lives, they might well have shown the resilience necessary to transcend it, because no single trauma is likely to prove decisive in the development of debilitating emotional damage. But they didn't experience just one trauma. Rather, they experienced an accumulation of traumas and other risk factors, and this tells their story. And they did so with little in the way of positive developmental assets to help compensate for the assaults on their psyches and thus provide the basis for resilience in the face of adversity.

RESILIENCE IS NOT ABSOLUTE

Resilience is not absolute. It is not a trait. It exists in counterpoint to the accumulation of risk factors and the deprivation of developmental assets. Despite differences among individuals in resilience to trauma, it is important to note that when the nature of the trauma is severe and prolonged enough, the casualty rates reach virtually 100 percent (if all forms of dysfunction are included).

That is what military psychologist Dave Grossman concluded from his review of research conducted more than half a century ago. A World War II study of American soldiers revealed that after sixty days of continuous combat, the rate of "psychiatric casualty" reached 98 percent (and those who did not break down were characterized as having psychopathic personality profiles to start with, which pushes the percentage that have some sort of serious mental health problem after two months of combat to 100 percent). However, as Grossman recounts in his book *On Combat*, what they made of the emotional damage they suffered in combat is a different story.

Many of these World War II psychiatric casualties were able to return to service after a relatively short period of safe rest and therapeutic processing. In the long run, the key lay in how positive their lives were before they went into combat, and the extent to which they had resources and support in dealing with the emotional damage they experienced in combat after they returned home. This is what shaped the postwar lives they led. Most recovered well. Some were plagued with lifelong recovery issues. Some were emotionally incapacitated by their experience.

A study conducted in Chicago by Patrick Tolan and his colleagues revealed that among abused male children living in the most violent and impoverished neighborhoods who were exposed to racism, 100 percent exhibited significant psychiatric and/or academic problems between the ages of thirteen and fifteen. As with the soldiers studied in World War II who faced continuous combat, the conditions of life for these kids were so inhospitable to normal human development that all were damaged as a result of their experiences. This does not mean that all received a "Go to Jail. Go Directly to Jail. Do Not Pass Go" card. All were casualties, but a majority found ways to cope that did not involve violent crime, and some eventually led exemplary lives. That's the good news. But it does caution us against definitions of resilience as a trait independent of context.

People who go to the gym and do aerobic exercise have more "resilient breathing" than couch potatoes. However, neither group can breathe on the surface of the moon, because the lunar environment is so hostile to human functioning that all individual differences are overridden and, in a sense, become contextually irrelevant. I've listened to killers who lived on the surface of the moon psychologically and socially.

THE TRAUMA OF PSYCHOLOGICAL MALTREATMENT

The traumatic impacts of physical and sexual abuse seem obvious to most people (except, perhaps, those who scoff at the idea that the experience of abuse is a mitigating factor in sentencing murderers and other violent criminals). Few doubt that beating or raping a child is likely to produce emotional damage. But what about psychological abuse and neglect? On the basis of my work as a developmental psychologist focusing on issues of child abuse and neglect in the 1980s, I developed one of the first professional efforts to understand the concept of "psychological maltreatment" as a source of trauma in the lives of children and youths and apply it to child protective services.

This effort to translate the general idea of "emotional abuse and neglect" into more specific terms relevant to understanding child development took the form of a book—*The Psychologically Battered Child,* published in 1986. At the heart of this analysis are five forms of psychological maltreatment as violations of the child's basic human rights. Each is grounded in an understanding of child development research:

Rejecting—Sending the child messages that convey worthlessness and
    fundamental unacceptability.

Isolating—Cutting the child off from normal social relationships or from
    forming such relationships in the first place.

Ignoring—Failing to provide the child with essential emotional nurturance
    and responsiveness.

Terrorizing—Using intense fear as a parenting technique to control the
    child.

Corrupting—Mis-socializing the child in the direction of values that are
    antisocial or self-destructive, particularly with respect to sexuality,
    criminal behavior, and/or substance abuse.

In the nearly three decades since I offered this analysis, researchers in child development have elaborated on and studied these concepts, and mental health and social work professionals have employed them in analyzing the destructive and traumatic effects of maltreatment on child and adolescent development. In response to suggestions by other researchers, I have added the concept of "degrading" to my list (as suggested by Stuart Hart and his colleagues). *Degrading:* Depriving a child of a personal sense of dignity and self-respect. These behaviors send the message that the child is inadequate, lowly, and inferior compared to other like-aged children.

The approach developed in *The Psychologically Battered Child* was offered as the framework for prosecuting cases of psychological maltreatment in 2004, by Victor Vieth in an article titled "When Words Hurt: Investigating and Proving a Case of Psychological Maltreatment." Vieth is the Director of the District Attorneys Association's National Child Protection Training Center and a great child advocate.

Even in the absence of physical and sexual maltreatment, psychological maltreatment is associated with developmental damage. As I read the research, and as I laid it out thirty years ago in my book, it is for the most part the *psychologically* abusive and neglectful elements of both physical and sexual maltreatment that are associated with most of the developmental damage to children.

The correlation between physical events in a child's life and that child's emotional and cognitive development is weak. Two children with the same physical injury (a broken arm, for example) react very differently as a function of why their injury has occurred and who is responsible.

In high school, I knew two boys who broke their arms in the same month. Ricky broke his arm playing football; Antonio broke his arm when his drunken, enraged father threw him down the basement stairs. Ricky's injury was, if anything, a badge of honor. Antonio's injury was a badge of shame, because it signified the rejection he experienced from his father. It was Antonio's experience of psychological maltreatment that was damaging to his heart, his spirit, and his mind.

I believe that comparisons like this attest to the concept that it is the psychological maltreatment component of other forms of abuse that is most significant in producing developmental damage. Physical abuse can produce neurological problems (with executive function and emotional regulation, for example) and even death, of course. But for the most part, messages of rejection, terror, humiliation, isolation, and degradation do the bulk of the damage, not the physical injuries or the pain inflicted. To rework an old folk saying, "Sticks and stones may break my bones but words will break my heart."

Difficult as it may be for some to believe, the same is true of sexual abuse. The physical acts that constitute sexual abuse have little *intrinsic* developmental meaning. What gives them meaning is the psychological messages they convey, whether directly from the perpetrator (e.g., "If you tell anyone about this, I will kill you and your whole family") or indirectly, because of the child coming to understand the cultural meaning of these acts (e.g., "You are damaged and unclean because you did this with an adult"). All these messages have developmentally damaging effects because they constitute or result in terrorizing, rejecting, isolating, ignoring, degrading, and/or mis-socializing. They have their effects through the psychological maltreatment associated with the acts.

The concept of psychological maltreatment often proves useful in understanding how human growth and development becomes emotionally warped, and thus constitutes a mitigating factor in death penalty cases. It certainly helped in understanding this next case.

THE ANDREW DIRKSON CASE

Twenty-four-year-old Andrew Dirkson* shot his pregnant wife in 2009, in Florida, and was convicted of killing her and her unborn child in 2012. During the sentencing phase of his trial, I testified to the role of psychological maltreatment in shaping the person who fired the gun that killed his young wife. It was clear from what I had learned about him that Andrew had experienced multiple and severe forms of psychological maltreatment during childhood and adolescence. Although in my testimony I spoke about the role of isolating and mis-socializing in Andrew's life, here I will focus exclusively and in detail on rejecting—because, as I noted before, it is usually the most important source of emotional damage in a kid's life, and I believe it was so in Andrew's case.

Furthermore, because some people are prone to dismiss any role of child abuse in explaining murder (disgracefully calling it "the abuse excuse"), I want to be as concrete and specific as I can about the psychological maltreatment in Andrew's life. One important thing to remember in looking at this report is that, while some of the specifics sound relatively "normal" when looked at separately and from a distance, it is the accumulation of instances into an ongoing pattern of psychological maltreatment that counts.

Andrew's family has experienced multigenerational abuse and neglect. For example, his maternal grandmother was sexually abused by her father and physically and psychologically abused by her mother, as was his mother by her grandfathers. The family's problems include substance abuse (e.g., alcohol problems on his father's side of the family, including his grandfather), dysfunctional relationships (e.g., domestic violence), and mental health problems (e.g., widespread depression in his immediate and extended family on both his mother's and his father's side).

There is an intergenerational pattern of rejecting behavior by parents in Andrew's family. For example, his Aunt Marilyn says of the home she shared as a child with Andrew's mother, Bobbie, and their sister, Tammy, "There was a lot of negativity. There was no type of love in that situation. We'd be called stupid and dumb. I never did well in school. We were never praised or helped." And his father, William, came from a family in which his mother died when he was seven years of age (apparently from a depression-related suicide) and his father "did not want any of the children," who were eventually placed with their maternal grandparents. William says, "My household growing up was very abusive, both physically and verbally abusive." This intergenerational pattern of rejection continued in Andrew's life.

He experienced multiple rejections during childhood and adolescence. For example, family members report that when Bobbie had a boy (Andrew) in 1989, instead of the girl she had wanted, she was extremely disappointed. When she did have a girl (Betty) in 1995, she showed acceptance toward her and rejection toward Andrew. As the paternal grandfather reports, "Naturally Betty gets whatever she wants and Andrew never did. Bobbie just wanted a girl, that was all. There was favoritism towards the girl." According to family members, after Betty was born, Andrew started smearing his feces on the walls of the home and hiding his soiled underwear. Andrew's attachment issues with his parents were clearly exacerbated by the arrival of a *wanted* sibling.

Aunt Marilyn reports that the family environment was full of rejection: "William never showed him affection. They were smothering his sister with affection. But Bobbie raised him like we were raised, without love. She didn't know how to show love to him. . . . William was mean spirited. He was cruel to animals. I heard him hitting a dog. William was bitter, complained he was never happy. He was always grumpy. William's a miserable, miserable person." Thus, Andrew "had no role model, no affection, no guidance. The only personality he dealt with was mean, and that Bobbie was passive and not an advocate" for Andrew.

Aunt Tammy also offers examples of the rejection Andrew experienced: "Bobbie was nasty to Andrew. Andrew didn't want to play football but his dad made him play. He was overweight. He was fat. He had to run. His face was red. He looked so sad. There was a lot behind Bobbie's house. His dad would tackle him and call him a 'fat pussy.' He looked so sad. His dad would tell him 'you're fat and stupid.' I told him to knock it off. . . . I remember how his face was, he looked at me like, 'God help me.'" She recalls that if Andrew made any kind of comment, or said he liked something, his father would insult Andrew for voicing his opinion. Andrew would not protest but would drop his head and internalize his emotions. "They did not have a father–son relationship at all."

When Andrew was a young child, he and his parents lived in his grandparents' home, and Bobbie's relationship with her son was weak. It is not surprising that Andrew was closer to his paternal grandmother, Charlene, than to his mother. Bobbie reports: "Andy bonded more with Charlene than with me. When we moved out she was still trying to tell me what to do. Like he had two mothers. This was not the case with Betty; she came home with only me. I did things my way. Betty is close to me."

A high school teacher and counselor of Andrew's says, "He would definitively tell me that he didn't think his parents cared about him. It was a constant theme that no one cared what he did; they just didn't care. That was a constant from day one."

According to a report prepared by John Sterling and Lisa Amaya-Jackson for the American Academy of Child and Adolescent Psychiatry, problems with "emotional regulation" are observed frequently among children who have been victims of maltreatment. They usually have few, if any, role models of effective emotional regulation in their families. Rather, they witness family members expressing extreme and erratic emotional responses to daily life. And in their efforts to find some way to cope with the incredible stress of living with maltreatment, children often develop strategies that do not serve them well in the larger, more normal social world of school and community.

Andrew has many issues with emotional regulation—anger management, impulsiveness, and depression. School reports from first grade indicate that even at that young age, he was struggling with emotional regulation. His teacher reports, "I also remember as a first grader he would come to school with his daily journal. He would draw pictures with blood and guns. I would have to tell him to stop." Reports also indicate that "at school he was touching other children's buttocks."

Andrew's second-grade teacher had taught his mother Bobbie as a child. She says of Bobbie and her sisters, "The girls it seemed to me enjoyed having the attention at school. I don't know if there was a lot of affection or anything shown at home. They seemed to be needy emotionally; they also didn't have a lot of encouragement to be participating in things, that sort of thing, like other kids. . . . It seemed like when she [Bobbie] married Andrew's dad she seemed to change also; just a kind of unhappiness and darkness. That is kind of what I saw happening with Andrew. If I remember correctly his father dressed in fatigues a lot and was not a very approachable person. It just didn't seem to be a very happy home life. . . . Mom just seemed to become very angry. . . . She just seemed to have anger about her."

Andrew had a chronic pattern of social difficulties that seem clearly related to the nature of his social environment at home. His third-grade teacher reports this: "Andrew's issues were more behavioral. He didn't know how to socialize with others. He wanted to be liked but he didn't have the skills to make it happen. He definitely had anger issues. You never knew when it would kick in. He would just boil over. He would fight with his peers in the playground constantly. He would throw fits in the classroom if he didn't like what we were doing. He just seemed to boil inside. He had a lot of playground issues. I would try to get in touch with Bobbie and William regarding his behavior but they wouldn't return my phone calls."

In high school, his difficulties intensified. He eventually was expelled (for bringing a knife to school, apparently a deliberate attempt to be expelled so that he might be placed in an Alternative Education program at another school). When asked by a teacher at his new school why he was there, Andrew told him that he had "an anger management problem." Andrew responded well to the special attention and messages of acceptance he experienced at this school, where he was awarded the "Alternative Education Spirit Award" and "Class Spirit Award" by the staff, thereby fulfilling the desire he expressed in his entrance essay: "I want to prove my girlfriend's mother wrong and be happy with my life."

Evidence of emotional regulation issues abounds in the reports and records. For example, according to the Director of the Alternative Education school: "I think Andy was a square peg in a round hole. . . . There is something about Andy that I like, but Andy's personality had a very hard edge. He is really rough and came off like he had a chip on his shoulder and he was angry at the world. . . . Andy was always complaining about something. Nothing in Andy's world was going right. He had the foulest mouth of any kid I ever met."

After Andrew was arrested for shooting his pregnant wife, a police investigator asked him about reports of verbal and physical aggression in the relationship. Andrew answered, "If you don't fight, is it really a relationship?" Given his family history, this conception of domestic relationships is not surprising.

In his emotional regulation issues, Andrew is typical of immature young adults who have had to cope with psychological maltreatment in childhood and adolescence. It seems likely that issues of emotional regulation contributed to the crime for which he was being sentenced when I testified. One special issue relevant to Andrew's life is that of extreme "rejection sensitivity" (which I mentioned in chapter 1, in the case of Marvin Tolman). While everyone is sensitive to being rejected, those with a history of parental rejection and psychological maltreatment are prone to develop a heightened sensitivity.

Research by psychologist Geraldine Downey and her colleagues has linked this heightened rejection sensitivity to domestic violence in men. Her studies show that "this cognitive–affective processing disposition undermines intimate relationships" in general. Of course, most relevant here is that it can stimulate domestic violence in vulnerable men. Actions of their partners that to these men signal impending rejection (even "normal" gestures of independence) are perceived as the prelude to abandonment. This produces a spike in aggression on the male's part.

Although there were no witnesses to the killing of Andrew's wife, from everything we know, it seems that his actions were prompted by rejection sensitivity. His friend Katie Treat alludes to this in her report: "He talked to me so much about how desperately he wanted to be with someone and couldn't stand to be alone." This suggests an issue with rejection sensitivity.

There are reports that Andrew's wife was afraid of him and wanted to leave. According to a statement made by a relative of Andrew's wife, "She told me, 'I am so tempted to just pack all my belongings up, but I'm deathly afraid of his reaction.' And 'He'll probably flip out and pull a gun on me, knowing him.'"

Any such hint of rejection on her part could well have precipitated the kind of panicked aggression associated with extreme rejection sensitivity. The presence of guns in their house allowed his panic to translate efficiently into lethal aggression, as is so often the case when extreme emotional reactions occur in the presence of firearms (e.g., the demonstrated link between having a gun in the home and both suicides and deaths of family members, which we will explore in chapter 7).

Andrew's onetime cell-mate reports: "Andy and I talked a lot during our time together in prison. He talked mostly about his wife and the baby. He told me that he wanted to be a dad in the worst way. I believed him because he cried. He cried a lot. Most days it would be two or three times a day. This went on regularly the first two months that Andy was incarcerated." Wanting to be a father "in the worst way" suggests the intensity with which he would have reacted to being threatened with abandonment by the mother-to-be of his child. It really is the *worst* way to want to be a father. Coupled with the other information available, it suggests how extreme his reaction would have been if his rejection sensitivity were stimulated by a real or perceived threat of abandonment.

In 2011, Andrew was a troubled boy, despite having attained the legally significant age of eighteen. I believe his second-grade teacher captured this in her comment that when she saw on television that Andrew had been arrested for the crime for which he was being sentenced, she thought, "Wow. I could still see the little second-grade boy in his face. I was surprised to see the little boy that I knew, but not surprised too, knowing what kind of environment he grew up in. . . . He didn't have an easy life."

Geraldine Downey and her colleague Scott Feldman report that the kind of difficult life Andrew experienced is likely to lead to problems with attachment relations in adulthood. They found that "early experiences of overt rejection (e.g., physical maltreatment) and covert rejection (e.g., emotional neglect) are internalized as sensitivity to rejection." They found that rejection sensitivity in the childhoods of adolescents and young adults provided the foundation for difficulties with attachment relationships in adulthood (both avoidant and ambivalent patterns of attachment behavior). To my mind, this was the back story to the murder Andrew committed. He was a psychologically battered child who developed a pattern of rejection sensitivity that set him up to kill his wife and unborn child.

I think that when all was said and done, the jury understood Andrew. They rejected the prosecution's request for the death penalty and sentenced him to life in prison.

PROBLEMS WITH EMOTIONAL INTELLIGENCE ARE AT THE HEART OF THE MATTER

Most of the killers to whom I have listened are emotionally damaged in matters of emotional regulation, in matters of depression, in matters of rage, and in matters of empathy. On average, and in general, research that has investigated the links between mental illness and aggression tells us that mentally ill people are no more likely to engage in criminally aggressive behavior than others. But the emotional damage that flows from child maltreatment, living in a violent community, and suffering social deprivation puts the killers I sit with at risk for violence because it creates a toxic brew of emotional-regulation difficulties, depression, rage, and diminished empathy.

Psychologist Daniel Goleman transformed public and professional discussions of "intelligence" with the publication of his book *Emotional Intelligence* in 1995. He marshaled evidence from a wide range of sources and settings to show that emotional competence—the ability to understand yourself and others and to act effectively on the basis of that understanding—is generally more important in life success than conventional, traditional measures of *cognitive* intelligence.

Among the elements of emotional intelligence is empathy. Researchers Stephanie Harris and Marco Picchioni have demonstrated the crucial importance of empathy in mediating the relationship between emotional damage and violence. They report that when the other mental-health risk factors for aggression and violence are present, empathy can inhibit an individual from moving down that pathway; when empathy is lacking, the odds of violence increase.

Developmental psychologist Laura Stockdale has reviewed the evidence linking difficulties with empathy and violent behavior. She finds that empathy is an important mediator between personality and community characteristics on the one hand and violent behavior on the other. For example, individuals from high-crime neighborhoods are significantly more likely to become violent only if they display lower levels of empathy. This connection extends to the finding that empathy is negatively related to aggressive behavior in childhood. For example, highly empathetic children were less likely to be aggressive during free play with peers, and empathetic children are consistently rated as less physically and relationally aggressive by their peers and teachers.

The greatest risk comes when lack of empathy creates a context in which emotional damage can join with the moral damage of the war zone mentality to produce lethal violence. In this sense, emotional damage is the other half of the equation that often leads to lethal violence, and empathy is the most powerful operator in that connection. We see this in the lives of killers.

PUTTING IT ALL TOGETHER

How do we put together all the elements that we have explored in the first four chapters of this book—the decision-making issues in chapter 1, the alienation issues in chapter 2, the issues of moral damage in chapter 3, and the issues of emotional damage in chapter 4? Some of the leading scholars in the field of criminology have devoted themselves to this task. For example, Rolf Loeber and David Farrington are famous for their work exploring the pathways from childhood aggression to adolescent violence (including murder). Their Pittsburgh Youth Study focused on thirty-three convicted homicide offenders, thirty-three arrested homicide offenders who were not convicted, and thirty-nine homicide victims. Utilizing a wide range of risk factors that are reported in their 2011 book *Young Homicide Offenders and Victims,* Loeber and Farrington attempted to differentially identify homicide offenders from nonoffenders in their urban inner-city sample of youths. The results speak to how difficult this is. They "missed" about 40 percent of the homicide offenders (i.e., incorrectly identified them as non–homicide perpetrators) and falsely identified as homicide perpetrators more than 10 percent of the youths who, in fact, did not commit a murder.

For improvement on this success rate, we can look to the work of Chicago psychologist Robert Zagar and his colleagues. Zagar has worked for more than twenty years with the Cook County Court in an effort to understand how violence arises in the city, how to predict which individuals are most likely to act violently, how to figure out which inmates are most likely to become repeat offenders if released, and how to prevent early risk factors from translating into violent delinquent behavior in the first place. It's very important work.

The key to Zagar's work has been developing a mathematical formula (an "actuarial model") for predicting which of the many kids "at risk" will actually end up killing someone (as well as predictions regarding sexual assault). Using a mix of psychological tests (the 823-item online version takes about two hours to complete) and records from social-service and health agencies as well as the courts, Zagar and his colleagues have come up with a statistical "actuarial" approach that is remarkably accurate.

The model identifies 97 percent of those who end up as killers (missing only 3 percent), and it misidentifies as killers only 3 percent of those who do not end up killing anyone. Thus, in statistical terms, this approach offers excellent "sensitivity" (also called the "true positive rate" because it represents the proportion of the actual positives that the model correctly identified as such—i.e., the 97 percent of the killers who were correctly classified as such). And it offers excellent specificity (also called the "true negative rate"—the 97 percent of the nonoffenders who are correctly classified as such). It is extremely hard to achieve such high rates of sensitivity *and* specificity at the same time, so this is a major achievement. It validates what I have been saying in Part I of this book and paves the way for Part II.

These are the factors in their formula:

Prior court contact(s) or arrest(s)

Poor executive functioning (decision making and related abilities)

Lower social maturity

Weapons possession conviction

Violent family

Gang membership or participation

Male

Academic underachievement

Serious illnesses

Low socioeconomic status

Substance abuse

Previous neurological disorder

Alcohol abuse

Head injury

Truancy/suspension or expulsion

Single-parent family or orphaned

Hyperactivity

Epilepsy and other illnesses

Unemployment

Antisocial personality

Physical abuse

Clearly, we have examined many of these factors in Part I. Thus, Zagar's work provides an important statistical validation of the conceptual framework I have been developing. What is more, because he has made his approach available as a package of tests and data-collection instruments (to mine the records for relevant information), the result is a cost-effective way to focus attention on the individuals most in need of investment (as we will see in chapter 8, when I return to Zagar's findings regarding prevention). Access to Zagar's approach is through him directly (doctorzagar@gmail.com) as well as through a website (www.standardpredictor.com).

One final note on Zagar's work. The technical specifications of Zagar's approach are very important—particularly given that other approaches are right only 75 percent of the time, at best. For that reason, I am including at the end of this book a brief appendix that offers a detailed summary of the research underlying the model—involving thousands of children, youths, and adults—which Zagar prepared and agreed to have included. I urge everyone with the necessary level of methodological expertise to read it and the published articles on which it is based (see Appendix: Zagar's Model).

Having laid out the dynamics of moral and emotional damage that flow from growing up with trauma and the war zone mentality in Part I, it is time to move on, in Part II, to a series of issues in "applied developmental psychology" that flow from this analysis. These are the special developmental issues we face in understanding and dealing with violent adolescents, the policy and program issues involved in rehabilitation and transformation, the special role of guns and the gun culture in the dynamics of killing in America, and a final integrating analysis of "What's next?"

PART II

The American Way of Killing

5

"If You're Old Enough to Do the Crime, You're Old Enough to Do the Time"

JOHN CHRISTIANSON* WAS THIRTEEN YEARS OLD in 1996, when he killed seventeen-year-old Mannie Richards, who, along with some of his friends, was threatening John and another boy as they walked home from school in the small town of Camden, Oregon. A few months later, the judge in the case ruled that John would be tried as an adult. A press report presented what happened in court this way:

> Christianson is the youngest child to face trial as an adult in county history, officials said.
>
> But the boy's lawyer contends Christianson shouldn't be treated as an adult. "He's completely frightened," she said. "He thinks his life is over."
>
> Christianson began to cry when the judge made his ruling. Christianson also is charged with two counts of first-degree assault, unlawful possession of a firearm, second-degree assault, brandishing a weapon and two counts of felony harassment. The charges were filed in response to the Richards shooting near Camden City Park and an encounter the night before when Christianson is accused of threatening other youths with a rifle. The boy will be held in the county jail pending arraignment and a trial. A deputy prosecutor was pleased with the judge's ruling and hopes it will send a message to others. "We hope that the impact will be through the school systems and law enforcement that juveniles with guns aren't being treated as youngsters," she said. "If the message passes that the penalties are severe, it will impact their behavior."

I met John later that year in the county jail, as he awaited trial. Interviewing him with me was Claire Bedard, who had conducted many of the interviews that I drew on for my book *Lost Boys*. That meeting with John was the start of a relationship with him that has lasted two decades.

John's young life was full of trauma and loss. His mother was a drug addict who went in and out of his life. His father (whom he had never met) was in prison. He was raised mostly by his maternal grandparents, but from time to time he spent vacations with his mother and her boyfriend in Los Angeles, where he was drawn into the world of gangs and drugs. It's a long story of confusion, sadness, anger, and escalating problems in school and with his peers that culminated in the events that landed him in jail, facing trial for murder.

There was something profoundly appealing about John. Maybe it was his earnest hunger for connection and guidance as he spoke of how he was influenced by the Christian preacher who visited him (and convinced him that he should plead guilty and accept punishment for his sins) and by the adult murderer in the next cell (who drew him further into the dark side of life with his tales of sexual violence). Maybe it was the fact that his hands reminded me of my own son, Josh. Whatever it was, I was hooked, and so was Claire.

John pled guilty to second-degree murder and received a sentence of twelve years in an adult prison—albeit in the juvenile wing of that prison until he turned eighteen. John and I corresponded over the years, and I was able to visit him every time my professional travel or vacations took me to the Pacific Northwest. He once sent me a Father's Day card in which he talked about "growing up in the land of the lost." When he graduated as valedictorian of the high school he attended within the prison, Claire and I were there to cheer him on. But he went directly from there to the dark world of the adult wing in that same prison.

Like many kids who have been abandoned by their parents, John was haunted by their ghosts. All John knew about his biological father was that he was Mexican, and the only Mexicans John socialized with were the boys he met when he visited with his mother in Los Angeles, who happened to be gangbangers. I don't think it is coincidental that he became a leader of the Mexican gang in prison. By all accounts he was good at it, a natural leader.

Soon after he began his sentence, John's grandmother died, and he grieved the loss of the woman who had been more of a mother to him than his biological mother ever was. To his credit, John's grandfather, Ron, stuck by him over the years, even though he was only his grandmother's second husband and not biologically related to John at all. Ron visited John as often as he could, and half hoped, half believed that the goodness in his grandson would prevail over the moral and emotional damage that he brought with him into the prison. But that damage was reinforced and amplified by John's experiences there, year after year of his adolescence, until he was integrated into the ranks of the adult inmates.

I shared Ron's hope, but over the years when I visited John and when we spoke on the phone or exchanged letters, I felt and saw his hardening identity as a criminal. He had a sense of this himself, often remarking that the norms and ethics of life in prison were very different from the norms and ethics of life on the outside. He told me of all that he had learned, spending his adolescence and early adulthood in prison, "growing up in the land of the lost." He learned how to fight, how to lie, how to intimidate, how to manipulate, how to protect himself from exploitation, how to exploit others. What he didn't learn was how to live successfully in the outside world. Research by psychologist Craig Haney confirms that in this, John was like many adolescents who receive lengthy sentences, particularly lengthy sentences in adult prison.

As he approached the end of his twelve-year sentence, John spoke of his dreams of making a good life for himself. But more and more, as that release date approached, it became clear that his terms of reference—money, cars, thrills, and sex—doomed him. As a felon, he had a hard time finding a job. When he finally did, it was with a business owned by his girlfriend. When that relationship ended, he was out of a job and at loose ends; before long, he was dealing drugs.

He was arrested and ended up back in prison. Eventually, we lost contact as he disappeared into the penal system and the "lifestyle" it represented. He told me in one of our last conversations that that way of living was familiar to him. He knew the rules. He knew how to make his way there. Having come of age in prison, he was so thoroughly "prisonized," as Craig Haney puts it, that he was more "at home" there than he had been in the outside world after his release.

I always wondered how John's life might have been different if the criminal justice system had treated him as the kid he was in 1996, rather than the adult it believed him to be, the "danger to the community" the judge called him in court when he transferred John's case to adult criminal court.

What if he hadn't moved John out of the juvenile system, where he might have had a better chance to forge a different path? What if the bullet he fired in 1996, as a way of threatening the older kids who were plaguing him, had missed? When you are confronted with a fourteen-year-old boy as I was in 1996, you have to wonder "What if. . . ."

This might have been the end of the story of my relationship to John Christianson, but as it turned out it wasn't. In late April, 2014, out of the blue, I received a long letter from him. It read, in part:

Jim:

It has taken me years to sit down and write you this letter. And even now the words fail me. There is so much I want to talk to you and Claire about, so many things I want to tell you. I miss the both of you. I miss our connection, our love and the sense of family we had together. It's very hard for me to write this letter. I feel so much shame, for sitting here in prison once again at 31 years old, and for allowing my life to turn out this way. . . . But through it all I am still filled with hope. This is not how my story will end. . . . Your lost son is still a work in progress. The journey continues. . . .

With Love,
John Christianson

I wrote back to John reaffirming my care for him and asking for more information. He wrote back quickly, describing how he had severed his ties with the gang and moved into a special unit in the prison, reserved for men who had broken with gangs, to create the social and psychological space he needed for rehabilitation and transformation—to redirect his "continuing journey." In my follow-up letter, I promised that I would visit him and keep the door open for him to become something more than my "lost son." I had begun to hope for John again, and would offer what support I could. There are no guarantees, but there is hope. I felt that when I visited him in October of 2014 and witnessed his emerging shift in consciousness. Time will tell where it leads him. He hopes, and I do too.

WHAT TO DO ABOUT KIDS WHO KILL?

The American Bar Association reviewed the history of our juvenile justice system and found its American origins in English common law. Traditionally, under the English common law that provides some of the foundation for American legal thinking, a child less than seven years of age was thought to be developmentally incapable of forming the state of mind (*mens rea,* or "guilty mind") necessary to be held accountable for criminal acts. That made a child immune from prosecution. Younger children were thus below the legal "age of criminal responsibility" (the age below which a child cannot be held legally responsible).

Children seven to thirteen years old were presumed to be mentally incapable of true criminal action, but this could be challenged in court, on a case-by-case basis. In such cases, the prosecution bore the burden of proof for opening the door to prosecution in adult court. Children fourteen and older were presumed to be criminally capable. This too could be challenged in court on a case-by-case basis, but here the burden of proof fell upon the defense (i.e., to prove that the adolescent was *not* mentally capable).

In the American legal system today, states differ in where they set the lower limit for the presumption of criminal responsibility; the age range is from six to twelve. In some cases, states that don't have mandatory minimums rely on the English common law age (i.e., seven); in other cases (e.g., Illinois) there is no minimum age. For federal crimes the minimum age is eleven.

The youngest age at which young killers can be tried *as an adult* (as opposed to the age at which they can be tried at all, ordinarily in a juvenile court) varies from state to state. Some states have no minimum age, which means that any child could be tried as an adult. Many states set a lower limit, generally somewhere between ten and twelve. Some states set an upper age limit (lower than the "bright line" of eighteen that the U.S. Supreme Court has set and to which all states and the federal government adhere), above which a child charged with homicide is automatically tried as an adult. For example, it is mandatory in Wisconsin that a killer ten years of age or older who has committed a serious violent crime be tried as an adult unless the court makes an exception, a policy that I have come to know firsthand.

These policies followed upon an earlier shift toward changing laws to permit the trying of young adolescents (as young as thirteen) for murder in adult court. The case that started the trend was the case of Willie Bosket (in New York State)—the very case that led Fox Butterfield to begin the research that led to his 1995 book *All God's Children* (which I cited in chapter 3 in regard to the southern culture of honor). The subtitle of Butterfield's book is "The Bosket Family and the American Tradition of Violence."

Willie had followed in the footsteps of his father, Willie Senior, through the juvenile system, and his violent intransigence (fueled by a cunning intelligence) persuaded lawmakers that they needed a more powerful response than the juvenile court system and its affiliated institutions could provide.

Therefore, in 1978, at the urging of then Governor Hugh Carey, they passed the Juvenile Offender Act, which made kids fifteen and older eligible for prosecution as adults in murder cases.

By the 1990s, there was public concern (one might say "hysteria") about the rise of what were then referred to as "superpredators"—a term coined and popularized by political scientist John Dilulio. In 1995, he predicted the rise of a "new breed" of offenders, "kids that have absolutely no respect for human life and no sense of the future.... These are stone-cold predators!" Murder rates had risen in the 1980s and early 1990s, and this fueled acceptance of Dilulio's thesis.

As James Howell pointed out in his 2009 book *Preventing and Reducing Juvenile Delinquency,* prominent criminologists like James Q. Wilson took the same approach in 1995, arguing that in the near future (five years), society would be flooded with tens of thousands of remorselessly violent youths: "Get ready," Wilson wrote. James Howell also identified criminologist James Fox's 1996 warning of "a bloodbath" of teen violence and a "juvenile crime wave" storm. And Howell cited others who joined this chorus, such as criminologist Al Blumstein, who echoed these themes in his work as well in the mid-1990s, tying these trends to the "crack cocaine epidemic." Many observers in the mid-1990s, beyond this small group, saw the same trends and were alarmed (myself included). But I and others did not see the affected youth through the diabolical lens that those in the "superpredator" camp did. In my book *Lost Boys,* I argued for an insistence upon their humanity, not their inhumanity. Alas, this message fell on mostly deaf ears.

Legislators took note of the diabolical superpredator model of youth violence (fear always sells in American politics), and there was a national push toward harsher, more adult-like punishments—life without parole for juveniles being one response. Along with this came a retreat from rehabilitation as a goal of incarceration, and a greater emphasis on punishment ("sending a message") and containment (a kind of "preventive detention" based on the principle that the longer criminals are locked up, the less time they have among the general public to commit more crimes).

As many observers of the juvenile justice system have noted, however, the epidemic of juvenile superpredators predicted by Dilulio, Fox, Blumstein, and others did not materialize. Howell and others came to define "the rise of the superpredator" as a destructive myth, destructive because it led to policies that violated the human rights of troubled kids and to policies and programs that were (and are) self-defeating. It illustrates one of my favorite cautionary slogans: "You can change the world . . . but unless you know what you are doing, please don't!"

Things now are generally much as they have been for decades (and some in the superpredator camp—like James Q. Wilson—ultimately admitted in public that their projections had not been confirmed, that their extrapolations from the youth homicide data of the early 1990s did not pan out). In fact, things got better after 1995, rather than worse, as youth murder rates dropped rather than increased, and those rates are now at historical lows, according to the Centers for Disease Control and Prevention. Where they will go as we move through the twenty-first century is an open question. Of course, this acknowledgment of the trends in numbers does not deal with the false dehumanization at the heart of the "superpredator" concept itself, a topic we will return to later.

As Mosi Secret reported in *The New York Times* in 2011, there has been a national trend to prosecute fewer adolescents as adults, but this affects only those on the borderline between fifteen and seventeen. It includes legislative changes that have raised the age of adulthood for purposes of criminal prosecution from sixteen or seventeen to the national standard of eighteen, as well as a trend toward prosecutors allowing the prosecution of juveniles *as juveniles* in the criminal justice system.

Innovations in the treatment of juveniles have helped reduce the numbers (e.g., the use of electronic monitors and improved counseling techniques such as "multisystemic therapy" and "trauma-focused cognitive–behavioral therapy"). What is more, demographic and economic changes of the late 1990s reduced the numbers of kids living in severe deprivation. Financial pressures on state governments have led to a willingness to consider less expensive "community" solutions over more costly lockup options. All these factors have resulted in a 41 percent decline since 1995 in the number of juveniles in detention, according to a report by the Annie E. Casey Foundation. To quote the report:

> Data from the U.S. Census Bureau and the U.S. Department of Justice Office of Juvenile Justice and Delinquency Prevention show that youth confinement peaked in 1995, at 107,637 in confinement on a single day. Since then the number of youth confined has dropped by nearly 37,000 to 70,792. Over the same period, the rate of youth in confinement dropped by 41 percent, from 381 per 100,000 youth to 225 per 100,000. . . . Despite this rapid decline, the United States still locks up a larger share of the youth population than any other developed country.

WHAT HAPPENS WHEN INCARCERATION IS
BIG BUSINESS?

At the same time, the rise of private prisons has created enormous political pressure to create clients for their businesses. The rise of for-profit prisons has injected into the public policy debate an actor with a financial incentive to increase incarceration—and a business interest that masquerades as concern for public safety (in a manner similar to the role of the National Rifle Association in the national debates about gun control, as we will see in chapter 7). Private prisons earn hundreds of millions of dollars for their investors and, like the gun industry, have taken to lobbying public officials as a way to increase sales. They do so very effectively.

A 2011 report by the Justice Policy Institute titled "Gaming the System: How the Political Strategies of Private Prison Companies Promote Ineffective Incarceration Policies" documents how the lucrative private prison industry (the two largest companies had revenue totaling three billion dollars in 2012) pursues its entrepreneurial agenda by influencing the governments that are its clients. The report reveals the private prison industry's three principal routes of political influence: direct lobbying, campaign contributions, and social networking.

Over a ten-year period, the three biggest private prison companies contributed more than $6 million to politicians at the state level (where most of the big financial decisions regarding incarceration are made). In addition, their direct lobbying efforts have cost them hundreds of thousands of dollars. What is more, industry leaders cultivate relationships with key political decision makers. The Justice Policy Institute cites as an example the fact that the cofounder of Corrections Corporation of America (an "industry leader") used to be the chairman of the Tennessee Republican Party.

I think that privatization of prisons is like privatization of hospitals, fire departments, police forces, and other public services. It injects a profit motive into the sensitive issues of helping and usually leads us into further problems. The Justice Policy Institute's report indicates that while the total population in prisons has increased by about 50 percent over the past fifteen years, the number of inmates in private prisons has increased by about 350 percent. Crime does pay—for the prison business.

One final note on this issue: Looking at the few studies available, there is no conclusive evidence that private prisons do any better on measures of recidivism than public prisons. An analysis conducted by Adrian Smith and published in 2012 on Corrections.com offered this review of the evidence:

> A study by the U.S. Bureau of Justice Statistics found that the cost-savings promised by private prisons "have simply not materialized." Some research has concluded that for-profit prisons cost more than public prisons. Furthermore, cost estimates from privatization advocates may be misleading, because private facilities often refuse to accept inmates that cost the most to house. A 2001 study concluded that a pattern of sending less expensive inmates to privately-run facilities artificially inflated cost savings. A 2005 study found that Arizona's public facilities were seven times more likely to house violent offenders and three times more likely to house those convicted of more serious offenses.

Moreover, "Evidence suggests that lower staff levels and training at private facilities may lead to increases in the incidence of violence and escapes. A nationwide study found that assaults on guards by inmates were 49 percent more frequent in private prisons than in government-run prisons. The same study revealed that assaults on fellow inmates were 65 percent more frequent in private prisons."

All of this is important for many reasons. From my perspective, it is important because anything that creates an incentive to see a man instead of a boy when a juvenile criminal presents himself is a problem. I worry about private prisons particularly on this score, because it's in their financial interest to see every possible young offender not as a boy who needs help, but as a *man* eligible for incarceration in their facilities, a "customer" either now or in the future.

LOST BOYS OR LOST MEN?

Important as the issue of reversing the trend away from juvenile to adult prosecution and incarceration is, my principal concern here is not with the legal position of children at the lower age of the "criminal responsibility" continuum. It lies rather with the upper end, the point at which boys become men. Every state's laws set eighteen as the upper limit of what it means to be a minor for legal purposes in the criminal justice system. Thus, killers who have turned eighteen are everywhere defined as men (or women) rather than boys (or girls). The FBI reports that of some fifteen thousand murders that typically occur each year, only about 2 percent are committed by kids ages thirteen to sixteen. Individuals ages seventeen to nineteen years old commit about 10 percent, and individuals twenty to twenty-four years old commit about 17 percent.

Of the killers whose cases I detail in this book, many were in the eighteen-to-twenty-four age range that accounts for more than one in four murders in our country. Robert Tallman was twenty; Junior Mercedez was twenty-three; Leonel Rivas was nineteen; Ron Richardson was twenty; Duke Jimenez was nineteen; Malcolm Jones was twenty-two; Jane Montero was twenty-one; Tim Bankovic was eighteen; Marquan Banner was eighteen; James Jackson was eighteen; Andrew Dirkson was twenty. All were legal adults as much as if they had been in their thirties (the group that commits 24 percent of all the murders in the United States).

But were they really adults? Were they lost *boys* or lost *men?* I have had some wrangles in court on this point. In the case of Jacquon Jones* in the late 1990s, during the prosecutor's cross-examination, he sarcastically commented on my use of the term "lost boy" when I referred to the nineteen-year-old defendant. "Isn't he really a man?" he asked rhetorically. I replied that given the trauma and social deprivation that Jacquon experienced growing up, he was psychologically immature, as were many so-called "young adults" like him—impulsive, socially inexperienced beyond the toxic world of the inner-city, drug-fueled gang culture in which he lived . . . and killed. To my mind he *was* a lost boy.

The World Health Organization defines "adolescence" as extending to age 19. The United Nations cultural organization, UNESCO, defines "youth" as the period between ages fifteen and twenty-four. All the young killers I noted earlier would fall into this category. Yet from the perspective of the criminal justice system, they were all fully adult.

Psychologists are starting to direct their research attention to what developmental psychologist Jeffrey Arnet, in a 2000 article in the *American Psychologist,* called "emerging adulthood" (offering "a theory of development from the late teens through the twenties"). He cites a wide range of evidence to support the view that "emerging adulthood is a distinct period demographically, subjectively, and in terms of identity explorations." Arnet reports that when asked if they have "reached adulthood," nearly 60 percent of those ages eighteen to twenty-five answer "in some respects yes, but in some respects no." Moreover, various forms of risk-taking behavior (unprotected sex, most types of substance abuse, and risky driving behavior) peak *not* in adolescence, but in this emerging adulthood period. There is even an organization devoted to studying this phenomenon (the Society for the Study of Emerging Adulthood).

In this chapter, I am concerned with how we understand and treat young killers, whether they are officially children (younger than ten), officially minors (younger than eighteen), or officially adults (if they are eighteen or older but still engaged in the transition to full social and psychological adulthood, which may not come until their late twenties). Perhaps they are not children, these young killers, but for the most part they are not men and women. As a developmental psychologist with forty years of professional experience, and as a man in his late sixties with grown children in their thirties, I do see them as boys, lost boys. Some of them, the younger ones, really are just boys, no matter how the legal system tries to redefine them.

THE CASE OF MARTIN TEFFLER

October 18, 1999: I am sitting across from fourteen-year-old Martin Teffler* in an interview room in the Juvenile Detention Center in Johnson, Ohio. Martin is at a crossroads in his young life—charged, as an adult, with conspiracy to commit murder. If he goes to trial as an adult and is convicted, he could face a sentence of life imprisonment without the possibility of parole. The charges stem from his arrest three months earlier on evidence that he and two other boys were planning to commit an attack on their school. Martin was joined in jail by Obedia Jones* (another fourteen-year-old, who was also charged as an adult) and a thirteen-year-old whose identity had been withheld because he was being dealt with as a juvenile. The boys had made a "hit list" of 165 targets, stole a plan of the school building from the custodian's office, and got their hands on Martin's father's gun so that they could steal other weapons. Their plot was elaborate and included stealing a van, forcing the principal of their school to play a rap song over the PA system, massacring students and others on their "hit list," and getting away in a blaze of glory, which included flying to New York City in a hijacked airplane. They were caught when another teen overheard them boasting of their plan. This was just months after the horrendous Columbine High School shooting in Colorado, in which two teenagers killed thirteen people before committing suicide, and with the rash of other school shootings in recent years, it is little wonder that many in Johnson responded with alarm, even hysteria.

When I listened to Martin, I heard a troubled, confused, angry, and hurt boy, not a young adult mastermind of a terrorist plot. I heard a boy who got carried away with melodramatic boasting, showing off in a way that was understandable if you listened to him closely. He was a boy immersed in military culture who had been "playing Army" avidly since he was a child, a boy whose father had been a soldier in the Army. I heard a boy who had long-standing and painful issues with his social status in school. He spoke of the hierarchy in his school as having the "preps" at the top, the "normal kids" in the middle, and the "scrubs" at the bottom. Although he was adamant about not being classified as one of the "scrubs," his peers identified him as such. He told me that he used the money he earned from his part-time job as a busboy at the K-Mart restaurant to buy "good" clothes (that his parents couldn't or wouldn't buy for him) so that he could fit in with the "normal kids." I heard a boy talk about his father's history in the community (public drunkenness and low-grade confrontations with the police), a history that reinforced the boy's need to "elevate" himself in the eyes and ears of his peers. I heard a boy who, at the time of the plot four months earlier, was in a period of crisis at home and at school. He had been suspended for mouthing off at a teacher. He had been suspended for wearing his military-style fatigues at school. He had been suspended for fighting. He was mad at his parents (having been involved in an intense confrontation with them in the days before his arrest). All these things heightened his boasting and posturing to meet his need to appear tough, to please his ex-soldier father, and to "elevate" himself in the eyes of his peers.

I heard how this troubled, vulnerable boy was caught up in the hysteria of post-Columbine America, excited by the media frenzy that brought attention to Dylan Klebold and Eric Harris in the wake of their attack and suicides in Colorado only months before. Of course, in this he was not alone. Across America, many troubled, melodramatic kids (one of whom I eventually interviewed) were similarly caught up and swept away by the dark fame earned by Klebold and Harris for their crazed, doomed attack on their school. When a teenager created a website called "www.thechurchof DylanandEric.com" (now defunct), kids from all over the country signed on to express their solidarity with the feelings that drove those boys to do what they did. Like so many young boys, Martin converted his sadness to aggression, living out the message boys absorb that it is "better to be mad than sad." I heard all this and more, and then wrote a report for his attorneys that concluded this way: "I believe it would be a miscarriage of justice to try Martin Teffler as an adult for conspiracy to commit murder. He acted as a tough-talking fourteen-year-old on the outside and a fragile child on the inside who liked to 'play' army, not someone with adult reasoning and emotional maturity creating and implementing an elaborate plan to commit murder."

Although Martin's plot was discovered and he was apprehended before he could carry out his attacks, I believe that his case tells an important story, as does the case that follows Martin's in this chapter—in which, once again, no one actually died. I start with Martin because, in many ways, his case illustrates the problems that the legal system, and we as a society, have in knowing how to approach violent adolescents. The fact that he could have been sentenced to life in prison if the local prosecutor's plan had been accepted by a jury says a great deal about the cultural and legal context of adolescent violence in America.

At the time I interviewed Martin Teffler in 1999, some twenty-five hundred individuals in the United States were serving life sentences without parole for crimes committed before they were eighteen years of age—nearly one hundred who were fourteen or younger. If the prosecutor in Johnson had stuck to his guns and had his way, Martin would probably have become one of them.

It was a day before jury selection began that the district attorney, confronted with my report, changed his mind (I would say "opened his mind" to the possibility that there was more to the story) and permitted Martin and his fourteen-year-old coconspirator to be tried as the juveniles they were. Martin pleaded guilty to a juvenile charge of "conspiracy to commit assault with intent to commit great bodily harm" and was sentenced to a juvenile facility where, over time, he could be assessed psychiatrically as he developed and matured, and where there would be time to help him deal with his emotional and social issues.

TIME CAN HEAL SOME WOUNDS

It's worth noting that the passage of time is often "therapeutic" for adolescents. The highly publicized case of Andy Williams (who shot and killed two students and wounded many others at his high school in Santee, California, on March 5, 2001) provides a sad example. Fifteen-year-old Andy had moved recently from a small town in Maryland and didn't fit in well in his California school. He was teased and bullied for many reasons, but particularly for being short, a "late-maturing boy" as he would be known if he were in a developmental psychologist's research project.

I never met Andy, although I was contacted by a group of individuals who organized to support him (and who have continued to advocate on his behalf in the years since the shooting occurred). From them I learned that in the fifteen months from when he committed the shooting until he went to court, this late-maturing boy actually did mature physically, and as a result grew by nearly a foot. The tall teenager who faced the court was no longer the shrimp who had committed the crime—for which he was tried as an adult and ultimately sentenced to fifty years to life in prison.

If only he could have waited a year! His shortness would have disappeared, and perhaps with it the characteristics that opened him up to the teasing and bullying that drove him over the edge. He might have matured in those fifteen months to the point where he found alternative ways to make his life more positive and less the living hell it seemed to be for him in March of 2001.

The passage of time can heal a great deal when it is given a chance. It can really change things for the better in a teenager's life—if the adult world and the criminal justice system give it a chance, and don't override the process of development by declaring that a teenager is an adult and then sentencing him to a lifetime in prison before there is an opportunity to demonstrate and observe the changes that maturation and therapy can achieve.

Things really did change for Martin Teffler, and for the better, because the prosecution gave up on charging him as an adult and rather let him be the 14-year-old kid that I sat with in October of 1999. He went to a juvenile facility and cooperated with the help they offered. I don't know the details of the treatment he was given, but no doubt it involved counseling and a chance to reflect on his motivations and his behavior in the months and days leading up to his arrest. The shock of it all, the reflection it stimulated, the counseling he received, and the passage of time were successful.

Martin went to a juvenile facility rather than a prison, and a couple of years later he was released. He graduated from high school on time, entered the Navy, rose to the rank of Chief, and married. Had he been tried as an adult, he might well have disappeared into the prison system and never been heard from again, like so many others who have gone that route—like John Christianson, perhaps, or Andy Williams, or any one of the other teenage shooters who survived their misguided assaults on their schools and were then sentenced to spend the rest of their lives in prison.

THE CASE OF DAN ARMSTRONG

I interviewed seventeen-year-old Dan Armstrong* on February 22, 2012, in my office in Chicago, with his distraught mother sitting outside. Dan was charged as an adult with attempted murder. As I noted earlier, in some states, kids ten and older are automatically charged as adults if they are charged with homicide—or, as in Dan's case, attempted homicide. Dan was unlucky enough to live in one of those states.

Dan was sixteen when he was charged. He and a teenage girl, Tanya, had made a suicide pact. Tanya was seriously depressed and had asked Dan to help her complete her suicide plan. As a show of solidarity with this girl whom he loved with all the passion of a misguided, naive, and melodramatic teenager, Dan had reluctantly agreed to kill himself as well, "so we could be in Heaven together forever," he told me. The two kids chose a nearby park to complete their plan.

Tanya asked Dan to help her cut her wrists with the knife the kids had stolen from Dan's mother. "She said, all I had to do was guide her hand," Dan said. And then he cut his own wrists. The cuts were not deep enough on either of the kids for them to bleed out, so Tanya asked for Dan's help in cutting her neck, and he obliged. Then Dan cut himself on the neck, and the couple waited for death.

Luckily for both kids, death did not come, and Dan used his cell phone to call his mother to come get him and help the girl. Tanya survived, but the local prosecutor charged Dan as an adult with attempted murder. That was the law. But the law did allow for Dan's case to be moved over into the juvenile system. The public defender assigned to the case petitioned to do that, but the prosecutor insisted that Dan be tried as an adult. This was over the objections of Tanya and her family, not to mention Dan's parents, the psychiatrist who assessed Dan, and me. (And, I would argue, anyone with even a modicum of understanding of teenagers in general and Dan in particular.)

The legal system, in the person of the local prosecutor, may have seen this as a clear case of attempted first-degree homicide. After all, Dan knew that his actions could cause Tanya's death, and he willingly chose to do them anyway. But from the perspective of the mental health professionals involved in the case (and many other observers), it was hardly a clear case in these terms at all. In a sense, it is best seen as two attempted suicides coupled with an effort at "assisted suicide."

In psychiatric terms, this case has elements of what used to be called "shared psychotic disorder" by the Diagnostic and Statistical Manual-IV of the American Psychiatric Association (and is now simply considered a specific variant of psychotic disorders in DSM-V). In this psychopathology, one party draws another into a delusional system (as, I think, happened between Harris and Klebold in Columbine). In the present case, Tanya drew Dan into a delusional system that had two primary elements. First, Tanya thought that committing suicide was a good solution to her situation (e.g., a better alternative than returning to a psychiatric facility). Second, Dan saw helping her do it, and joining her in death, as a demonstration of his loving commitment to her. In this he was offering a contrast to the way she was treated by other boys, including her boyfriend at the time of the suicide pact, Tom (who was planning to turn her in to her parents or the police).

When I interviewed him, Dan explained to me that he tried to help Tanya kill herself out of positive feelings of mercy, compassion, and love for her. When I asked him what he thought would have happened if they had died, he replied, "We would be together in Heaven." When I asked what he feared most (as he faced the possibility of a very long period of incarceration), he replied, "That I won't get to see her again." And then he started to cry. When we finished the interview, I gave him a big hug. Sometimes, simple humanity has to trump professional objectivity.

As an impressionable, love-struck, somewhat troubled, and socially isolated boy with no previous romantic experience, Dan was highly vulnerable to being drawn into Tanya's world. I met Tanya (and the rest of her family) the day I testified on Dan's behalf on July 14, 2013. She came across as perhaps the most depressed young person I have ever met, a kind of emotional black hole. But for Dan she was irresistible.

Here is what the child psychiatrist who interviewed Dan had to say about him in court: "Though it appears on paper that Dan should be culpable for his actions in willfully helping another person to end their life, the reality is that Dan is a kind, compassionate boy with immature problem solving, and minimal experiences in complicated human relationships. He has in many ways been a victim of another person's significant mental health troubles and drive for death, combined with his own extreme naivety."

In helping Tanya slide the knife across her wrists and cutting her throat, Dan was not motivated by any conventional criminal intent—no money, rage, or revenge was involved. This case was, first and foremost, a mental health crisis involving two troubled teenagers whose behavior incidentally crossed over into the criminal domain of killing. Moral and emotional damage was present, of course, in what Dan did, but not of the severity and nature of the cases described in chapters 3 and 4. He was not poor, nor living in a setting dominated by community violence, nor the victim of traumatic maltreatment. I think the criminality in this situation was incidental to the larger, more pressing mental-health issues besetting these two kids.

Any rational response would have included taking the time to assess who Dan really was, and where this particular incident fit into his past behavior. More importantly, it would have focused on what might be true of his *future* behavior. He was, after all, just a kid, and by all indications not a kid on the pathway to a long-term pattern of antisocial, criminal, violent behavior. Dealing with Dan as the juvenile he was would only recognize realistically the nature and origins of his behavior. Trying him as an adult would fulfill some fantasy worldview in which he was a mature criminal actor.

The issue came to a head when I testified at the hearing to decide whether Dan should be tried in adult court, as the law provided, or have his case moved to juvenile court. It is called a "reverse waiver hearing," and it was necessary in order to waive the legal default option of trying the case in adult court. It was necessary to engage in this reverse process because of the state's law—and the prosecutor's intransigence.

In his cross-examination of me, the prosecutor kept referring to Dan as "Mr. Armstrong," as is common in the way the criminal justice system deals with kids. I saw this as an opportunity to highlight the underlying issue contained in the expression "If you're old enough to do the crime, you're old enough to do the time." I was profoundly disturbed by the thought that we were in a court-room arguing about the legal presumption that kids should be tried as adults.

To make this point, the next time the prosecutor referred to Dan as "Mr. Armstrong," I responded: "That's part of the problem, that you keep referring to Dan as 'Mr. Armstrong.' Mr. Armstrong is the man sitting in the third row of seats in this courtroom, Dan's father. We are talking about Dan, a sixteen-year-old kid at the time of this terrible incident."

From her reaction to my testimony and that of the child psychiatrist, I thought that the judge got the point. Later, when she issued her ruling, it indicated that legally, her hands were tied. She said that Dan would be tried as an adult because his case did not meet the strict criteria for a reverse waiver to juvenile court—most notably, that the adult system could not meet his mental health needs; the other criteria were that the move would not affect the likelihood of others doing what Dan did and that the move would not undermine the seriousness of the crime. It was a sad day for everyone on the defense side of the courtroom (and I think for almost everyone else involved, with perhaps the exception of the prosecutor). It looked like Dan might follow John Christianson's path, rather than Martin Teffler's.

As it turned out, the prosecutor ultimately agreed to let Dan plead to charges *as an adult* that allowed him to escape prison in favor of mental-health interventions and probation. I was told that this was the result of political pressure put on the prosecutor to avoid the public outcry that would have ensued if Dan had been sentenced to adult prison. Dan's mother told me she was planning to make such an effort ("I'm going to raise hell about this until someone pays attention!" were her words to me).

I cannot verify the prosecutor's motivations, only the result of his action. The judge sentenced Dan to two years of probation. Thus, Dan was given a chance to follow the path that Martin had walked, rather than being cast into the dark hole of prison as John was. Granted, Dan was a "typical teen-ager," as his lawyer called him, with near perfect school attendance and an otherwise spotless record, whereas Martin and John were troubled and aggression-prone boys. But is the happy fact that Dan and Martin failed in their attempts to kill people while John succeeded enough to justify the radically different paths their lives have taken? I don't think so.

THE SUPREME COURT RULES ON THE FATE
OF YOUNG CRIMINALS

In 2005, in a five-to-four decision, the U.S. Supreme Court ruled (in the case of *Missouri v. Christopher Simmons*) that it was unconstitutional to pronounce a death sentence for crimes committed while the defendant was still a juvenile (younger than eighteen). Speaking for the majority, Justice Anthony Kennedy wrote, "The age of 18 is the point where society draws the line for many purposes between childhood and adulthood. . . . It is, we conclude, the age at which the line for death eligibility ought to rest."

In a harsh dissenting opinion, Justice Antonin Scalia said that the majority opinion did not reflect American values and principles, but only "the subjective views of five members of this court and like-minded foreigners." The reference to "like-minded foreigners" is instructive. The United States remains only one of two nations that have failed to ratify the United Nations Convention on the Rights of the Child, which, among other things, bans the execution of minors. The only other UN member state that has failed to ratify the convention is Somalia. Somalia's excuse is that it doesn't have a functioning central government. Of course, sometimes it seems we don't either—witness the debt crisis/government shutdown fiasco of 2013.

In 2010, the Supreme Court followed up on its decision about capital punishment for juveniles in the case of *Florida v. Graham,* by deciding that it was similarly unconstitutional to sentence juveniles to life without the possibility of parole for crimes other than murder. Seventeen-year-old Terrance Graham was on probation for robbery when he committed another robbery. The judge in the case sentenced him to life without parole because he was a "threat to society."

Writing for the majority in *Florida v. Graham,* Justice Anthony Kennedy said that juveniles "lack maturity and have an underdeveloped sense of responsibility." These two five-to-four decisions by the court, one banning execution and the other life sentences without parole for crimes other than homicide, brought U.S. legal policy closer to conformity with the rest of the modern world. This, of course, is exactly where Scalia and others like him *don't* want us to be. It's as if the rest of the world is debating Twitter versus email, and the United States is just getting its head around the concept of the fax machine. And Scalia and company believe we are the better for it.

Underlying the movement to try children and adolescents as adults in criminal cases is the proposition that "If you're old enough to do the crime, you're old enough to do the time." This might be dismissed as simply a misguided platitude, were it not so terrible in its consequences. As I said before, American prisons contain some twenty-five hundred individuals who were sentenced to life imprisonment (or death) for crimes committed as children or adolescents. The Supreme Court decisions regarding life imprisonment for juveniles have stimulated review (and possible change of status) for many of these individuals, but the issue of over-incarceration of youth remains. It's an uphill battle.

ADOLESCENTS ARE NOT ADULTS

As I see it, the underlying problem that puts kids in prison for life is the fundamental miscarriage of justice attached to routinely trying juveniles as adults on the basis of the acts they commit (whether completed or just intended) rather than an appreciation for who they are developmentally.

Would it have made a difference if John Christianson had been tried as a juvenile and placed in a stable adolescent treatment program that would have helped him deal with his emotional and conduct problems, as Martin Teffler was? Would it have made a difference if he *knew* that being successful in that adolescent treatment program would enable him to leave the facility at eighteen or twenty-one and enter adulthood as a free young man without an adult felony conviction, as Martin Teffler did? Who knows? I can't say for sure that I do. But because he went to adult prison rather than to a more age-appropriate program, we will never know.

No doubt, my relationship with John Christianson has affected my view of trying juveniles in the adult criminal justice system, but my objection to trying kids as adults goes beyond my beliefs and my experiences. It is also founded in the scientific concerns of developmental psychology. The available evidence tells us that the adult system is not well prepared to deal with juveniles, most especially juveniles with significant mental health issues—which, it turns out, is most of the juveniles incarcerated in both systems.

A study by Linda Teplin and her colleagues, published in 2002, found that the majority of incarcerated youths (nearly two-thirds of males and nearly three-quarters of females) were troubled enough to meet the official criteria to be diagnosed with one or more psychiatric disorders. The study found high levels of mental health problems even after excluding kids with "conduct disorder," that pattern of chronic aggression, bad behavior, and acting out that is likely to get a young person incarcerated in the first place. Among the group without a diagnosis of conduct disorder, nearly 60 percent of males and over two-thirds of females met diagnostic criteria and had diagnosis-specific impairment for one or more psychiatric disorders. These included "a substance use disorder," "affective disorders" (like depression), and various other "disruptive behavior disorders."

My point is that the centrality of mental health problems is not true only in cases like Dan's, where the offense in question is so clearly and directly related to an emotional crisis. It is also true in the much more common cases like John's, where the offense comes out of a chronic pattern of aggression, bad behavior, and violating the rights of others, a pattern which, in mental health terms, is labeled "conduct disorder." And it is even true among kids whose mental health problem is not itself the immediate cause of incarceration (e.g., depression or substance abuse).

Although their treatment needs are different, the evidence is clear that most kids who are incarcerated require the kind of high-quality psychological services geared to adolescents in a safe, supportive, and nurturing environment that Martin Teffler received, and which he used to recover his life and get back on track. This precious commodity is scarce enough in many juvenile programs, but it is sorely lacking in the adult prisons, to which juveniles may be sentenced when they are treated like adults in the legal system.

Within the field of psychiatry, it is understood that child and adolescent psychiatry is a subfield, distinct from adult psychiatry, and such professionals are not generally found in adult facilities. Staff in juvenile facilities are more likely to define their mission as rehabilitative and to pursue efforts to accomplish that goal in a manner appropriate to adolescents. Indeed, that goal was a major reason why juvenile courts were created in the first place: to provide a setting where the focus is on understanding and treatment, not merely classification and punishment (albeit with some attention to rehabilitation), as is largely the case in the adult system.

It is difficult to protect adolescents (particularly those like Dan, with no history of "street smart" violent behavior and toughness) from the predatory behavior of older inmates. And research compiled by psychologist Craig Haney shows that the younger individuals are when incarcerated, the more likely they will develop severe adjustment reactions to prison life that will impede the normal development of social skills, appropriate values, codes of behavior. And that's not all.

DETERRENCE DOESN'T WORK WITH JUVENILES

Research on the lack of a deterrent effect of dealing with juveniles in the adult criminal system is clear. An authoritative review conducted in 1996 for the federal government by Jeffrey Fagan, a well-respected expert in these matters, concluded: "Most of the evidence on general deterrence suggests that laws that increase the threat of sentencing and incarceration as an adult have no effect on youth crime rates. Research on specific deterrence consistently finds that adolescent offenders transferred to criminal court have higher rates of reoffending than do those retained in juvenile court. Rarely do social scientists or policy analysts report such consistency and agreement under such widely varying samples, measurement, and analytic conditions."

Of course, higher rates of reoffending for juveniles transferred to adult criminal court could be related to the seriousness of the crimes committed by the juveniles who are transferred, as well as "who" those juveniles are in terms of their background and antisocial history. But Fagan and others who have studied this issue conclude that those factors are not really the issue at hand. The issue is much more the way adults think about the motivations and actions of delinquent kids than it is significant differences in the kids themselves. That's why the supposed deterrent effect doesn't happen.

The prosecutor who argued for trying John Christianson as an adult said in court, "If the message passes that the penalties are severe, it will impact their behavior." But Fagan's research attests to the fact that this just isn't true. Martin Teffler knew that the two boys who attacked Columbine High School a few months before had died (at their own hands). That did not deter him. Nor did it deter the other kids who attacked their schools with guns in the months and years after the events in Littleton, Colorado. After all, most of these kids were so depressed or hopeless or narcissistic or deluded that they wanted to die. That was part of their plan.

Were there kids who wanted to make war against their schools and peers but declined to do so because of the deterrent effect of long prison sentences for those who did? It's possible, of course. But research on the psychology of adolescent thinking suggests it is implausible that criminal penalties have much of a deterrent effect on adolescent behavior. Larry Steinberg and Elizabeth Scott's 2003 state-of-the-art review came to this conclusion. Their report has become a definitive review of research on this topic, a report to which I made reference in my testimony on Dan Armstrong's behalf.

In Dan's case, there was absolutely no reason to believe that dealing with him in the adult criminal justice system would have a deterrent effect, either on him or on other juveniles. At the time he tried to help Tanya kill herself and accompany her in death, all that mattered to him was his misguided and melodramatic juvenile love for her.

The psychological reality underlying Fagan's research is that the factors that motivate teenagers who kill (or try to kill) are highly unlikely to be affected by the punitive messages of the legal system that are meant to deter them. For the most part, as was seen in earlier chapters, young people who kill tend to be in a state of moral and psychological crisis at the time of their deadly actions. In such situations and in such states, rational calculations of risk–benefit do not operate (for adults as well, not just kids).

While this is true for almost all of us, for adolescents it is a particularly powerful factor. In Dan's mind, he was operating out of love and compassion, and other considerations were absent. In John's mind, it was a matter of self-defense, pride, and compensation for the pain he felt as a boy abandoned by his parents. In Martin's mind, it was a matter of desperate need for peer affirmation and proof that he was not a loser.

Research has revealed that adolescents generally do not make good risk–benefit calculations, particularly when strong emotions are involved. This research finds that adolescents generally emphasize benefits and rewards over risks when faced with a situation that contains both. This is one of the conclusions of Steinberg and Scott's 2003 review of the research. This is part of the larger set of problems that adolescents face in dealing with the social world around them.

Deborah Yurgelun-Todd and her colleagues have found that adolescents tend to demonstrate less ability than adults to assess accurately the emotional meaning of facial gestures, seeing "shock, surprise, and angry" faces where adults (correctly) see "fearful." And adolescents tend to use more primitive parts of their brains (the amygdala) in processing faces, whereas adults use more sophisticated parts of the brain (the frontal cortex).

Laura Thomas and her team took this research a step further. They investigated how teens and adults respond to subtle emotional differences displayed on faces. A special software program allowed them to present faces as they morphed from one emotion to another (e.g., from fear to anger). Adults were more efficient than adolescents (and children for that matter) in detecting the shift. All in all, this growing body of research validates the idea that in social situations, adolescents may be prone to behavioral choices based on faulty information.

Because they tend to process this information in the amygdala rather than the frontal cortex, they tend to respond impulsively and "emotionally" rather than reflectively and "thoughtfully." It's worth noting here that in this, psychopaths are the extreme opposite of adolescents; to an extreme degree that differentiates them from normal adults, psychopaths tend to process emotions exclusively in the frontal cortex rather than in the amygdala. Neither adolescents nor psychopaths reflect the balance that is required in humane adulthood, in which emotional processing takes place in both areas in a manner that combines genuine feelings (and thus empathy) and reasoned emotional regulation (and thus socially productive behavior).

Steinberg and Scott's review also shows that teenagers sometimes make better decisions acting alone than they do in the presence of their peers. For example, young people in driving simulators commonly choose to stop at yellow lights if such cautious behavior will lead to rewards they value. In the presence of their best friends, however, youthful drivers often "choose" to drive through those lights in the same simulator. This finding testifies to the frequently negative role of peer *presence* (as opposed to the more commonly understood peer *pressure*).

What is more, as I argued in my testimony in Dan's case, it is not as if there is a large pool of troubled teens (boys and girls sharing delusions about suicide) waiting on the verdict in his case to calculate whether or not there is a "free pass" for the actions involved in assisted suicide. Nor is there a pool of teenagers ready to shoot their peers if the courts give them the go-ahead by sentencing school shooters to juvenile facilities rather than to life sentences in adult prison. To the contrary, if there were to be any effect of granting a reverse waiver in Dan's case or of keeping John's in juvenile court, it would be to send a *positive* message to teenagers.

What message? The message that adults are capable of responding to the mental-health complexities of adolescent suicide and aggression against others with compassion and understanding, rather than in ways that are developmentally inappropriate and punitive. As it is, adolescents are reluctant to share information about the mental struggles of their friends. A national poll of high school students a year after the attack on Columbine High School found that 60 percent of the respondents said that if a peer talked about killing people, they would not report it to an adult. A big reason is that they fear adults will take punitive action rather than offer a compassionate, therapeutic response. Kids don't want to get their friends "in trouble."

Are there "cold-blooded" juveniles out there who calculate the odds of adult prosecution before committing violent acts? I suppose there are. More likely, there are chronically criminal *adults* out there who employ underage youths to commit violent crimes on their behalf with the expectation that these younger offenders will be treated more leniently than they, the adult criminal mentors, would be. I believe this does happen, mostly in the case of adult criminal enterprises that involve the sale and distribution of illicit drugs. Can these individuals be deterred? There are situations in which targeted enforcement efforts can have a deterrent effect, but most of these situations do not involve juveniles directly, particularly juveniles who qualify as "affective" rather than "predatory" killers (to employ the terms used by Adrian Raine and his colleagues in their study of emotional regulation, which I mentioned in chapter 4).

One example of successful deterrence is to be found in the Boston Gun Project/Operation Ceasefire, which I will discuss in more detail in chapter 7.

This Boston effort was successful in reducing youth gun violence by targeting the youth gangs who were responsible for about 60 percent of all youth homicides in the city (although they comprised just 1 percent of the city's youth population and just 3 percent of the youth population in the most violent neighborhoods).

As a report by Anthony Braga and his colleagues put it: "The Ceasefire crackdowns were not designed to eliminate gangs or stop every aspect of gang activity, but to control and deter serious violence." By focusing resources on this group, the project achieved a 60 percent reduction in youth gun killings. The interventions enhanced deterrence for a group that was well defined and able to receive and act upon the message directly—namely, youth gang leadership.

What happens when we move beyond the confines of groups like youth gangs, which have a leadership structure and an antisocial criminal agenda (e.g., selling drugs)? I believe that a more consistently "adolescent friendly" justice system would only increase the likelihood that teenagers would report suicidal and homicidal thoughts and gestures on the part of their peers to adult authority figures. But I believe it would also increase the odds that kids would seek help for their friends (like John) who were spiraling out of control and into a pattern of potentially lethal aggression. When troubled teenagers are cut off from adults who demonstrate compassion and insight, bad things can happen, and often do. Creighton McFarland's case speaks to that issue.

THE CASE OF CREIGHTON MCFARLAND

Like John Christianson, Michigan native Creighton McFarland* actually did kill someone, another teenager, when he was sixteen years old. It happened on May 13, 1995, when a dispute between two other teens over a girl got out of hand. Creighton's troubles started with a traumatic brain injury when he was seven years old; he experienced a life-threatening fall while hiking in the mountains with a friend. All accounts indicate that this event so destabilized Creighton emotionally that he withdrew socially and emotionally from the life he had known before.

I met Creighton in 2011, after he had served sixteen years of his life sentence. He was coming up for parole, had read my book *Lost Boys,* and thought I might be able to help persuade the parole board that he was rehabilitated and therefore safe to release. Creighton told me about that accident and the resulting head injury that had started his downward spiral: "Emotionally, it felt like I fell from a mountain top. This impacted me psychologically. It changed the way I operated in the world. I soon started to live my life to avoid injuries (real or imagined)." He told me that by the time he was twelve, "Every choice I made, from abandoning childhood friends, to quitting sports, operated to isolate me from living. Not living meant not getting hurt. The new friends I did make were running from life like I was."

This disconnection set in motion the alienation that, in turn, led to his issues with substance abuse: "It wasn't long before I began using marijuana on a regular basis. It was an even shorter time before I learned getting 'high' could help me 'avoid' reality." Thus, like many young substance abusers, he used drugs (and alcohol) as a form of self-medication to deal with his anxiety. The downward spiral continued as he began hanging out with "the wrong crowd" (which contributed to his substance abuse—recall the negative effects of "peer presence"). His disaffection from school grew (despite his high intelligence). He started getting in trouble in the community (including a juvenile placement for stealing marijuana from a friend's parents' house). This path led to the killing that eventually brought me into his life.

Here is what Creighton told me about the event (sixteen years and a lot of reflection later):

> The day of the crime I had been drinking. . . . My friends and I were in one of our usual hang-out spots. That is where Bobbie found me. He asked me to go with him to Jim's house. Bobbie wanted to confront Jim over his girlfriend— Bobbie's girlfriend. I agreed to go. On the way over, Bobbie claims I stated, "I'm going to cap that motherfucker." I do not remember saying those words. However, based on my lifestyle and my attitude and my lack of empathy I probably did say it. Once we got to Jim's place we all assembled in the living room. That is Jim, Bobbie and myself. Jim and Bobbie began arguing over Jim bothering Bobbie's girlfriend. In fact, they were involved in a physical altercation the prior night. Each one wanted an apology from the other. Each one attempted to have me validate their argument. Before I continue, there are two items I need to mention. First, Jim knew I carried a gun. Second, I was standing between both Bobbie and Jim as the argument began. Each was standing on opposite sides of the room, with Jim standing near the door. At that point I had enough. I felt the intensity of the room was increasing. . . . I stood up and walked toward the door, where Jim was standing. As I did this, I noticed Jim had pulled out his knife. Then, Jim and I got into an argument. He told me what he thought of me. I got angry. In my mind, this outburst was unacceptable. He challenged my pride and my manhood. My mentality was he challenged my manhood, so I'm going to get him first. I didn't feel

threatened by the knife, but by the perceived challenge. After shooting Jim, I fled from his place.

I believe that like Martin Teffler, Dan Armstrong, and John Christianson, Creighton McFarland *should* have been dealt with as the troubled juvenile he was, not the adult that the court ruled him to be. But he *was* treated as an adult, and given a life sentence (with the possibility of parole—the results of which I will share in the next chapter).

THE ROLE OF DRINKING IN ADOLESCENT VIOLENCE

Creighton told me that his drinking was "no excuse" for what he did. That is true, but it is relevant. Understanding the role of substance abuse in the behavior of juveniles is important because it is often part of the equation that leads juveniles to acts of violence. As such, it can be important in understanding why there is both a moral and a scientific basis for responding to kids who kill as *kids* first and *killers* second.

Research has revealed that alcohol tends to make kids more susceptible to peer influences and cultural expectations than they would be if sober. And kids who kill are usually surrounded by peers who engage in aggression—and are flooded with beliefs and attitudes that promote violence. When Creighton shot Jim in 1994, he became a terrible case study for this research (which was reviewed and summarized by science journalist Malcolm Gladwell in a 2010 article in *The New Yorker* magazine).

Before 1958, the prevailing view was that alcohol had a general, and generic, physiologically based effect on perception and behavior: it reduced inhibitions in a uniform way, across cultures and social situations (the "disinhibition model"). Then came anthropologist Dwight Heath's research, which began a process that changed this understanding. In contrast to the disinhibition model, Heath offered (and others confirmed) the "myopia model." At the core of this body of evidence is the finding that the principal behaviorally relevant effect of alcohol is not to disinhibit generally but, as Gladwell put it, "to narrow our emotional and mental field of vision."

"Disinhibition suggests that the drinker is increasingly insensitive to his environment—that he is in the grip of autonomous physiological effects. Myopia theory, to the contrary, says that the drinker is, in some respects, increasingly sensitive to his environment: he is at the mercy of whatever is in front of him." The preponderance of evidence at present favors the myopia approach.

It certainly does a better job of explaining what Creighton McFarland did. It wasn't that the alcohol in his body revealed some underlying murderous impulse (disinhibition), but rather that it focused his attention on the aggression between Bobbie and Jim, and that put him, in Gladwell's words, "at the mercy of whatever is in front of him"—namely, the aggressive behavior of the youths in the same room with him.

What else was in front of him? Researchers Craig MacAndrew and Robert Edgerton concluded that "Persons learn about drunkenness what their societies impart to them, and comporting themselves in consonance with these understandings, they become living confirmations of their society's teachings." The disinhibition model remains current in North American society and culture despite the challenges of researchers like MacAndrew and Edgerton. Thus, Americans are taught by their culture to *expect* to be disinhibited, and to some degree they act that way in response. In an odd way, the myopia theory explains the power of the disinhibition model.

To be used in court, the new understanding of the myopia theory must meet the criteria for "novel science" established by the *Daubert* rule (which I presented in the Introduction). It is making inroads.

I served as an expert witness in a case in North Dakota in which three boys with a history of fighting got drunk while watching mixed martial arts on television at the house of one boy's uncle. By the end of the evening, the sixteen-year-old member of the group was in critical condition because one of the other boys had hit him in the head with a club he found in the basement TV room. The myopia theory helped explain why, for these boys in this situation, getting drunk was a critical element in the equation that produced the nearly lethal assault.

The relevance of the myopia theory to Creighton's case is clear, because the cultural expectation most common in North America is that young men will become aggressive when drinking. Thus, it becomes a self-fulfilling prophecy: when males get high, they get violent.

The boy who did the hitting with the club was sentenced to prison, and the uncle who sponsored the underage drinking was held financially liable for dealing with the sixteen-year-old's injuries. I think that my report's presentation of the myopia theory was persuasive in explaining why it was irresponsible to allow teenagers to drink heavily and watch violence on TV, and that it contributed to establishing a precedent for employing this model in legal proceedings, thus building a base for eventually meeting the criteria for the *Daubert* rule in the United States. Time will tell.

When Creighton witnessed his friend engage in an aggressive conflict, he joined in. When challenged, he responded violently: he pulled his gun and fired. It was an emotionally stupid thing to do. But that's often what adolescent brains tell kids to do—stupid things, particularly when those brains are impaired by psychoactive substances like alcohol and drugs, and while those brains are also responding to messages from the social environment that promote violence. The damage done by the kids acting on behalf of those brains that are under these influences can be catastrophic: Jim died, and Creighton was sent to jail, possibly for the rest of his life.

THE CULTURAL INSANITY OF PUNISHING KIDS AS IF THEY WERE ADULTS

In my opinion, as disturbing as what troubled and drunk sixteen-year-old Creighton McFarland did is the fact that the presumably saner brains of responsible adults in the legal system did not prevail in the wake of Jim's death. These adult brains did not seem to understand Creighton as the troubled sixteen-year-old that he was, and treat him accordingly. That would have meant dealing with him as a juvenile rather than as a fully formed criminal adult. Sentencing Creighton, as an adult, to a life sentence for what he did was, I think, a form of cultural insanity.

Most recognize this quote from Albert Einstein: "Insanity is doing the same thing over and over again and expecting different results." Our approach to violent juveniles is "insane" in that we ignore what developmental science tells us about who teenagers are and punish them as if they were fully functioning adults. Then, when that doesn't work, we repeat the process of punishment, over and over again.

As Jeffrey Fagan concluded after reviewing the available evidence, sentencing juveniles as adults increases rather than decreases the recidivism rate. Other researchers have buttressed his conclusion, including a group that focused intensively on the State of Florida. Donna Bishop and her colleagues looked at nearly three thousand juveniles in Florida who were transferred to adult court and compared them with a matched sample of juveniles who were not. Recidivism was greater for the transferred youths. Lawrence Winner and his colleagues looked at some of the same data and found that the negative effect of transfer was most noticeable for non–property crimes (including violent crimes).

Kathleen Heide and her colleagues tracked fifty-nine Florida juveniles involved in homicides in the early 1980s who had been sentenced to adult prisons. By 1999, nearly 70 percent of them had been released from those prisons. Despite (or more likely *because of*) being sentenced to adult prison rather than being dealt with in the juvenile justice system, 60 percent of them were returned to prison, mostly within the first three years of release. I have worked on the cases of many such individuals—Simon Dalton and John Christianson being two such cases.

But there is a counterforce of lucidity in our society, even if only a weak one. The march toward sanity in our society's legal treatment of juvenile killers started in 2005 with the *Simmons* case, which banned the execution of minors. It continued in 2010 with the *Graham* case, which banned life sentences for juveniles convicted of crimes other than murder. And in 2012, in the case of *Miller v. Alabama,* the court ruled (again five to four, with Scalia, Roberts, Alito, and Thomas once again dissenting) that it was unconstitutional to give mandatory life-without-parole sentences to any young killers, period. Justice Alito spoke for the four dissenters when he said, "When the majority of this court countermands that democratic decision (by state legislatures), what the majority is saying is that members of society must be exposed to the risk that these convicted murders, if released from custody, will murder again."

Before proceeding, I should note that, as it turns out, research reveals that murderers are *less* likely to be recidivist than other criminals. The federal government's Bureau of Justice Statistics provided this report on recidivism: "Released prisoners with the highest re-arrest rates were robbers (70.2%), burglars (74.0%), larcenists (74.6%), motor vehicle thieves (78.8%), those in prison for possessing or selling stolen property (77.4%), and those in prison for possessing, using, or selling illegal weapons (70.2%). Within 3 years, 2.5% of released rapists were arrested for another rape, and 1.2% of those who had served time for homicide were arrested for homicide."

Not surprisingly, however, a study of recidivism among murderers in New Jersey conducted by criminologist Albert Roberts and his colleagues in 2007 found that the highest rates of recidivism among murderers (defined as subsequently committing a new violent or drug crime, in almost all cases not another murder) were for those who had killed during the commission of a felony: about one-third. The lowest rates were for those who had killed as part of an incidence of domestic violence: about 10 percent. But even these numbers are much lower than the rates for other criminals (e.g., 70 percent plus for thieves of one sort or another).

And these figures include mostly adults (who commit the bulk of all killings), not mostly juveniles. According to a New York State Parole Board study published in 2011, of 368 convicted murderers granted parole between 1999 and 2003, only 1.6% had returned to prison within three years for a new felony conviction (none of them a violent offense).

Speaking for the majority in the *Miller* case, Justice Elena Kagan said, "The mandatory sentencing schemes before us violate the Eighth Amendment's ban on cruel and unusual punishment. Why? Because life without the possibility of parole for young killers ignores the possibility that these kids might some day be rehabilitated."

Justice Kagan is right. Kids like Creighton McFarland who kill *can* become rehabilitated, and they sometimes do. I know that because I have listened to some of these kids later in their lives, when they have become adults. The process may take years, and the fruits of the process may not be apparent until after they are well into adulthood. But it can and does happen. That will be our focus in the next chapter: the path to transformation and rehabilitation that some killers travel.

6

Tales of Rehabilitation, Transformation, and Redemption

FROM TIME TO TIME, I RECEIVE letters from men in prison who have read my book *Lost Boys,* which is often available in prison libraries or is given to them by counselors, friends, relatives, or attorneys. Mostly they report and reflect on how reading *Lost Boys* has illuminated their own experience and the path that brought them to prison, typically for life or for very long sentences. Sometimes these letters ask for my help. One such letter arrived in 2009, dated April 6.

It came from Frederick Hill, a thirty-four-year-old serving a life sentence in a California prison. Eighteen years earlier, Fred was involved in a series of crimes in which he and his partners robbed video-store employees at gunpoint as the stores were closing for the night. They kidnapped the employees and threatened to kill them. He didn't kill anyone, but he certainly could have if one of these kidnapping-robberies "went bad," as such situations sometimes do, particularly when adolescents are involved. As a result, Fred was serving a life sentence (but with the possibility of parole).

In his letter, Fred told me that he had been turned down by the parole board before, on the grounds that he "lacked insight." In the interim, he had read *Lost Boys* in the prison library and, since he was coming up for parole again soon, was turning to me for help in gaining the "insight" that the board had said he lacked. He included several reports on his progress written by professional staff at the prison. I wrote him back to say, "I was moved by your letter and your situation. Thanks for including the professional reports. It sounds like you are a good candidate for parole." Thus began a relationship that continues to this day. It wasn't just Fred who contacted me. Before long, I was talking on the phone to Naomi Hill, Fred's wife.

Naomi and Fred had been friends in high school but had lost touch. Some years later, Naomi discovered through a mutual friend that Fred was in prison, and she began to correspond with him in 2007. The correspondence turned into visits, the visits turned into love, and eventually the couple married on June 17, 2008. It is natural and appropriate to be skeptical of such "prison romances," of course. But the more I heard from Naomi (and Fred), the more convinced I became that the relationship was genuine and legitimate on both sides.

I also became convinced that Fred might well be one of the few individuals who get involved in very serious violent crime as a teenager and then go to adult prison, but find a way to rehabilitation, transformation, and redemption rather than the despair and further violence that is so common among inmates. I agreed to fly out to California, and on February 10, 2011, I interviewed him at Chuckawalla State Prison. I told him that I would listen to his story and, if everything went well, I would write a report on his behalf for his next parole hearing (to be held a few months later). I heard a true story of rehabilitation, transformation, and redemption from a young man who had flirted with the dark side as a teenager but, over the succeeding eighteen years, against all odds, had found his way back to the light while in prison—in the "land of the lost," as John Christianson had described it years before. I wrote a report about Fred Hill that concluded: "Based upon my twenty-five years as a developmental psychologist studying violent youths as a researcher and an expert witness, I am confident to the best of my abilities that releasing Frederick Hill is a safe and humane course of action, and I strongly recommend the parole board do so."

ASSESSING THE RISKS OF RELEASING A PRISONER

When an inmate who is serving time for a violent crime asks to be released, the parole board faces some very difficult challenges. Any decision to parole an individual who committed a very serious violent crime represents a risk for the parole board. The consequences of a mistake are grave. If it releases an individual who is not prepared for a prosocial postrelease life, the board runs the risk of being complicit in future harm to innocent persons (and being the target of public and political criticism for being "soft on crime," with headlines like "Parole Board Releases Murderer Who Kills Again").

As I noted in chapter 5, Justice Alito spoke to this (in the *Miller v. Alabama* case that outlawed mandatory life in prison without parole for juveniles) when he said, "[W]hat the majority is saying is that members of society must be exposed to the risk that these convicted murders, if released from custody, will murder again." These same voices embraced this line of thinking in *Graham v. Florida,* when they opposed the majority's ruling that *any* sentence of life without the possibility of parole for juveniles who had not committed murder was unconstitutional. There is always a risk when an inmate is released (more on how this risk is assessed later).

But if the board refuses to release someone who *is* ready, and who will succeed in his postrelease life, it runs the risk of wasting the resources of the state in incarcerating that individual (in California, about $48,000 per year, according to the Vera Foundation) and wasting the human potential of a person who might make a positive contribution to society (priceless).

Of course, this second kind of result rarely gets the kind of attention that the other kind of error does in the mass media and the political arena. Rarely does anyone other than the inmate and his family even know that this has happened (unless an advocate takes on the case and makes of it a public cause célèbre). Have you ever seen a headline like "Parole Board Keeps Reformed, Formerly Violent Criminal in Prison"? At one level, it is all about calculating risk—the risk of mistakenly releasing someone who is actually still dangerous versus mistakenly denying parole to someone who is truly rehabilitated.

ASSESSING THE RISKS OF A BAD DECISION TO RELEASE AN INMATE

Identifying which inmates are good candidates for release and which aren't is a tough scientific (as well as moral) problem. Systematic efforts to do so began with the work of Ernest Burgess in the 1920s. His decision-making test was the standard for many decades, across the United States and more broadly in the Western world, including the British Commonwealth and the European Union. Current efforts are focused on improving the Burgess model. Nonetheless, the success rate of judgments by psychiatrists and psychologists asked to predict future violence ranges from 30 to 50 percent, according to research reviewed by Robert Zagar and his colleagues. It's fundamentally a difficult statistical problem, in addition to the clinical assessment issues it reflects.

I should point out that this assessment—predicting postrelease violent behavior—is different ethically (and perhaps scientifically) from the growing movement to base initial sentences on a statistical model of future criminal behavior. Writing for *The New York Times,* law professor Sonja Starr has examined the growing trend toward what is called "evidence-based sentencing" (some twenty states now do it) and concluded that the risk factors employed in the prediction contain a bias against the poor and minorities that undermines the constitutionality of the practice. As she sees it, the fatal flaw in this approach is that "It contravenes the principle that punishment should depend on what a defendant did, not on who he is or how much money he has."

Of course, the whole process of introducing "mitigating" and "aggravating" factors into sentencing for killers, in which I participate routinely, is exactly that—*and should be.* No one seems to be challenging that aspect of the process. In a sense, the whole point of this book is precisely that "who" you are and "why" you committed a criminally violent act are relevant for sentencing. It is certainly behind the Supreme Court's decision that all minors should be immune to the death penalty because of a group characteristic, namely their age.

That being said, sentencing decisions involve a complex set of ethical, constitutional, and scientific considerations that are not really at issue here. We are considering individuals who are already incarcerated and awaiting release. It is all about predicting future behavior. And it is fair if the decision-making process for parole incorporates the assessment of enough "group" factors to make it essentially a decision based on an individual rather than on some generalized assessment of group characteristics (e.g., "poor people" or "minorities"). The more powerfully predictive the assessment, of course, the closer it gets to being completely individualized. If it were 100 percent accurate, there would be no "faith" in the prediction, only scientific certainty. Can we have that kind of certainty?

When I studied statistics as a graduate student, I found that among the various concepts we were taught, one of the most practical and influential was "Type 1 versus Type 2 error." Type 1 error occurs when you think the evidence before you warrants the conclusion that two groups really are different, but it turns out they really aren't. An example of Type 1 error: you flip a coin one hundred times and get sixty-five heads and thirty-five tails and conclude the coin is "rigged," but it turns out it isn't. Type 2 error occurs when you conclude there is no real difference between two groups but it turns out there really is. Concluding that a coin is fair after getting sixty heads and forty tails is Type 2 error if it turns out the coin actually is rigged. How is this possible? It flows directly from the fact that statistics reflect probability, not certainty.

To say that a result is "statistically reliable" means that an observed difference is most likely a real one (typically, 99 or 95 percent of the time), and not due to chance variations, *but only most likely, not certainly.* It indicates that the risk lies within the margin of error you are willing to accept in making the decision. In chapter 4, I presented the remarkable results achieved by Robert Zagar in handling this problem with respect to predicting which kids will become killers—correctly identifying 97 percent of the killers (missing only 3 percent) and correctly identifying 97 percent of the nonkillers (falsely identifying only 3 percent). Zagar and his colleagues have also brought this "actuarial" approach to the matter of determining when an inmate is ready for release as well. "Actuarial" here refers to the construction of a mathematical model based on computation of statistical links between the various inputs (the life and times of the individual inmate) and the outcome (whether or not individuals are likely to succeed in the outside world if they are released).

The results are impressive. Using an eighty-two-item list of risk factors results in significantly more accurate identification of which inmates are at highest risk for violent offenses if released than previous efforts (Zagar and his colleagues reviewed a wide range of previous efforts). Their eighty-two items provide a map of experiences at home and at school, relationships with peers and family members, educational and vocational history, neuropsychological vulnerabilities, experience in the adult and juvenile justice systems, and other measures of who the inmate is, where he comes from, how he has related to society in the past, and how well his brain functions. Below are some examples:

Home Considerations

Not living with parents until age sixteen
Violent family
Physical abuse
Low family socioeconomic status
Young age when leaving home
Poor reason for leaving home
Young age when parents died

Young age when parents separated or divorced

Many siblings

Low family birth rank

Home mobility

Low family interest/contact while in jail

Individual/Medical Considerations

Parental, teen adult alcohol and substance abuse

Illnesses

Asthma

Adult opiate/heroin use

Birth, pregnancy, or perinatal disorders

Antisocial personality disorder

Psychopathy

Epilepsy

Minor physical anomalies, some congenital

Estimated ability, attitude, character, honesty

Jaundice

As Zagar puts it, "Despite any limitations, probation-parole tests have been shown to be more accurate than police records, clinical judgment or single psychological tests." The 82 items capture the developmental history of the inmate—the factors and forces that brought him to prison in the first place—as well as his specific history of offending and antisocial behavior generally. Thus, these items provide an assessment of the state of his mind and character as he is being considered for release from prison. They give accurate guidance about 90 percent of the time (compared with the 30–50 percent accuracy rate for "clinical judgment"), and I have focused on many of these factors in my own assessments of readiness for release.

When a parole board is reviewing applications for release, the members have to decide who among the applicants are really rehabilitated and ready for release and who are not, always with incomplete information, and knowing that the inmate's self-interest lies in convincing the board that he really is safe to release. Truman Capote wrote a compelling account of two men who murdered a whole family in Kansas in 1959 (in his bestselling book *In Cold Blood*). He reports asking one of the men why he didn't tell the prison psychiatrist that he was having murderous thoughts before he was set free. The answer: "If I told him that they never would have released me."

A 5 percent chance of being wrong may be acceptable if the stakes are low. For example, what if the inmate involved was in prison for a short time for a minor crime and had a good record before and since being incarcerated? Would a 5 percent chance of error be acceptable? A 10 percent chance? Perhaps. But what if the stakes are higher? What if, for example, the inmate had committed a murder? How sure would you want to be then?

Certainty is impossible, because professionals who assess the inmates may make mistakes, information is sometimes uncertain, and, to top it all off, inmates may lie and misrepresent themselves—whether intentionally, in an effort to deceive, or inadvertently because they lack insight into their past, present, and future actions. Furthermore, *of crucial importance in the eventual accuracy of any prediction are the postrelease conditions faced by released prisoners (and, to his credit, Zagar addresses some of these factors in his actuarial equation).*

As I mentioned in my rendering of Michelle Alexander's analysis in *The New Jim Crow,* being a convicted felon imposes a terrible burden after release from prison (and the disproportionate imprisonment of people of color thus has far-reaching social and economic consequences beyond the immediate and direct effects of incarceration per se). Having a felony conviction on one's record may severely affect one's prospects for employment. If a former felon can't work, he is more likely to return to criminal activities, because of both financial stress and the blow to self-esteem that comes with rejection in the job search. Issues of substance abuse not treated effectively in prison can lead parolees back to criminal activities. Ongoing associations—such as membership in gangs that exist both inside and outside the prison walls—can make it difficult for released inmates to "get a new start," no matter how motivated they are to stay clean. The list is long, and all these factors can have an effect on how accurate any prediction of postrelease success versus recidivism seems at the time it is made, while the individual is still in prison.

Research conducted and compiled by Lisa McKean and Charles Ransford for the Center for Impact Research on programs designed to reduce recidivism "outlines three major elements of programs that successfully reduce recidivism: treatment for substance abuse or mental illness can help remove barriers that prevent employment and integration; education provides the skills necessary for inmates to obtain the types of jobs that lead to more successful outcomes; and employment provides released inmates an income as well as supporting integration by increasing stability and self-confidence." McKean and Ransford go on to elaborate on these program directions in ways that are demonstrated to reduce recidivism.

So how much risk of error should the parole board accept? One in one hundred? Five in one hundred? And how do the odds change as a function of the crime for which the inmate was sentenced in the first place? As the data reported earlier indicate, the irony is that murderers generally have very low recidivism rates compared with thieves and other, nonviolent "petty criminals."

Parole boards face this kind of risk assessment decision every time they review an inmate's case, because in almost every case, they can't know everything. They have only a sample of the information they would need to be sure, because no matter how detailed the records, how sophisticated the professionals who provide assessments, and what the inmate says in a face-to-face interview, there is always doubt and room for error. What is more, things can change internally and externally for an inmate once he (or she) is released.

As I said before, in statistical terms, Type 1 error is when you decide on the basis of your imperfect information that an inmate is rehabilitated, but it turns out he isn't. Type 2 error is when the inmate really is rehabilitated but you decide he isn't, and thus prevent his release. When people first come to these concepts (Type 1 and Type 2 errors) they often say, "Why don't you just take steps to minimize both?"

The problem is that the two types of error are generally "reciprocal": as you reduce the chances of one happening, you increase the odds that the other will happen. If you are highly conservative about making Type 1 errors (in the sense that you try to avoid *any* cases where you inaccurately conclude that an inmate is rehabilitated when he isn't, by setting a very, very high standard of proof), you increase the chances of a Type 2 error (that is, in trying to avoid releasing anyone who isn't rehabilitated, you mistakenly keep incarcerated people who should be released). And vice versa. This is what makes the results of Zagar's predictive model all the more extraordinary; it effectively minimizes *both* Type 1 and Type 2 errors to an extraordinary, perhaps unprecedented level.

Decisions made by parole boards are a struggle to find an appropriate balance between mistakenly letting unrehabilitated inmates out of prison (Type 1 error) and unjustly denying parole for prisoners who really are rehabilitated (Type 2 error). I could see this process at work in the following case.

I met Mannie Townsend* because his lawyer knew of the work I had done on behalf of Frederick Hill and Creighton McFarland and hoped that I might help in Mannie's efforts to get paroled, after nearly two decades in prison for a crime committed when he was a teenager. I interviewed him at Arizona's Tompkins State Prison. The prison has multiple facilities within its borders, and it houses some eight thousand inmates—half the population of the entire community.

Tompkins is located about sixty miles southwest of Phoenix, in a rural area, and the two biggest employers in the area are the farms and the prison (which employs about a thousand people). Data show that the local community's crime rate is about half the national average (I think that doesn't include the eight thousand inmates of the prison). The city's motto is "Oasis in the Desert." As I drove up to the prison, the cynic in me had to smile at the irony. It hardly seemed an oasis of any sort, but from reading Mannie's records, I knew that some good things do happen there.

The staff were very friendly and helpful as I was processed for admission and led to the room where I was to listen to Mannie's life story—a story I knew something about from reading his records. A gangbanger as a teenager, he had hooked up with a group of his friends to commit a series of armed home invasions. In the course of one of these robberies, the elderly man of the house panicked, fell into a fish pond, and drowned. In another, one of Mannie's friends shot and killed the homeowner. Mannie was sixteen at the time. In our interviews twenty years later, he said he was surprised and shocked when the shooting happened, but he acknowledged that he was part of the group, that he was into the burglarizing, and that he should not have been surprised that his friend had a gun. For his role in the murder, Mannie received a life sentence with the possibility of parole. That was eighteen years before I met him, by which time he was thirty-six years old.

The young man I interviewed was very different from the gang-affiliated, narcissistic armed robber who went to prison. He was serious, thoughtful, respectful, and reserved. Mannie's rehabilitation began when he joined Alcoholics Anonymous in 1997 (which he was still attending) and Criminal Gangs Anonymous in 2008 and began to get an education (he received his GED in 1997). But the real turning point in his transformation came on September 11, 2001. As he put it, "9/11 shocked me. It was a real eye-opener. I never saw myself as an American until it happened. Soon after the attacks, I saw a woman on television talking about how the gangs in her neighborhood were like the terrorists. It all clicked for me then: I was a terrorist in my community. After that I looked at things differently." In the wake of that insight, Mannie dissociated himself from the Duke Street gang, which had been his primary social identity since he was fifteen, and really started on the road to rehabilitation, transformation, and redemption. He even says that "If I wasn't in prison I would probably have died already, the way I was living back then."

The prison's website states that at the heart of rehabilitation activity in the Department of Corrections are efforts to do two things. First, to provide effective evidence-based programming to adult offenders; and second, to create strong partnerships with local government, community-based providers, and the communities to which offenders return in order to provide services that are critical to offenders' success on parole. These elements are consistent with what McKean and Ransford found to be effective in reducing recidivism.

Mannie had taken advantage of many of a bewildering array of opportunities for education and self-improvement; in addition to AA, he participated in many workshops and courses: "life plan recovery," "Bible study," "anger management," "parenting," "victim awareness," "Crossroads—a course on grief," "group therapy," "insight and drugs," "self-worth," "stress," "insight and drugs," "insurance and money management," "auto body," "construction," "graphic arts and printing," "small engine repair," among many others, and, by the time I met him, he had completed thirty-three college credits from the local community college.

Critical Issues in Deciding Mannie's Fate

But assessing Mannie's readiness and worthiness for release was not a simple task for the parole board. In addition to his participation in educational and self-development programs, there was also a less rosy side to his history while in prison. He had been written up for twelve offenses during his early years at the prison, before his 9/11 insight—mostly fights with other inmates and "disobedience to prison rules." However, most troubling for any parole board would be the official early diagnosis of "antisocial personality disorder."

Antisocial personality disorder is the adult version of conduct disorder, and it is often the kiss of death for an inmate seeking parole. This is partly because it is so often seen to be synonymous with being a psychopath, although (as I reported in chapter 1), the godfather of the study of psychopaths, Robert Hare, believes it should be understood as a distinct, though frequently overlapping, condition of being.

Antisocial personality disorder is the diagnosis you get as an adult if you are a conduct-disorder case grown up: "a pervasive pattern of disregard for, and violation of, the rights of others that begins in childhood or early adolescence and continues into adulthood ... [a lack of] remorse, as indicated by being indifferent to or rationalizing having hurt another," to quote from a report written about Mannie by a prison psychologist in August 2010, in preparation for the parole board meeting at which my own report was directed.

The prison psychologist's report acknowledges that this assessment reflects mostly his adolescent gang membership and his prison record prior to 2001. As a result of including Mannie's ten-year process of rehabilitation, the "overall risk assessment" by the prison psychologist reads as follows: "After weighing all of the data from the available records, the clinical interviews, and the risk assessment data, it is opined that Mr. Townsend presents a relatively MODERATE RISK for violence in the free community." This validates one reason for Hare's distinction between psychopaths and sociopaths. The first is a deeply engrained trait, while the second is a pattern of behavior—and patterns of behavior are generally much more amenable to change than deeply ingrained traits.

This assessment presented the parole board with a classic Type 1–Type 2 error dilemma. There was enough negative stuff in the report to reinforce doubts that Mannie's transformation from violent, antisocial person to peaceable, prosocial person was complete and genuine. That would reinforce the concern that releasing him would produce a Type 1 error (they let him out, he is still violent and antisocial, and he commits another violent crime).

On the other hand, my report was very optimistic about Mannie, asserting that his rehabilitation and transformation is complete and authentic enough to make him a good candidate for release *(particularly given the significant social support from family and friends he had lined up in anticipation of parole).* I believed that Mannie looked good on the factors that Zagar and his colleagues included in their actuarial model to predict postrelease success.

The calculation of risk in Mannie's case exemplifies the challenges parole boards face: the stakes are high, and the intellectual challenges for applied psychology daunting, when Type 1 and Type 2 errors come out of the laboratory and into the real world, as they do in parole board decisions. Beyond the technical challenges and legitimate concerns raised by trying to be fair while keeping the community safe, there is the darker side of the decision-making process. This includes the fact that the various actors involved in the process are human beings, with egos, memories, unconscious and conscious bias, and reputations to protect. Some of them have political or ideological axes to grind. All of these things can get in the way of the truth, as happened in the following case.

THE CASE OF ROBERT HARRIS

Robert Harris* was up for parole—for the second time—in 2011, when I met him. He was not eligible until eight years earlier according to the terms of his sentence—life with the possibility of parole after twenty years. He was seventeen when he went to jail for his involvement in a murder. When he first came up for parole, he was denied, largely on the recommendation of a prison psychologist. She opposed parole on the grounds that Robert "does not accept responsibility for his actions, and denies that he killed anyone, saying he didn't pull the trigger on the gun that killed the old woman he and his friends were robbing," as she wrote in her report. It's a classic case of sending the message "You must accept responsibility for your actions and show remorse before the community will consider reinstating you."

Fair enough. However, it turns out that the reason Robert denied shooting the old woman during the robbery is that he didn't do it. A clerk in the prison's main office mistakenly cut and pasted the records of one of Robert's codefendants into Robert's file. The other young man is the one who actually did the shooting, although Robert was participating in the robbery. And at the time of the incident, Robert had expressed his shock, anger, and sadness that his partner in crime killed someone.

It took months of legal action on the part of Robert's attorney to get the record rectified. Finally, a judge ordered that the record be corrected to show that Robert did not pull the trigger. Now it was clear in the record that his denial of responsibility for the killing was not based on dishonesty or refusal to accept the reality of his actions, but rather on his insistence on accuracy and truth. What happened next is the really bizarre part of the story.

When Robert came up for parole again, the prison psychologist still argued against it. She claimed that despite the fact that she had based her negative recommendation on Robert's denial of being the shooter in the first hearing, and although his denial had now been shown to be truthful, she believed that fact was irrelevant and that Robert should stay in prison.

(And the truth shall make you free?) As it turned out, Robert did get parole, despite the self-serving actions of the embarrassed prison psychologist, in part on the basis of the report I filed on his behalf.

Sometimes even the truth is not enough, because values take precedence over intelligent and informed compassion. Duke Jimenez* was twenty when he killed Roberta Teebee, and twenty-three when I interviewed him and wrote a report for the court in which he was sentenced. The judge in the case recognized the developmentally devastating accumulation of risk in Duke's young life, but nonetheless sentenced him to seventy years in prison.

According to a press report, "The judge said Duke, the youngest of five children, grew up in an 'urban war zone' with no family structure, but had taken responsibility by pleading guilty and has taken steps to improve himself in the nearly four years he's spent in jail since his arrest. 'His mother was an alcoholic. His father was a convicted murderer (of Duke's older sister),' the judge said. 'This young man had no chance.'"

Outside the courtroom, Teebee's daughter, Sylvia, said the family wanted Duke to get natural life in prison. "I'll settle for seventy," Sylvia Teebee said, thanking the prosecutors for their efforts. "He'll be an old man by the time he gets out. It still doesn't justify what he did. For what he did, there is no punishment. It's over, but it's not over."

SENTENCING FOR HOPE?

A seventy-year sentence for a twenty-three-year-old could be a life sentence, or a sentence to "death in prison," as most "life" sentences really turn out to be. The trend toward life sentences without parole is testimony to this same cultural perspective on the meaning of justice and retribution. According to a report from The Sentencing Project, a research and advocacy group, by Ashley Nellis and Ryan King, "The number of individuals serving life without parole sentences increased by 22% from 33,633 to 41,095 between 2003 and 2008. This is nearly four times the rate of growth of the parole-eligible life sentenced population."

I don't disregard or minimize the moral issues involved. If one of my loved ones were murdered, I know it would be difficult to respond with compassion for the killer (as Mary in chapter 2 did, reaching out to the youth who had murdered her niece). And I don't belittle the good-faith efforts of parole boards to avoid the mistake of releasing someone who will commit another violent crime. I worry about making that kind of mistake myself when I testify as an expert witness. Sometimes it keeps me up at night. However, from my experiences visiting prisons and reading the letters I get, I think the bigger problem at present is that too many killers are being kept in prison long after they have been rehabilitated, transformed, and redeemed, even if this number represents a minority of those who are convicted of murder.

ANSWERING THREE QUESTIONS ABOUT RISK

In considering the cases of young offenders who are up for parole, I try to answer three questions. Each connects with the variables assessed in what Zagar and his colleagues have found to be the best predictors of future offending among inmates being considered for release. In a sense, like the discussion I presented in chapters 3 and 4, these questions are an attempt to open up the "black box" of the actuarial equations and illuminate why the eighty-two variables identified in Zagar's research make human sense. Addressing these questions is my attempt to overcome the weaknesses of "clinical judgment" identified by Zagar and others and to relate my observations to a body of theory and research in developmental psychology that explains how and why Zagar's actuarial model works so well statistically. Answering these three questions is a big part of what I can bring to the process.

Was this individual so psychologically damaged as a child that by the time he entered adolescence he was irreparably harmed developmentally and thus at high risk for a lifelong pattern of antisocial behavior and crime? When such harm is embedded in consciousness (and unconsciousness) and patterns of behavior in childhood, it generally does not just disappear automatically through the process of maturation and reflection that tends to occur with aging. Rather, it tends to become a permanent feature of life.

Was he so psychologically damaged while incarcerated that he could not take advantage of and profit from opportunities for rehabilitation and spiritual development available in prison? When moral and emotional damage is profound, it can resist conventional treatment programs for mental health problems, substance abuse, and anger management (if they are even offered in prison). It can resist the ameliorative effects of educational programs. It can persist even though years pass and the individual matures. It can even thwart the potentially transformative effect of opportunities for spiritual development. And if the individual is victimized in prison—perhaps raped or forced into sexual slavery in return for not being violently attacked—even if he was "normal" when he entered prison, he may be profoundly damaged by the time he is scheduled to be considered for parole.

Does he have the psychological resources and the social support necessary to make a successful transition from prison and succeed in a positive life after he is released? If there is no positive structure of support—family, friends, organizations—in which the released inmate will be embedded, the risks of recidivism increase. The consistency of the structures and values of postrelease relationships with the goals of in-prison rehabilitation programs goes a long way toward determining the odds of recidivism. For example, sociologist Christopher Uggin found that having a job reduced recidivism for parolees age twenty-seven or older, and criminologist Charis Kubrin and her colleagues found that parolees released into economically disadvantaged neighborhoods had higher recidivism rates, even controlling for individual characteristics of the parolee.

Many individuals who come to prison as adolescents for committing a violent crime had childhood experiences that resulted in their entering adolescence with very serious developmental damage. As I explained in chapters 3 and 4, the childhood of these individuals is typically characterized by severe abuse and neglect in the family, violently traumatic experiences in the community and/or school, high levels of family disruption (often including abandonment and rejection), and exposure to antisocial lifestyles. Often this results in childhood onset of a chronic pattern of aggression, bad behavior, acting out, and violating the rights of others (which may be diagnosed as "conduct disorder"). By the time they reach age ten, children characterized by this pattern are so well established in it that they enter adolescence at very high risk for later antisocial criminal behavior (perhaps diagnosis with antisocial personality disorder).

After reviewing the research on this topic, David Farrington and Rolf Loeber reported that, on average, some 30 percent of youths who demonstrated childhood onset of conduct disorder end up in serious violent delinquency as adolescents. However, as I reported in chapter 1, this figure is not 30 percent but rather 60 percent in some particularly antisocial neighborhoods, and only 15 percent in some "good" neighborhoods (as defined by Felton Earls and others, "good" describes a level of collective support in the neighborhood for prosocial versus antisocial values and behavior). This is testimony to the power of the social situation facing a child as he becomes a teenager. Among individuals with childhood-onset conduct disorder who bring that disorder to adolescence, few "get better" spontaneously, but many get better with intensive intervention designed to change the way they think and feel about things (see chapter 5). However, most individuals whose conduct disorder does not start until adolescence do get better (often spontaneously, by a process in which social consequences and psychological maturity displace the negative behavior—what is called "aging out"). Farrington and Loeber's review of the evidence makes this clear, and this was one reason I was optimistic about Mannie Townsend: judging from the information I had seen, his conduct disorder was of the adolescent-onset type.

CREIGHTON MCFARLAND: THE REST OF THE STORY

Creighton McFarland* (whose story I began in chapter 5) grew up in Michigan and was, like Mannie Townsend, eighteen years into his life sentence when I met him. I decided to act as his advocate because the evidence available to me indicated that he had not experienced the classic toxic influences associated with moral and emotional damage in childhood (abuse, violent trauma, social deprivation, the war zone mentality, etc.; see chapters 3 and 4). He did experience father absence (his biological father left the family when Creighton was two), but as compensation he had at least one stable father figure while growing up (a long-term partner of his mother). On the other hand, he had experienced a traumatic accident as a seven-year-old, a life-threatening fall while hiking in the mountains with his assigned Big Brother.

As I reported in chapter 5, all accounts indicate that Creighton's fall and injury so destabilized him emotionally that he engaged in social and emotional withdrawal in the wake of that traumatic event. This disconnection set in motion the alienation that, in turn, led to his issues with substance abuse (some of which appears to have been a form of self-medication to deal with his anxiety), hanging out with "the wrong crowd" (which contributed to the substance abuse), disaffection from school (despite his high intelligence), and ultimately his involvement in the shooting of another teenager for which he was now incarcerated. It is important that, like Mannie Townsend, Creighton did not begin to display conduct disorder until he was twelve. Thus, his problem was of the adolescent-onset type, rather than the childhood-onset type. This history suggests that when Creighton committed his violent crime at age sixteen, he was in a state of adolescent crisis compounded by substance abuse, rather than a chronic condition of profound developmental damage linked to a toxic childhood.

The good news in adolescent-onset cases is that the individual is likely to become rehabilitated as he moves into adulthood and matures, assuming that he receives social and psychological support and avoids committing acts that lead to incarceration. Of course, if he commits a serious violent crime and enters the criminal justice system (particularly as an "adult"), a whole new set of issues arises. In any case, though, the nature of the individual's adolescence should be a mitigating factor in assessment for parole. In Creighton's case, it was used in exactly the opposite way: his very youth when he committed murder was taken as an aggravating factor arguing against parole. What should have been a positive (he was young and therefore potentially receptive to rehabilitation) became a negative (committing such an act as a teenager predicted an irreversible career as a violent criminal and danger to the community). The evidence presented in chapter 5 makes a good case that courts ought to keep options open for *any* youth being sentenced. *Regardless of the crime,* individuals should be eligible for parole when they can demonstrate that they have moved out of adolescence and along the path of rehabilitation rather than the path of antisocial hardening.

As I mentioned in chapter 4, one of the most important issues in understanding trauma is whether it is a single incident (acute trauma) or an ongoing pattern of experience (chronic trauma). This distinction is relevant in predicting those young offenders who will be good candidates for eventual parole (like Creighton) and those who will not. Single incidents of acute trauma are amenable to resolution through some combination of "psychological first aid" in the form of reassurance and the passage of time as things return to normal.

Chronic trauma is not so amenable to resolution: there is no possibility of a simple therapy of reassurance because a "return to normal" is not a solution, in that the problem *is* the norm. War zones, neighborhoods with high levels of community violence, and abusive families are all prime examples of chronic trauma. While this does not disqualify them completely, it does put many young killers from such environments at a severe disadvantage when it comes to rehabilitation, transformation, and redemption. But this should not lead to hopelessness and inaction on our part. Rather, it should only tell us that retrieving them from the path of criminal violence will be an uphill battle, requiring all the resources we can bring to bear on their behalf. And it may take a long time.

But there is more than just the individual's preincarceration experience to be considered in assessing the risks associated with release from prison. The second question has to be answered: What did he experience in prison, and how has he responded?

Creighton McFarland provides a positive example. His experience in prison was notable for three reasons. First, he was able to avoid some of the most traumatic experiences associated with incarceration for a juvenile, namely sexual and physical assault. As Craig Haney has found in his research, adolescents who are subject to the trauma of violent sexual assault are likely to develop rage and/or social withdrawal that both damages them psychologically and disinclines them to take advantage of opportunities for educational and social improvement that may be available in prison.

Second, Creighton McFarland had access to a competent psychotherapist (retained and paid for by his mother) for a period that began shortly after his arrest and continued for more than three years. This therapeutic resource was invaluable in helping Creighton deal with the underlying emotional issues that were linked to his substance abuse and delinquent behavior. This paved the way for taking advantage of educational and social development programs during his incarceration. Aided by therapeutic intervention, Creighton was able to make good choices and avoid being drawn into the negative side of prison life.

Third, Creighton had the ongoing support of his mother. She was a positive influence on his life throughout childhood and continued to be supportive even during his adolescent delinquent phase. Once he went to prison, she continued to stick by him. As my mentor, Urie Bronfenbrenner, liked to say, "For human development to move forward in a positive way, you need to have someone who is crazy about you."

Shortly before I traveled to visit Creighton, I received a letter from his mother, Loretta. After outlining Creighton's history as a member of her family, she wrote this about her son: "I am very proud of the man my son has become. He has grown reflective, insightful, compassionate, and attached to his niece and nephews, sister, and to me—acting on this in the ways he can (e.g., letter writing, remembering birthdays). Since his move ten hours away, I visit every three months and speak to Creighton on the phone once a week. He never tires of the letter writing—to all family members! (I thought the art was dead!)."

As a result of the many positive aspects of Creighton's incarceration, he presented himself to the parole board as a mature young man with a lot of constructive educational and social experiences in his portfolio, and with the fruits of effective long-term psychotherapy—not as an angry, traumatized, oppositional, and uneducated individual. Creighton was well positioned developmentally and socially to make the transition from prison to success in the outside world for four reasons.

First, the results of psychotherapy had helped him resolve emotional and conduct issues that led him to the situation in which he committed his violent crime, and the same therapist was available to assist him with psychological support after release.

Second, he had achieved a high level of self-awareness—including appreciation for the dynamics of his crime. His high intelligence had been harnessed on behalf of self-understanding. He had mobilized empathy in a way that boded well for the future. Empathy is such an important mediator of the relationship between personal and community characteristics and violent behavior that several researchers have called for intervention programs targeting youths at risk for violent behavior that specifically seek to increase empathy. As noted in chapter 4, Laura Stockdale's research review makes it clear that building up empathy is an effective way to weaken the causes of violent behavior, by weakening the links between risk factors and violent behavior.

Third, his intellect enabled him to profit from the educational opportunities he had seized while in prison, and this equipped him with marketable skills. When psychologist Emmy Werner reviewed research on resilience, she identified "at least average intelligence" as one of the foundations. Having at least average IQ in facing challenges is like having both hands free, whereas less-than-average intelligence is like having one hand tied behind your back. Beyond his intelligence and the skills he had developed as a result of taking advantage of programs in the prison, Creighton had a clear sense that no job would be too "low" for him upon release; thus, he would not likely feel aggrieved by less-than-lucrative financial prospects.

Fourth, he had a supportive family awaiting his release (most notably his mother, who was a fully functioning, prosocial individual). He was committed to a transitional living arrangement that would provide a high level of support for his sobriety, positioning him to avoid the negative effects of substance abuse that plagued his preincarceration adolescence.

Despite all this evidence on the plus side, the parole board decided that Creighton should spend eight more years in prison. This seemed a travesty to me. He was ready to leave the prison and make a positive life as a young adult on the outside. I suspect it was the moral issue that did him in. The parole board's vote answered the question "Is sixteen years enough time to spend in prison for killing another human being as he did?" with a resounding "No."

The good news was that they gave him a release date. The very bad news was that they pushed that date so far into the future that it opened him to many dangers that he would not have faced if he had left prison in 2011. I hoped and prayed that he would make it.

As it turned out, this was not the end of the story. Three years later, out of the blue, I received this email from Creighton:

> Dear Dr. Garbarino:
>
> I don't know if you remember me, but you flew out to interview me back in 2011 . . . to conduct an evaluation of me in order to present your findings to the Board of Parole hearings. I was found suitable at my 2011 hearing; however, the Board set my release date far in the future. Since that time the state legislature has passed a law recognizing and codifying the importance of youthfulness when making parole decisions for someone in my position. As a result of this law, I was released on May 7, 2014. I believe a huge part of my case being processed smoothly, without any legal hiccups, [is] in large part due to your efforts on my behalf. My family and I want to say thank you. Freedom is wonderful!!!

Wonderful indeed. The kind of legislation that led to Creighton's release is a glimmer of lucidity from the Michigan legislature. It holds out hope that other states will come to their senses on this issue and pass their own version of this law, aptly named "Justice for Juveniles with Adult Prison Sentences." It offers hope for the thousands of inmates in our country's prisons who were under eighteen at the time of their crimes and were tried as adults and sentenced to adult prison terms.

The decisions that parole boards make involve tough choices beyond the technical concerns. They involve a frightening moral calculus. While a full consideration of this is beyond my scope here, and more suited to a philosophical treatise, I can't ignore it completely.

For many people, the calculations of risk that I have been reviewing here are not the only concern. For some, there is a transcendent moral issue. There are those who find it morally objectionable that *anyone* who commits a violent crime, particularly a murder, should ever be released. This is one reason why prosecutors often show up at parole board hearings to argue against release (as they did in Mannie's case, and in Frederick Hill's case as well). For those who see things this way, the prison door should never swing open for those who have taken a human life (or even threaten to do so, as in Frederick's case—terrifying robberies of store clerks at gunpoint). In the terms of this moral calculus, such acts permanently put the offender outside the realm of normal society, beyond the circle of caring.

Such is the cultural context of even many compassionate and humane judges when they approach sentencing in murder cases. I think it is one reason why they can hear the mitigating stories I tell in court, about how some killers have been innocently victimized by profound moral and emotional damage, and still pronounce death sentences. Or sentences without parole for troubled young offenders.

TWO CONTRASTING PATHS

Some killers will never leave prison alive, and even when they die they may not leave, if they are buried in the prison cemetery. But some who are given life sentences do, in fact, make a life for themselves while in prison. As I see it, there are two basic paths open to someone sentenced to life in prison (or to any long-term incarceration). Many, if not most, individuals walk a path that is some mix of the two.

The first, and perhaps most common response, is to become a savage, a barbarian. Those who follow this path take on the violence of prison life as their own. They sink to its lowest common denominator and stay there, perhaps reinforced by their merging with a brutal prison gang. Indeed, some of the most violent individuals in America live out their years in prison in a constant state of warfare with those around them. I have interviewed some of them—for example, Danny Samson, whose record of violent and antisocial behavior while in prison is long, discouraging, and scary.

Perhaps better than anyone else, these "savages" exemplify the state of barbarism captured in the classic words of the seventeenth-century philosopher Thomas Hobbes, who wrote in *Leviathan* of life without political civilization: "In such condition there is . . . no knowledge of the face of the earth; no account of time; no arts; no letters; no society; and which is worst of all, continual fear, and danger of violent death; and the life of man, solitary, poor, nasty, brutish, and short." That is the first path available to those incarcerated for long periods, but it is not the only path.

The second path is to live as if one is a cloistered monk (or nun) bound by vows of poverty, chastity, and humility and committed to learning, self-improvement, and spiritual development, *even though you will never leave prison alive.* Such individuals do exist in prisons. Jarvis Masters is one. I have met others over the years, including Creighton, Mannie, and Fred. Indeed, the first prisoner in whose case I was asked to serve as an expert psychological witness—Felicia Morgan (the seventeen-year-old who killed Brenda Adams for her jacket)—is in many ways another such individual.

Recall from the Introduction that when Felicia Morgan was sentenced to life in prison, the judge left the door open for possible parole after thirteen years. That was in 1992. She came up for parole in 2005 and was denied. She has been denied four times since then, despite evidence that she has undergone the kind of transformation and rehabilitation envisioned by the judge who sentenced her.

A report filed by *Milwaukee Journal Sentinel* writer Jim Sting indicates that the family of her victim has advocated on Felicia's behalf at the parole hearings, and says that Felicia has accomplished a great deal: "In 2001, she earned a high school equivalency diploma, and in 2008 she completed a dental technician program through Moraine Park Technical College. She also was trained in computers, had a wide range of jobs in the institution, and received certificates for anger management, victim awareness, life coping skills and Bible study, among other classes." Her attorney, Robin Shellow, has stayed in touch with Felicia all these years and says of her, "She has grown up into a bright, strong, sensitive and kind young woman. Coming of age in an adult prison is not easy." But Felicia is still in prison.

As for Mannie, his parole board gave him an early release date. He got the news the day before Christmas in 2011. What a gift it was for his parents, who had stuck by him all those years while he was in prison! What a gift for him, that all his work to get his head on straight and be persistently well behaved had paid off. And what a gift for me, to know I played a role in bringing compassion to life through my efforts to make sense of how Mannie had arrived at the point where he went to prison for murder. Eighteen years later, he emerged not just intact, but better off than one could ever have expected, given the struggles of his early years.

THE TRIUMPH OF PROMISE

While Creighton McFarland was originally told to wait eight more years before being released, the news for Frederick Hill and his wife Naomi was much better. Fred was approved for parole on March 25, 2011, and released on September 26 of that year, just a month before Naomi's thirty-fourth birthday. I couldn't stop smiling at the news; the excitement in Naomi's voice when she called to tell me was contagious.

We have stayed in touch. Fred and Naomi are doing well, and Fred has become a loving father to Naomi's three children from a previous relationship. Here's an email Naomi sent me in April of 2012:

> Our family will always be so grateful for your help, and Fred continuously wants to show the people who helped him that he is worth it. He is a full time student at the local community college, which helped him get this job he has for the city (who would have thought he could work for the city . . . LOL). We attend church every Sunday (despite him saying he would only go once a month), and we have a full day of soccer games for all the kids on Saturdays and just enjoying each other. Fred has changed my entire family's views about men in prison and they accept him with open arms now. During spring break, his parole officer allowed us to go on a trip to Orange County, where we went to the Discovery Science Center, and to the beach. Fred was like a big kid, playing in the sand with the kids, burying each other and splashing in the water. He says he can't remember the last time he even went to the beach. His parole officer has lightened up a little bit. I believe he sees Fred is doing the best he can . . .
>
> God Bless,
> Naomi

She included two photos: Naomi and Fred with her three kids in one (all beaming with big smiles), and a sonogram of the baby girl they were having together in the other. The baby was born in August of 2012, and they named her "Promise."

Rehabilitation, transformation, and redemption. It does happen. Promises are fulfilled. I knew this for sure in February of 2013, when I was in Los Angeles to speak to a professional conference and had a chance to have dinner with Fred, Naomi, and the children. They showed up at the hotel in a minivan and we went to dinner at a pizza place. The utter normality of it all was overwhelming. At one point they handed me baby Promise, and I thought again, "Rehabilitation, transformation, and redemption. It does happen." It really does. I held it in my arms.

7

Guns Don't Kill People—People with Guns Kill People

STEPHEN WALTON HAS A LOT TO SAY ABOUT GUNS. "If you were walking down the street unarmed, you knew to avert your eyes in order to not provoke a fight." Stephen got his first gun when he was eleven, from a friend. It was a .22 automatic, and he recalled how he used to play with it and clean it. It felt cool to have a gun and see how people reacted to having it pulled on them. He did not need to be as timid about looking people in the eyes when he walked down the street.

Once, when he was thirteen, he wore a new jacket out to the store. When he came out of the store, a guy with a gun came up to him and took the jacket away. Stephen did not have his gun with him at the time, so he surrendered the jacket. But when he got to where he was going, he called his cousin, and they went to their house, got their guns, and went looking for the guy with four of their fellow gang members. When they found the guy who stole Stephen's jacket, they beat him badly—kicked him, punched him, and got the jacket back.

He was wearing that same jacket months later when he was shot on the street. The cycle of violence continued. Stephen reported that he had been in multiple shootouts. When he was fifteen, he saw his friend Kevin shot in the head, dead, right in front of his face. His friend Bonzo was also killed. He told me, "In my world I knew that if you were timid you got walked over. I did not have to be timid once I got a gun."

WHY DO KIDS CARRY GUNS? WHY DOES ANYONE?

A study conducted in Cleveland by psychologist Jeremy Shapiro and his colleagues revealed that a set of four motives play a crucial role in whether a youth will be drawn to guns. The first is what they called the "aggressive response to shame." This refers to the code of honor that says, "If someone insults you, you have to fight." Kids who have incorporated this belief are more likely than other kids to be drawn to guns. The second motive is "comfort with aggression," meaning that a kid is not worried or upset about being around other people with guns. The third motive is "excitement," when guns evoke positive feelings of emotional arousal. The final motive is the "craving for power and safety"—associating power and a feeling of security with carrying a gun and being with other people who carry guns.

Shapiro and his colleagues found that less than 1 percent of the kids studied who had none of these motives possessed a gun, while fully one-third who possessed a gun appeared to have all four of these motives. Stephen Walton articulated all four motives in my interview with him. In that, he is not unique. Most of the murderers I have listened to over the years resemble Stephen in that respect.

Of course, the package of motives that Shapiro and his colleagues identified is not confined to kids. By most estimates (e.g., according to GunPolicy. org), although fewer than one in three Americans owns a gun himself (or herself, in growing numbers), somewhere between a third and half of us live in households in which someone owns a gun.

It's worth noting that because of multiple gun ownership in the United States, the actual number of guns is about the same as the total population of three hundred million—which would average out to one gun per person or about three guns per household if these weapons were spread evenly through the population. There are so many guns in our society that no treatment of killing in America can be complete without considering the larger context in which killers operate, namely the American gun culture.

Shapiro's results make sense only in the context of a society in which guns are readily available and are culturally normal. Most of us can appreciate this only by having international comparisons. It's like the old question "Could fish describe water?" Assuming that fish could describe anything, they could appreciate the nature of water only if they had exposure to air. Awareness and understanding lie in the contrast between this and that.

Asking many Americans about guns is like asking a fish about water, in the sense that they/we have accepted the ocean of guns (this) to the extent that it doesn't register for them/us how strange it is by international standards (that). Estimates of the number of guns per capita for entire countries are notoriously sketchy in many cases, so all these data have to be taken with a grain of salt (in some cases, a very large grain). But virtually every possible charting of guns in private hands puts the United States at or near the top. If we confine ourselves to affluent, highly modernized countries around the world, the contrasts are striking.

The United States contains about one hundred guns per one hundred population. The second-highest figure in this group of nations is for Switzerland, at forty-six. The Swiss are considered a special case, however, mostly because all Swiss men serve in the national militia and are encouraged to keep their rifles at home even after they leave active military service, *although in most circumstances they are prohibited from keeping ammunition at home.* Even with that special condition, the rate of households with guns in them in Switzerland is about half that in the United States. As Americans, we pride ourselves on our country's exceptionality in many ways; when it comes to loaded guns in private hands, we truly are "Number One!"

How many news stories about a little kid killing his friend or sibling or parent—in which the neighbors say something like "His dad had four guns in the house, but they were a perfectly normal family"—does it take before it registers that the fact of having the guns in the first place is intrinsically related to the problem, not some irrelevant detail? I don't think you can understand murder in America unless you understand guns in America. Guns don't kill people. American people with guns kill people—others and themselves.

Even as I write this, I know that simply raising the issue is enough to elicit hostility and rejection among a significant number of my fellow citizens. When, after the Sandy Hook mass shooting in December of 2012, I wrote an essay for CNN.com about the origins and dynamics of youth violence, the only negative responses I received (a couple of which were quite nasty) came from people who were offended by what I said about guns. In this book, devoting a chapter to discussing guns is necessary, however. This is not just because most of the killers I have interviewed used guns to commit their murders. It is also because the gun culture in America provides a critically important aspect of the context in which these murders were committed—and, as in all aspects of human development and behavior, context is crucial to understanding cause and effect.

Several studies by psychologists have explored the cultural psychology of guns. Leonard Berkowitz and Anthony LePage got it started with their classic study published in 1967, on what they called "the weapons effect." They induced anger in people who were then placed in a room with guns. These angry people acted more aggressively (by administering electric shocks) toward others, when given the opportunity to do so, than angry people who were exposed to "neutral" objects such as sports equipment.

But it's not as simple as that. Not by a long shot. Subsequent research found that just exposing people to "weapons-associated words" could stimulate more aggressive behavior, but mostly among people who as individuals had little experience with weapons or who lived in societies in which firearms are not very available. Thus, for example, in other laboratory studies, hunters showed less of the "weapons effect" than nonhunters. One interpretation of this finding is that hunters are already desensitized to the violence implicit in guns. Hunters are familiar with the death that guns cause, in the form of dead deer, squirrels, pheasants, and other creatures killed at their own hands.

The 1995 science fiction movie *Powder* contains a scene that speaks to what would happen if this desensitization were replaced with empathy. A teenager in the movie (named "Powder" because he is an albino) has the ability to induce empathy in others, whether they like it or not, even in those who have been desensitized to killing. On a hunting trip with his schoolmates, a sheriff's deputy who is hunting with the boys has shot a doe, which is now dying.

Anguished by the animal's death, Powder touches the deer and then the deputy sheriff. Powder's special ability to induce empathy means that the deputy sheriff suddenly feels the pain and fear of the dying deer. As a result, the deputy sheriff says, he cannot bring himself to take another life (much as he would like to), and so he reluctantly and bitterly gives up hunting. Would that this were possible in real life.

In research on the "gun effect," the other group (beyond hunters) who did not exhibit as much of the weapons effect in lab studies as did novices were people who viewed firearms mainly as defensive weapons. Data from the real-world use of weapons show that in some situations, the presence of a weapon in the hands of a potential victim may deter a would-be attacker. Even a casual Google search of the news turns up many such cases.

In a limited way, in those specific situations, that is a good thing for the potential victim. But that is not the whole story. This bit of individual personal safety comes with heavy costs to the society at large (and sometimes to that specific gun owner at a later point in life, perhaps when that same gun is used in a suicide, in a domestic murder, or to shoot an innocent person mistaken for an intruder, as we will see below). In fact, one estimate (by physician Arthur Kellerman) is that for every one intruder "legally" shot by someone in a household defending self, property, or family, three times as many people are shot in their homes. This includes incidents of domestic violence, suicides, accidents, kids murdering their parents, loved ones mistaken for intruders (etc., etc., etc.). Of course, the gun lobby disputes the validity of Kellerman's analysis. But as we will see, whether or not the exact ratio (one to three) is correct, there is scientific consensus that having a gun in your home produces a net decrease in safety.

DO SO MANY GUNS MAKE US SAFER?

Like many kids, thirteen-year-old John Christianson thought that having a gun in his hand would make him safer when he ran home to get his rifle after being threatened by some older boys in 1996. When he came back outside to confront the boys, he fired what he told me he thought of as a "warning shot" to scare them off. Unfortunately, one of the seventeen-year-olds was hit and died. John spent twelve years in prison for what he did, and I think the experience solidified him as an antisocial young man.

The reality that *sometimes* having a gun *does* make you safer when you are confronted with an aggressor has provided the rationale for some people to believe that they are *generally* safer being armed than being unarmed. *Overall and in general,* this is not true. According to an analysis of data published by Kellerman and his colleagues in *The New England Journal of Medicine* in 1993, keeping a gun in the home increases the odds of a homicide in that home by 60 percent. And, as I said before, these homicides are *not* mainly the killing of intruders, they are mostly the killing of loved ones, friends, and self. The net effect is negative, not positive. Of course, most gun owners firmly believe they can handle their gun responsibly and that, therefore, they will not become one of those homicides.

The bottom line is that while there are some circumstances in which having a gun will reduce your chance of getting killed, you are safer, on average, without one. This is a reverse parallel to the wearing of seat belts when driving. Although there are some circumstances in which you may be safer not wearing your seat belt (e.g., if your car goes off a bridge into a river and you can't get the belt undone), the net effect of wearing seat belts is to reduce injuries by 60 percent and fatalities by 90 percent, according to the Centers for Disease Control and Prevention. People who don't wear their seat belts so that they will be able to escape their flooded car if it runs off a bridge are making a big mistake individually. If millions and millions of people were to join them in that mistake, what was an individual phenomenon would become a cultural phenomenon. So it is with guns.

THE CULTURAL DIVIDE

Anyone who has been paying attention in America knows that there is a cultural divide about guns in our country. Ideas that seem reasonable on one side of that divide seem crazy on the other. This is compounded by the lobbying effectiveness of the National Rifle Association and its allies, who continue to support legal inaction to improve gun control, even in cases in which public-opinion polling is clearly on the other side of the issue. This included arranging in 1993 to have federal legislation passed that prohibited the Centers for Disease Control and Prevention from conducting work that would "advocate" on behalf of gun control. This provision effectively halted research because it was ambiguous enough to worry those making funding decisions that if a study produced evidence that supported the validity of gun control measures, it would be seen as advocacy. Knowledge, after all, is power. The ban was finally lifted in 2013, in the wake of the Sandy Hook Elementary School massacre.

Similarly, the Bureau of Alcohol, Tobacco, Firearms and Explosives (ATF) was prohibited from operating a sophisticated central registry for collecting, collating, and publishing data about the exact role of guns in crimes in America. Thus, federal researchers have been forced to assume the position of ostriches with their heads in the sand, where they can't see what is happening.

The first part of the "having a gun makes you safer" equation has led to some ideas that seem strange to most non–gun owners and most people in countries not "hooked" on guns. For example, a 2011 law in Iowa allows people who are legally blind to be licensed to carry guns in public. Press coverage in 2013 featured both criticism and defense of this legal provision. A report on National Public Radio (NPR) contained this item: "A legally blind 84-year-old man who has a permit to carry a gun and was featured in the paper says he welcomes the attention. 'This interest is good,' Quintin DeVore tells *The Register*. 'It shows we're like anyone else and we don't want to be left behind.' He added, 'I think it might also help people realize that blind people aren't sitting in the corner twiddling our thumbs.'"

I mentioned this at a conference shortly after this report appeared, and at the break a retired FBI agent approached me to say that "a lot of blind people are more responsible with their weapons than many sighted people and shouldn't be deprived of their Second Amendment rights." Others in the audience laughed in disbelief when I made mention of the Iowa law. A great cultural divide.

In the wake of school shootings like the Columbine attack in 1999, and again in the wake of the Sandy Hook massacre in 2012, some gun advocates seriously suggested that every teacher should have a gun in class (some saying that at least the principal and custodian should be armed). This seems reasonable to some and preposterous to others. A great cultural divide indeed.

After the Aurora, Colorado, movie attack in 2012, the same voices advocated that every theater should have armed guards watching the movies (a bit like sky marshals on airliners), and that patrons should be encouraged to bring their personal weapons into the theater with them in case of an attack. Days after the Newtown shootings, in San Antonio, Texas, an off-duty sheriff's deputy working security at the Mayan Palace movie theater actually did shoot a gunman in the theater, perhaps fueling the idea that guns in theaters make theaters safer. Of course, the shooter in this case was a trained police officer, Sgt. Lisa Castellano, not simply a gun-toting civilian. What is more, it was not a matter of multiple armed civilians firing at the gunman (which most likely would have resulted in multiple innocent casualties), but rather one trained professional in a well-defined situation.

GUNS KILL PEOPLE, ESPECIALLY GUN OWNERS

The real-world data on guns indicate that not only are you more likely to have a homicide in your home if you have a gun there, but the risk of killing yourself is heightened even more. Research published by Kellerman and his colleagues in *The New England Journal of Medicine* reports that suicide rates for people who have a gun in the home are anywhere from two to ten times higher (depending on the underlying suicide risk of the groups being studied). Nearly forty thousand of us kill ourselves each year, and thousands attempt it but "fail."

The overall suicide rate for Germany is ten per hundred thousand. For Switzerland, the rate is twenty-five per hundred thousand. But a study compared the suicide rates of ethnic Germans living in Switzerland (where the proportion of households with guns is nearly 30 percent and the number of guns per hundred residents is forty-six) with those of ethnic Germans living in Germany (where the proportion of households with guns is about 9 percent and the number of guns per hundred residents is thirty). The suicide rate among ethnic Germans in Switzerland is four times that among Germans in Germany—directly proportionate to the difference in the prevalence of households with guns in them. More evidence of the great cultural divide is that this kind of study is readily accepted as "causal fact" by some Americans and dismissed as "purely correlational" by others (meaning there is no causal connection, only a coincidental statistical artifact of the data).

As a compilation of data by the Harvard School of Public Health's "Means Matter" project reported, when guns are available, sad people use them against themselves. I think that much is clear, but then I do stand on one side of the great cultural divide. In the United States, the fifteen states with the highest rates of household gun ownership have a suicide rate roughly double that of the six states with the lowest rates of household gun ownership. Of course, other factors may be in play in creating this difference (for example, differences in the social conditions that lead people to own guns in the first place), but I think it is hard to dispute the proposition that having a gun in your home increases your risk of suicide, whatever other risk factors may be present. Consider that the Israeli military used to require its soldiers to bring their guns home with them when off duty. After they changed this policy, there was a 40 percent decrease in weekend suicides by Israeli soldiers.

Other methods of attempting suicide are much less likely to be fatal and thus give many attempters a "second chance." Gun-linked attempts constitute 5 percent of all suicide attempts but are fatal 90 percent of the time and thus constitute about half of the total number of suicides. Taking pills is the method chosen in 75 percent of suicide attempts, but these drug overdoses are fatal in only 3 percent of the cases. Research reveals that about 90 percent of those who survive a suicide attempt will *not* try it again, so this is very important in the long run, even though the single best predictor of successfully killing yourself is a prior suicide attempt.

The case of Dan Armstrong and Tanya presented in chapter 5 illustrates this point. When Tanya persuaded sixteen-year-old Dan to join her in a suicide pact—and ultimately begged him to help her kill herself, and then take his own life—the weapon chosen was a knife. It's hard to kill yourself—or, under normal circumstances, someone else for that matter—with a knife. And when Tanya could not do it, neither could Dan, even though he was motivated to help her. Is there any doubt that if Dan had brought a gun to that lonely beach rather than a knife, the odds that both he and Tanya would be dead today would be dramatically higher?

GUNS ARE US

According to the ATF, there are more than five thousand gun shows each year in the United States, and with the rise of Internet sales and marketing, access to guns has increased dramatically. For example, the website eHow. com ("Discover the expert in you") offers instructions in the form of four easy steps:

1. Figure out what type of gun you are interested in purchasing. Search the internet and read different reviews of firearms and their benefits.
2. After you have a good sense of which type of gun you want to buy, head to a local gun supply store and check the real thing out. Occasionally large gun surplus stores even have indoor firing ranges where you can squeeze a couple rounds off.
3. Talk to a gun store near you about having an online gun shipped to them. United States federal gun laws say that if you purchase a gun online you have to ship it to a federally licensed gun store. This is to make sure you follow the appropriate gun laws and pass a background check.
4. Place your online gun order at one of the many online firearm retailers. At the time of purchase you will need a valid drivers license and the gun store's name and address for shipment.

I must say, I am particularly intrigued by the sentence "Search the internet and read different reviews of firearms and *their benefits*" (italics added, I must confess). When I Googled "best weapons to commit a massacre" in the summer of 2012, my search turned up mostly news stories about the massacre committed by James Holmes at the movie theater in Aurora, Colorado. Months later, references to James Holmes subsided, and more generic massacre stories took his place. When I tried it again in September of 2013, I got Aaron Alexis and the Navy Yard shooting in Washington, D.C. By October, it was back to mostly generic historical stories. The more things change, the more they remain the same?

Through it all, when I Google "how to buy an assault rifle," there is no shortage of sites willing to help me accomplish that goal. To be fair, I should note that of the top five (nonmilitary) massacres by an individual in modern history, the United States contributed only one. This is according to the website top50fanything.com, which makes the top ten in my Google search with the "Top 5 Worst Gun Massacres by an Individual." But we do get our own "Top 5 Gun Massacres in Recent U.S. History" from that site.

Since we know that unloaded guns don't kill people, and that would be frustrating for prospective killers, I suppose it is reassuring for those who want to be armed to know that they can buy ammunition online even more easily than they can purchase guns themselves. James Holmes bought six thousand rounds online (and his guns at gun shops) as he prepared for the massacre in Aurora. But like everything else in the American way of killing, the impact of guns and ammunition is hardly a simple matter. In fact, all the data presented thus far on the dangers they pose underestimate their true impact on our society.

THE TRUE TOLL OF SHOOTINGS IN AMERICA

The state of medical trauma technology is an important factor in assessing the impact of gun violence on homicide rates. The military recognizes this. Because of improvements in battlefield trauma care, soldiers in Iraq and Afghanistan survived wounds that even a decade or two earlier would have been fatal. In his book *On Combat,* military psychologist Dave Grossman reports that a wound sustained by a soldier in World War II that would have been fatal 90 percent of the time was, by the Vietnam war, fatal only 10 percent of the time. And trauma care has only improved since then. Thus, the ratio of deaths to injuries in combat has declined dramatically. According to the Department of Defense, in World War II, 30 percent of the Americans injured in combat died; in Vietnam, the figure was 24 percent; in the wars in Iraq and Afghanistan, about 10 percent. And this is despite enhanced firepower.

Each year, about thirteen thousand murders occur in the United States. A study team led by Anthony Harris reported that if we had the same level of medical trauma technology today that we had in 1970, the murder rate would be three or four times higher than it is. The mortality rate from gun assaults was about 16 percent in 1964; it is about 5 percent now (this despite the greater use of automatic and semiautomatic weapons). More dramatically, the FBI says that if medical trauma technology today were at the same level it was in the 1930s, the murder rate today would be eight times higher than it is. Thus, more than one hundred thousand people come close to being murdered in our country each year (by 1930s standards; sixty-five thousand using 1964 standards). If each of those assaulted has only ten friends and family members, that's between half a million and one million of us who are directly affected by even the local, unknown murders committed across the country each year—setting aside the spectacular killings that affect us all by their prominence in the mass media that envelop us on television, on radio, on the Internet, and in print.

While our non-gun murder rate is comparable to those of most other modern, affluent, industrialized countries "at peace," our gun-related rate is extraordinarily high, by far the highest in the modern, affluent world. The numbers wax and wane, but typically we have about ten thousand gun-related murders per year—compared with *several hundred* in countries like the United Kingdom, Canada, and Australia. For all the talk we hear about "the American way of life," what is really striking when we look around the world is "the American way of *death*—by shooting."

GUN SAFETY ACROSS THE CANADIAN BORDER

When speaking to an FBI conference in the wake of the Columbine school shooting in 1999, I was asked for something "practical and immediate" we could do to make our schools safer. "Yes," I replied, "jack them up, put them on wheels, and drive them to Canada." At that time, the youth homicide rate in Canada was one-tenth that in the United States.

There are guns in Canada, to be sure. Overall, there are about twenty-four guns per hundred people (versus 101 per hundred people in the United States). Canadians have about one million handguns (in a population of about thirty-five million). Americans have about one hundred million handguns (in a population of about three hundred million). Thus, while there are enough handguns in America that each of us would only have to share one gun with two other people, in Canada each person would have to share one gun with thirty-four others. That is one reason why news reports of shootings by kids so often include a line that goes something like this: "He obtained the gun from his [parents, uncle, grandfather, brother, friend, etc.]." There are enough guns to go around in America, even if you can't buy one yourself.

Moreover, guns are very tightly regulated in Canada, in ways that seem politically inconceivable in the United States. Let's remember that the political slogan of the United States is "Life, Liberty, and the Pursuit of Happiness," but in Canada it is "Peace, Order, and Good Government." And this difference makes a difference.

On April 20, 2000, the first anniversary of the Columbine school shooting, I happened to be in Canada when a fifteen-year-old boy went on a rampage and attacked people at his school. His thoughts and feelings were, by all reports, much like those of the adolescents who attacked their schools on our side of the border (press reports said that fellow students described him as "a loner who was often bullied and teased about his appearance"). But in this case, the results were "five people taken to the hospital and all released later that day." Why? Because all this troubled boy could come up with was a knife, and it is extraordinarily more difficult to commit a massacre with a knife than with a gun, any gun. American kids who attack their schools routinely use guns, not knives. It's part of the cultural script that has been in place since the early 1990s, if not before.

WHAT TO DO ABOUT MURDER?

When it comes to murder rates, we are doing better than the poor, disorganized countries that are always on the brink of political and social chaos. Our official rate is about six per hundred thousand, whereas Guatemala and Mexico have official rates of thirty-four and eighteen, respectively (and the actual rates may well be higher than that). Recently, Honduras has taken the lead, with a rate of ninety-four per hundred thousand.

But when we compare ourselves with more appropriate cultural and socioeconomic counterparts—Western and Northern Europe, Japan, and the like—things look pretty grim. Their rates are generally less than two per hundred thousand (e.g., Canada and the United Kingdom), and some are even less than one per hundred thousand (e.g., Norway and Japan). This discrepancy is mostly the result of flooding the civilian population in the United States with lethal weapons, particularly handguns (coupled with the cultural and social issues of racism and economic inequality identified in chapters 3 and 4).

Our higher homicide rate remains despite the sophistication of medical trauma technology in the United States that "artificially" depresses the rate of deaths from potentially lethal assaults. And this partly explains why we have a lower murder rate than many other societies that have a lot of violence but lose more victims to that violence. They have the kind of murder rate we would have if we didn't have the medical system we do, which saves the lives of so many shooting victims (e.g., the rate in Guatemala is about what ours would be if we had 1960s medical trauma technology—which is what is available for many people, particularly poor people, in Guatemala). Without our level of medical technology, the death toll in the Aurora movie theater attack, for example, would likely have been much higher than it was. Given the nature of the weapons used and the wounds suffered, at the least, most of the victims who were in critical condition days after the assault occurred would have died.

Guns don't kill people; people with guns kill people. And people with guns that shoot a lot of bullets in a short time kill the most people (not overall, of course, but in a given incident). The fact is, our society has not even made serious efforts to limit ownership of the kind of assault weapon James Holmes used to kill and wound almost a hundred people in a shooting spree that lasted only a few minutes. New rule: if you think it's OK for civilians to have easy access to and carry around semiautomatic weapons and large caches of ammunition, you must simply acknowledge that periodic massacres are part of the cost of doing business in our gun-crazy society, and you do not have the right to express shock and surprise when someone uses such weapons and such ammunition to quickly kill and wound a large number of people.

Guns don't kill people; people with guns kill people—particularly if those guns can fire fifty bullets in a minute. After each mass shooting using these assault weapons, we repeat the same process: people buy more guns, and elected officials mostly wring their hands and bow to the pressure of the gun lobby, and we hear again that "guns are not the problem and gun control is not feasible at this time." And "this time" becomes the next time, and the next time becomes always.

THE ROLE OF FEAR

In 1993, I was interviewing kids in California who lived in a dangerous neighborhood. Nine-year-old Robert particularly intrigued me. He was bright, talkative, and eager to give me the details of his life. After hearing him talk for a while about the ins and outs of what happened in his "tough" neighborhood, I asked him what it would take for him to feel safer where he lived. He thought for a moment and then said, "A gun of my own." He spoke for many kids in neighborhoods that are similarly "objectively" dangerous, in the sense that violence on the streets and in the schools and in the homes is common.

Given the war zone realities of inner-city urban life, it should not be surprising to find that many kids who live there would want to have access to guns and, indeed, that many do. But the extent of the saturation of America with guns reaches everywhere, even into environments that many would presume to be gun free. For example, not long after I spoke with Robert in California, I interviewed a group of middle-class, White eight-year-olds in Illinois. Their lives were very different from Robert's, safe and protected in their suburban community. Nonetheless, when I asked about it, around a third of them related how and where they could get their hands on a gun.

I hope they never feel the need, but the prevalence of fear, even in the suburbs, argues differently. Andrew Dirkson, the young man I presented in chapter 4 (who killed his pregnant young wife), didn't live in a dangerous community. He lived in the hamlet of Tapersville, Florida, hardly the inner city. But he was part of the American gun culture that runs from inner city to suburbia to rural small-town America and back. In fact, the gun he used to kill his wife was one the couple had bought at a gun shop only days earlier. It was "her gun," and they purchased it for her safety. And he killed her with it.

Fear is a powerful element in the American obsession with guns. In the days following the Aurora attack, gun sales increased by 25 percent, as they did after the Columbine school shooting and after almost every other high-profile massacre. People fear that a "crazy" person like James Holmes will ambush them at the mall, at school, at work, at the movies, at church, and anywhere else in the social landscape. It's extremely unlikely to happen, of course, but fear is not about objective risk, it's about perceived risk. At the extremes, it is called being paranoid, and by global standards it is a fact of life in America.

Lack of trust in the forces of law and order is another element that feeds the gun culture. More and more, opponents of gun control have cast their arguments in terms of the need to protect themselves from the federal government. When the Senate Judiciary Committee held hearings on gun control in the wake of the Sandy Hook shooting, this message was clear, as an NPR account of the session makes clear:

Seated at the witness table was Wayne LaPierre, CEO of the National Rifle Association. Sen. Dick Durbin, D–Ill., had a question for the NRA chief: Did he agree with the point of view that people needed firepower to protect themselves from the government? "Senator, I think without any doubt, if you look at why our Founding Fathers put it there, they had lived under the tyranny of King George and they wanted to make sure that these free people in this new country would never be subjugated again and have to live under tyranny," LaPierre said. The same argument is being made by a smaller, more strident gun lobbyist, the Gun Owners of America. "I think principally the Second Amendment deals with keeping the government from going astray in a tyrannical direction," says Larry Pratt, the group's executive director.

ARE OTHER COUNTRIES ANY DIFFERENT?

Compare our society's response with what the United Kingdom did when faced with a mass shooting. On March 13, 1996, a forty-three-year-old man attacked the Dunblane Primary School in Scotland. Armed with four handguns, he shot and killed sixteen children and one adult before killing himself. How did the Brits respond? Within five weeks, a million people signed petitions supporting a ban on guns. Within a year, the Parliament had enacted the Firearm Amendment Acts, which effectively made private ownership of handguns illegal in the United Kingdom, and more than one hundred and sixty thousand guns were turned in to police.

Of course, the United Kingdom was starting from a different place than we are in the United States. By the mid-1990s, the number of households in Britain that had guns was small compared with the figures in the United States. And we can assume that Brits seem generally more trusting of their government, indeed of their fellow citizens, than Americans are. They don't have a Second Amendment with its protection for "well regulated" militias, let alone unregulated private individuals.

Although Australia is like the United States in many ways, Australia's handling of guns is more British than American. In 1996, Martin Bryant used semiautomatic weapons in the killing of thirty-five people in Port Arthur, in Tasmania. Australia's political leadership—in the form of *conservative* Prime Minister John Howard—decided that a powerful gun control initiative was a moral imperative, regardless of the political costs. Under Howard's plan, gun owners were compensated for turning in their (formerly legal) guns. Some seven hundred thousand guns were taken out of circulation (equivalent to forty million in the United States, based on the smaller population of Australia). The result was to halve the number of households with guns. Results? Gun-related homicides are down 59 percent, there has been a 65 percent decrease in gun-related suicides, and there have been no new mass shootings (after thirteen in the eighteen years preceding the gun ban). Not everyone is pleased (and initial opposition nearly toppled Howard's government). But Australia is safer for the change. Although if someone else besides the killer had been armed at the site of the massacre in Port Arthur, Australia, when Martin Bryant staged his attack, there might have been fewer fatalities, the net effect of reducing the prevalence of guns in that country has been to save many, many lives.

By contrast, lack of trust in government rules in America. In his analysis of declining social engagement in America, *Bowling Alone*, Robert Putnam reports, "The proportion of Americans who reply that they 'trust the government in Washington' only 'some of the time' or 'almost never' has risen steadily from 30 percent in 1966 to 75 percent in 1992." Twenty years later, it has reached even higher levels. American distrust of institutions and each other is at an all-time high. Guns fill the void for many people in our country.

A Canadian friend tells of driving his camper from trailer park to trailer park across America, and at each stop being advised by newly made American friends that he was crazy to travel without a gun in his camper. Twenty years ago, a Canadian friend and I were on the subway in Toronto when a very disturbed man boarded the train, muttering to himself, gesticulating, and then shouting. When my American vigilance kicked in and I went on high alert, my Canadian friend reassured me, "Relax. This is Canada, not the United States. And he won't have a gun."

On a visit to an inner-city Chicago middle school some years ago, I was asked by the school social worker—I'll call her "Mrs. Smith"—to visit her special project for "at-risk" kids. It was her pride and joy, this group of thirteen-year-olds upon whom she lavished her love and attention, even using her own money to purchase things they needed but couldn't afford. It was lovely to see how much the kids—boys and girls—beamed back at her the love she showed them. At one point during the visit, however, Mrs. Smith was called out of the room, leaving me alone with her precious charges. We talked a bit about the neighborhood and how much violence there was, and how getting to school sometimes was like walking a gauntlet of threat.

At that point, one of the boys asked me if he could show me something and walked over to his locker. He opened it and pulled out a gun that he said he carried to and from school for protection. "Mrs. Smith is a wonderful person," he said, "but you wouldn't want to put your life in her hands, not in my neighborhood." It was a sobering testament to the relative power of fear and love in a dangerous world.

As it did in the nuclear arms race between the United States and the Soviet Union in the decades after World War II, fear (along with profit for the manufacturers of weapons) drives the American arms race today (as it did during the Cold War with the Soviet Union). But even amid that fear, even though we are not Australia, we could make some progress in disarmament, as we did in the U.S.–Soviet arms race. One such bright spot is to be found in the Boston Gun Project (now called "Operation Ceasefire").

The Boston Gun Project—and efforts like it around the country—sought to transform the community of violence by a coordinated approach that involved as many of the "players" in the gun-violence equation as could be induced to cooperate. Inducements and "levers" included strict and swift enforcement of gun-law violations and a commitment to monitor the violent activities of the youth gangs that were the principal force driving the youth homicide problem in Boston in the 1990s. The goal was to target the use of guns by young people and take steps to reduce it substantially.

An evaluation team led by Anthony Braga documented the success of the project:

- 63 percent decrease in the monthly number of youth homicides in Boston
- 32 percent decrease in the monthly number of citywide shots-fired calls
- 25 percent decrease in the monthly number of citywide gun assault incidents

What is more, there was a 44 percent decrease in the monthly number of youth gun assault incidents in the neighborhoods where youth gang violence was at the highest levels before the start of the Boston Gun Project/Operation Ceasefire intervention.

Further analysis of the data confirmed that the timing of the drop in gun violence coincided directly with the implementation of the program in 1996 (rather than as a result of unrelated changes in youth gang activities). Finally, the study was able to rule out the role of underlying economic trends (e.g., unemployment rates) as the cause of the decrease in gun violence.

The success of the program *could* serve as an inspiration to us all in the face of the pessimism that has crept into public debate on the issue of gun violence in America. Perhaps the lesson is this: Gangs don't kill people; gangs that use guns kill people.

WHERE YOU STAND DEPENDS ON WHERE YOU SIT

In the wake of the Columbine shooting in April, 1999, I was asked to participate in a panel on "Youth Violence." The panel was chaired by journalist Charlie Rose and included the principal of Columbine High School, the head of a major urban police force, the head of a major movie studio in Hollywood, and an official representing the National Rifle Association. The audience was definitely a VIP group—from Martha Stewart to Alan Greenspan (head of the Federal Reserve Board) to MSNBC's Chris Matthews to Senator John Glenn to Michael Eisner (the head of Disney) and so on. They were all invited by our host, Ted Forstmann, a Wall Street investor and billionaire who at that time bankrolled a similar high-profile program each year in Aspen.

My role as the panel's academic was to provide some background on the developmental psychology of youth violence, of the sort we had just witnessed when Eric Harris and Dylan Klebold attacked their high school in Littleton, Colorado, and killed thirteen people before killing themselves. After each panelist had made an opening statement, I was asked this question: "Who do you point the finger of blame at for youth violence?"

I responded that rarely, if ever, was there a single cause. Rather, it is an accumulation of risks that builds up to the point where violence occurs, like building a tower of blocks—the tower gets higher and higher until the addition of one more block causes it to tumble. "So, you need two hands' worth of fingers to point," I said, "to reflect the fact that so many factors contribute to the end result—and then save one for yourself, because each of us contributes to the problem in some way."

The Hollywood executive next to me responded, "When you put it that way, I think we in Hollywood must accept a finger of blame because I recognize that the violence in our movies does contribute to the problem." Then it was the NRA official's turn, and he responded with words to this effect: "No, we don't accept any responsibility for what happened. Guns don't kill people, people kill people." It was vintage NRA rhetoric.

In the audience that morning was the actor Kevin Spacey. He responded to the NRA official's comment by raising his middle finger and saying, "Here's a finger of responsibility for you." It was a great moment that, of course, had no effect on the gun debate in America. Sometimes it seems that nothing does.

Each time there is a high-profile shooting in America, the NRA and its minions wait it out. The short-term tactics may shift according to each specific incident, but the overall strategy remains the same: aggressive stonewalling that exploits the ambivalence that many Americans feel about gun control issues. Beyond that public face, they effectively threaten lawmakers who might vote for gun control.

After each shooting incident, there are news reports that "the NRA's power has waned in recent years." But the numbers of guns and bullets increase, and the killing goes on: murders, suicides, accidents, little kids killing people with guns they found under a mattress, in a closet, behind the TV, in the glove compartment of the family car, or even in plain sight on the coffee table.

GUN MONEY TALKS

As with so many issues related to crime in the United States, a big part of the story is economic self-interest, according to a report prepared by Liz Bartolomeo for the Sunlight Foundation. Social ideology, such as the "right to bear arms," is often appropriated by groups and individuals with a financial interest in promoting those views. The organized gun lobby is an example: it outspent gun control advocates by a factor of two to one in 2004, by ten to one in 2000, and by thirty to one in 2006. In recent years, the gap has widened still further.

Bartolomeo's report provides data on relative spending by the NRA versus the Brady Campaign to Prevent Gun Violence, and this is its conclusion: "The NRA has spent 73 times what the leading pro-gun control advocacy organization, the Brady Campaign to Prevent Gun Violence has spent on lobbying in the 112th Congress ($4.4 million to $60,000, through the second quarter of 2012), and 3,199 times what the Brady Campaign spent on the 2012 election ($18.6 million to $5,816)."

By targeting their efforts at members of Congress who threaten their business, the gun lobby effectively shuts down public action to limit access to guns. They are so good at it, that even after highly publicized massacres like the one that took place in Aurora, the main story in the mass media is, in effect, "Gun control is not only not the solution, but it is not even a legitimate topic of public debate."

Where you stand depends on where you sit. I know that where I sit is not where many other Americans sit, and I know that it affects where I stand on guns in America. I stand against guns. I support domestic disarmament.

There is a killer in each of us. As I said in chapter 2, my experience in simulated combat on a dark night in 1966 taught me that much. That's when I became an advocate for gun control, and I remain one today. Getting close to killers for the past twenty years has only strengthened me in that position. I need only remember that night in 1966 and what I was prepared to do with a gun in my hands. Horrible as it was (luckily no one got hurt), it was an invaluable lesson. I wish more Americans understood it. Guns don't kill people; people with guns kill people. Even *innocent* people with guns kill people.

TWELVE MONTHS

In 2012, there were nine thousand homicides (and twenty thousand suicides) in the United States in which guns were used, according to the FBI. Most of the murders were done by the kinds of killers I interview. Some were the result of domestic violence. Some were instances of workplace violence. A few were homeowners defending themselves or their loved ones. A very small number resulted from true accidents. Some were American tragedies, in which "innocent" people killed other "innocent" people, a sad fact of living in a society in which so many people are armed with lethal weapons that translate mistakes into dead bodies so quickly and efficiently:

June 2012, Houston: A man in northwest Harris County says he fatally shot his son Tuesday after mistaking him for a burglar trying to break into his house, Harris County detectives said. Derrick Casson told detectives that he confronted two men in his home that he believed were breaking in."

July 2012: "A 14-year-old New Orleans boy was shot in the head early Friday morning after a homeowner said the unarmed teen was trying to break into his house. Homeowner Merritt Landry, 33, who lives in Marigny, allegedly shot Marshall Coulter after fearing for his safety, and told friends and family he thought the teen had a gun."

September 2012: "In New Fairfield, Connecticut, a popular fifth-grade teacher fatally shot a masked, knife-wielding prowler outside his house during what appeared to be a late-night burglary attempt, only to discover he had killed his 15-year-old son, police say."

October 2012: "A Sacramento, California, man shot and killed his 34-year-old girlfriend in his home early Monday morning, because he mistakenly thought she was an intruder. Homicide detectives are still investigating the boyfriend's story, and the man has been cooperating with detectives, though he is very shaken up, police said."

October 2012: "Authorities say a retired Chicago Police detective shot and killed his own son in an 'accidental tragedy' early Tuesday morning. Police say the man's son entered the Far Northwest Side home wearing a skull cap, and the father thought he was a burglar when he shot him."

Sometimes such accidents don't involve "innocents" shooting "innocents." Sometimes both parties to the accident are "guilty."

THE CASE OF MARVIN BENSON

I interviewed eighteen-year-old Marvin Benson* at the Cook County Jail in Chicago on May 19, 2006, as he sat shackled, awaiting trial for killing another teenager (John Dicky) in a conflict at school that had escalated from words to fists to guns on January 21 of the previous year. Marvin's attorney from the public defender's office pled self-defense to the murder charges filed by the government, using the same strategy as was used in the breakthrough case of Leonel Rivas in Colorado ten years earlier—namely, that in *his* world and from the perspective of *his* life experience growing up in the urban war zone, he had a reasonable expectation that his life was in danger.

The public defender told the court that although Dicky ended up dead, Marvin was the one in peril on January 21, 2005, and for weeks before. "Every day he went to school, every time he left his house, he had to ask himself, 'Is this the day? Is this the day they're going to get me?'" she told the jury.

The fatal incident of January 21 was the fruit of a decades-long "war" between two rival neighborhoods—Westend and Hemmingway. Marvin Benson had little choice in the matter. As he told me when we met: "Even if you don't want to be in the beef, it comes from where you live." In this environment, as in any war zone, loyalty is a prime virtue. As Marvin put it: "Coming from where I come from, you know that where you're from is who you're with when it comes to a fight." Marvin had to venture into enemy territory in order to go to school—a condition that left him in a state of chronic fear: "A lot of fear. I had to ride the bus to school in their territory." I think this is the essential context for understanding the events that led to the shooting at Central High School in 2005.

In Marvin's case, there were personal dimensions to his community war zone experience that went beyond the neighborhood rivalry. His older brother had been shot and killed. He had numerous friends who had been shot and killed. He had been shot at himself. Marvin told me that he often had dreams in which he was shot and killed. The rap group that Marvin organized was named "Man-Down" in honor of a man Marvin knew who had been killed on the street.

In the months, weeks, and days before the fatal shooting on January 21, the chronic conflict between the two warring neighborhoods was escalating, so far as Marvin was concerned. He and his closest friend put their money in together to purchase one gun and left it near the school (where they felt most threatened) so that either of them had access to the gun to respond to the heightened sense of threat they were experiencing.

Marvin reported that in a prior incident involving some of the same boys involved on the day of the fatal shooting, he was held back by a group while the subsequent shooting victim beat up a younger kid from Marvin's neighborhood. Marvin was told by the boy, "We're gonna fuck you up if you don't stay out of it!"

On the day of the incident, I believe he was in a state of hypervigilance. The ethos of the "culture of honor" dominant in his environment (in which acts of disrespect are experienced as psychological and socially intolerable) compounded the general risk connected with teenage boys carrying guns, to produce a lethal incident. A fight broke out at his school. In the ensuing scuffle he was shot (not, it turned out, by one of his enemies, but inadvertently by himself, with his own gun). Thinking he had been shot by someone else, he fired his own weapon.

Marvin's action in using his weapon was reckless, but understandable given his traumatic history and his state of mind at the time: intense fear and the belief that he had been shot by one of his enemies. Anyone who has been in a combat situation can relate to this sequence of events. In such an environment, you tend to believe that "Shoot first and ask questions later" is a wise strategy when you feel threatened. You quickly move into a state of arousal in which reflective thought is subjugated to primitive survival and aggressive impulses. The military offers extensive and intensive training to its soldiers to prepare them for dealing with such situations. Youths like Marvin must face these situations without the benefit of such training. His reckless behavior is indicative of that fact.

He felt intense fear (and perhaps shame, because as a male he was trained to disparage fear). He was provoked by a powerful "enemy" ("The three of us was jumped and there was quite a few of them.") He had been assaulted before and knew Dicky to be an aggressive enemy. In this hyperaroused state, there was a rapid escalation from verbal aggression (taunts like "pretty boy" and "asshole") to physical aggression (punches thrown and scuffling) to lethal aggression (drawing a gun). As Marvin reported it to me, "I was getting pushed around and I saw him make a move. Then it dawned on me that I have a gun in my coat pocket. So I pulled it and I was shot [not realizing that it was by his own gun, as was later determined]. So I started shooting."

How did the jury respond to this line of argument from the defense? They acquitted Marvin of the first- and second-degree murder charges brought by the prosecution and of assault with intent to kill, but could not reach a verdict on the manslaughter charge. Marvin was convicted only of three lesser charges: assault with a dangerous weapon, possession of a firearm, and carrying an unlicensed pistol. He was sentenced to sixteen years in prison on those charges in the shooting of John Dicky. The shooting was an accident, but neither the shooter nor the victim was "innocent." It was, in a sense, a "guilty accident," and Marvin will spend more than a decade paying the price for it. Had he not felt he needed a gun, perhaps he would not have had one. Had he not had one, perhaps Dicky would still be alive, and both he and Marvin would have had another chance to figure things out. But he did have a gun, and his misperception of who had shot him resulted in the death of a seventeen-year-old boy and the long imprisonment of his eighteen-year-old killer.

After the sentence was pronounced, the mothers of Marvin Benson and John Dicky rose from their opposite sides of the courtroom. They approached each other, embraced, and prayed. Both women understood, I think, that their two sons were casualties of the gun culture. Tanya Dicky held Sybil

Benson and said, "I'm here every step of the way. You're not going through this by yourself. It's okay, it's okay." But it's not.

LIVING IN LETHAL AMERICA

Innocent mistakes. Guilty mistakes. Accidents. Crimes of passion. Self-defense. Suicide attempts. Criminal assaults. What increases the lethality of all these actions is the use of a gun. What makes all of these events so likely to be lethal is the saturation of America with guns.

When suburban eight-year-olds can explain to me how they would *get a gun* and inner-city eight-year-olds can explain to me why they *need a gun* and blind people in Iowa are legally *eligible to carry a gun* in public and seven out of ten murders *involve a gun* and there are *as many guns as people* in the country and *more places to buy a gun than to buy gasoline,* America truly has a "gun culture." Our country shows no sign of trading that culture in for something less lethal. Guns don't kill people. People with guns, especially American people with guns, kill people.

8

Making Sense of the Senseless

UNDERSTANDING AND PREVENTING
KILLING IN AMERICA

FOR THE PAST TWENTY YEARS, I have listened to killers, reviewed their records, and sought out research from developmental psychology and other social and biological science disciplines in an effort to figure out what leads them to commit these horrible crimes, to make sense of the senseless. I listen to killers. I don't listen passively; I listen actively, with empathy and compassion. Instead of distancing myself from them in my goodness and their evil, I get close to them and establish a human connection.

I try to find some basis for connecting through our shared humanity. I listen for the human story behind the monstrous act. As an expert psychological witness grounded in the science of human development, my mission has been not to excuse killers, or somehow minimize or glamorize their lethal crimes, but to bring forth understanding, and sometimes even compassion. It's a hard thing to do, and it requires all my emotional and intellectual resources. It makes me cry sometimes. But we have to do it if we are to make progress in understanding and preventing killing in America.

Although it is scientifically and morally risky to view all killing as psychologically the same, in a real and profound sense, virtually all murder is the consequence of disconnection—actually, a series of disconnections—which psychologists call "dissociation." Murderers are dissociated from life—from their own lives, and thus from human life. And they are not alone. Threat, trauma, and stress lead them to dissociate, just as the fear and loathing they inspire in us causes us to dissociate from them—and that is one way we permit state-authorized executions to continue when most of the "modern" world has forsaken them. Perhaps being awash in media violence, as we are, helps along that process of desensitization to violence.

Watching *Law & Order, CSI, NCIS,* and the many other television shows and movies that feature killing engages our interest—sometimes a prurient interest—but it also disconnects us from the real killing that is actually taking place around us. Maybe this protects us from ourselves. Perhaps if we weren't so dissociated, we would be unable to take in all the violence and continue to function, and it would not take some spectacular killing such as occurred at Sandy Hook Elementary School in 2012, or the movie theater shooting in Aurora, Colorado, that same year, or the massacre at Columbine High School in 1999, to get our emotional attention. But I have to pay attention. I can't dissociate. I have to connect, and in connecting with the killer, I have to break that cycle of dissociation.

REACHING ACROSS THE TABLE

Twenty-five-year-old Barry Lodi* was on death row in a prison in rural Mississippi, and I was interviewing him as part of an effort by the public defender's office to get him a new sentencing hearing. Six years earlier, when Barry was nineteen, he killed an old woman and her two dogs. He invaded the old woman's house in a remote corner of the state so that he could rob her and use the money to support his new girlfriend and her child. After a year of being homeless and drugged up—meth, crack, heroin—Barry had met the young woman and her son and, as he put it, "finally found a family to belong to." Armed to the teeth, Barry took over the old woman's shack so that he and his new family would have a place to stay and money to feed "their" child— and their drug habits.

Like the stories of so many killers, Barry's story was one of multiple and overlapping insults to his development. He had experienced parental rejection (his mother abandoned him when he was five, leaving him to live with his father, who introduced him to drugs and alcohol when he was ten years old). He had experienced abuse (his father beat him with belts, extension cords, paddles, and almost anything else that was around and forced Barry to sleep nude in the same bed with him—"to keep me close," as Barry put it—and to use him sexually). He had experienced social isolation, profound feelings of worthlessness and depression, and school failure that started in childhood and escalated in adolescence.

At one point in the interview, Barry said that when he was fourteen, he noticed that other kids had it worse than he did. I thought, what could be worse than the life Barry led as a child and a teenager? So I asked him what he meant. "At least I had a home," he said of the house of horrors he inhabited with this father—a shack on a geographically isolated fifteen-thousand-acre farm. When Barry was sixteen, his beloved cousin Sally, his confidante and principal emotional support, was raped and killed. This was followed a few months later by the death of his favorite uncle, Bobby-Joe, in a drunk-driving accident. When he spoke about Sally's death, Barry said, "When Sally died, the light went out in my life." Then he started to cry. I reached across the table and put my hand on his, and my eyes leaked tears of compassion for this young man on death row who struggled every day to make sense of what he did and who he was. And what he would become.

MAKING SENSE

Three questions guide my professional work:

What path takes killers from childhood innocence to homicidal violence in adolescence or adulthood?

Once they have murdered and gone to prison, are they inevitably and irreparably damaged, or can they ever be transformed and rehabilitated?

How can we learn from these killers to prevent others from following in their footsteps?

Those are big questions, but my work has forced me, as a person and a citizen, to confront bigger ones as well. What is it about American culture that gives rise to so much murder? Why are we so afraid of each other that we incarcerate and execute people at rates that astound the rest of the civilized world? Why do we hold on to our guns and the death penalty, when so many other modern societies have given up both? Why must we dehumanize and separate ourselves from the killers among us, quick to define them as monsters, evil, or simply crazy? And why does our racist history and present racist consciousness make us so ready to see evil, not hurt, in violent Black and Hispanic men, and to incarcerate them at rates higher than those in any other country? These questions are always there, even as I examine the specifics of a particular case, and they help me make sense of the strange things I hear sometimes when I listen to killers.

There have been times over the past twenty years when my experiences as an expert witness in the American criminal justice system caused me to feel a bit like I had landed in Lewis Carroll's *Alice's Adventures in Wonderland* or its sequel, *Through the Looking-Glass, and What Alice Found There*, where delusion and reality are inextricably mixed. Sometimes the alien and surreal character of these experiences had me feeling a bit like Alice as she tried to make sense of her experience with the Queen of Hearts, the Mad Hatter, and the smiling caterpillar and find her way home. But in reflecting on these strange and sometimes bizarre encounters, I have come to realize that rather than simply being weird, isolated experiences, they actually can move us along the process of understanding, of making sense of it all, and thus aid in efforts to achieve prevention and effective treatment.

THE CASE OF ROBERT NAVARRO

The concept of resilience has become a staple of developmental psychology. While there is the usual debate over the fine points, researchers and clinicians alike have come to use the term *resilience* in recognition of the fact that human beings are not wimps. We humans have evolved the capacity to deal with adversity, to bounce back from potentially damaging events, experiences, and conditions. We can barely imagine the risks and dangers faced by early humans—predatory animals, predatory hominids, accidental injuries, widespread death among infants and young children. The list is long. My point is that there is a good case to be made that the human race would not have survived without developing the capacity for resilience. This is the context for understanding the bizarre courtroom discussion that followed my testimony in the next case.

Robert Navarro's* case exemplified many of the issues that are at the core of my testimony and that I have addressed throughout this book. He presented an extraordinary accumulation of risk factors in his young life: poverty, abuse, social deprivation, neurological damage, and gang-based community violence. Like that faced by early humans on the planet, the list was a long one. My point in reviewing this massive accumulation of risk for the jury was to demonstrate that it was not surprising that he had become morally and emotionally damaged by the life experience and social conditions that had been thrust upon him, experiences and conditions that he had not chosen willfully for the most part.

After laying all this out in the direct examination by the public defender representing Navarro, I was faced with the prosecutor for the inevitable cross-examination. "Other young men have faced difficult circumstances and not killed anyone," he said. "What's wrong with the defendant that he is not resilient?" I was at first a bit taken aback, because "resilience" was developed as a positive concept, to explain why kids *overcome* adversity, and here was a prosecutor using it as a negative concept, to explain why Robert had succumbed to adversity. He was attributing the moral and emotional damage Robert experienced not to an overwhelming accumulation of risk factors, but to his lack of some trait of resilience. Diverting attention from what had happened to this boy, he wanted to focus on Robert's "giving in" to massive adversity as but one more deficiency, one more negative trait, that this beleaguered young man possessed.

It occurred to me then that in an America that is so keen on diagnosing new conditions (and giving them acronyms to boot, as in the case of RLS—restless leg syndrome), a new diagnostic label could come into existence. We could call it "RDD—resilience deficiency disorder." This would aid in the process of absolving society from responsibility for dealing with the socially toxic environments in which many kids live. "Sorry, ma'am," I can imagine an official telling a mother, "your son is suffering from RDD. Add that to his ADD, and I'm afraid we have a classic case of EAS—excessive alphabet syndrome."

· · ·

The larger point, and the reason I include this case in my concluding chapter, is that there is an underlying message here about how we think about killers (and, thus, how we can improve our efforts at prevention).

The dominant way of thinking about human development in our country (perhaps particularly in our legal system) focuses on individualistic explanations in which the causes of behavior are sought in the cataloguing of positive personal attributes like "honesty" and negative personal attributes like "impulsiveness." However, this doesn't correspond with the reality of human behavior and development in real life. It doesn't correspond with the way things really are in the human ecology in which individuals live.

AN ECOLOGICAL PERSPECTIVE ON HUMAN
DEVELOPMENT: A REALITY CHECK

How can we best approach these issues? To do so effectively, we need a perspective on human development that begins with the realization that all development and behavior arise "in context" and that, as a result, there are few hard-and-fast, simple rules about how human beings develop; complexity is the rule rather than the exception. Rarely, if ever, is there a simple cause–effect relationship that works the same way with all people in every situation. Rather, we find that the process of cause and effect depends on the child (or adolescent, or "emerging adult") as a set of biological and psychological systems set within the various social, cultural, political, and economic systems that constitute the context in which developmental phenomena are occurring.

This insight is the essence of an "ecological perspective" on human development articulated by scholars such as my mentor, Urie Bronfenbrenner. It is captured in these words: If we ask "Does x cause y?" the best scientific answer is almost always "It depends"—it depends on all the constituent elements of child and context:

Gender—for example, the amount of infant babbling predicts childhood IQ in girls but not in boys, according to research conducted by developmental psychologist Eleanor Maccoby.

Temperament—for example, about 10 percent of children are born with a temperamental proneness to becoming "shy," but this predisposition can be overcome in most children with strong, supportive, and long-term intervention, according to research conducted by developmental psychologist Jerome Kagan.

Cognitive competence—for example, abused children who exhibit a pattern of negative social cognition were found to be eight times more likely to develop problems with antisocial aggressive behavior than abused children who exhibited positive social cognition, in research conducted by psychologist Kenneth Dodge and his colleagues.

Age—for example, on average, "unconditional maternal responsiveness" at three months of age predicts "obedience" at twelve months of age, but such unconditional maternal responsiveness at nine months of age does not, as reported by Eleanor Maccoby.

Family—for example, although home visits by a nurse that began prenatally were effective in reducing child abuse in first-time births to single mothers from 19 percent to 4 percent among a high-risk sample, this effect did not occur when there was an abusive man in the mother's household, as documented by psychologist David Olds and his colleagues.

Neighborhood—for example, the correlation between poverty and infant mortality is conditioned by neighborhood factors, being "higher than would be predicted" in some areas and "lower than would be predicted" in others, as a function of the degree to which prenatal services are accessible, as was found in research that Kathleen Kostelny and I conducted in Chicago.

Society—for example, a study conducted by psychologists Marie-Eve Clément and Camil Bouchard comparing the United States and Canada found that the correlation between low income and child maltreatment was significantly higher in the United States than in Canada.

Identity—for example, although Americans have elected a Black president, racial identity remains a powerful negative predictor of life experience and expectations, with overt bias, institutional racism, and the legacy of slavery and Jim Crow reverberating across the decades, remaining a powerful force in American life, according to research by Michelle Alexander.

Culture—for example, native Hawaiians see the goal of child rearing as producing an interdependent person, whereas most non-Hawaiian Americans ("haoles" as Hawaiians call everyone else) are seeking to create rugged individualists; Hawaiian mothers place a high value on infants sleeping with parents, but haoles discourage the practice, as reported by anthropologist Jill Korbin.

MAPPING THE ACCUMULATION OF DEVELOPMENTAL RISKS AND ASSETS

The ecological perspective is frustrating: we all would prefer a simple "yes or no" to the question "does *x* cause *y*?" I know from testifying in Congress that our elected officials would prefer a simple answer, and from testifying in court that judges would too. But reality is not obliging on this score. One important corollary of our ecological perspective is the fact that generally, it is the accumulation of risks and assets in a child's life that tells the story about developmental progress, not the presence or absence of any one negative or positive influence. For example, Arnold Sameroff's classic study included eight risk factors: both parental characteristics—educational level, mental health status, absence of a parent, and substance abuse; and family characteristics—economic status, race, maltreatment, and number of children.

The results of Sameroff's study indicated that the average IQ scores of children were *not* jeopardized by the presence of one or two risk factors. Given that research compiled by Emmy Werner has told us that what matters for resilience is that children reach an "average" level of cognitive competence, about 100, it is highly significant that children with zero, one, or two risk factors averaged 119, 116, and 113 on IQ tests, respectively. But in Sameroff's study, IQ scores declined significantly, into the dangerous range, with the presence of four or more (averaging 92 with four risk factors and 85 with five). In this research, each risk factor weighed equally in the effect; it was the *accumulation* of risk factors that accounted for the differences.

Thus, by mapping the environment of a child in terms of risk accumulation, we can know whether that child is doing "as well as can be expected," given the social environment he or she faces—or, perhaps, better or worse than the average child facing those same circumstances. Consider sad Barry, described earlier in this chapter. He clearly faced six of the eight risk factors identified in Sameroff's research, and, not surprisingly, his tested IQ ranged between 73 and 83 (depending on when the test was given). In this he was average, not in the sense that his IQ was average, but in the sense that the average kid with six risk factors scores at about the level Barry did. He did not suffer from "resilience deficiency disorder." He suffered from being dealt a lousy hand in life.

It goes beyond this, however. The Centers for Disease Control and Prevention have endorsed an approach to risk accumulation developed by Vincent Feletti, Robert Anda, and their colleagues that focuses on the impact of ten "adverse childhood experiences" (ACE). These risk factors are assessed through a series of ten questions, including inquiries about childhood experience of physical, sexual, and psychological maltreatment, poverty, domestic violence, household substance abuse, parental separation or divorce, depression or suicide in a family member, and incarceration of a family member. While not encompassing all possible negative influences on development (e.g., racism and educational impairment are not included), these ten factors have proved to be powerful in accounting for differences in negative outcomes extending into adulthood—for example, they account for 65 percent of the variation in suicide attempts, 40 percent of the variation in depressive disorders, and 56 percent of the variation in drug abuse, all three of which are relevant to understanding the lives of many killers.

For the purpose of understanding the lives of the "general population," it may be sufficient to report measures of health and well-being in which the lives of adults who had a score of zero (some 36 percent of the general population), one (26 percent), two (16 percent), or three ACEs (10 percent) are compared with those who had four or more (13 percent). But to understand the developmental damage experienced by many individuals in prison, it is necessary to appreciate the impact of extraordinarily high scores that are rare in the general population but common among killers. Only 4 percent of the general population have a score of five ACEs. Only 2 percent have a score of six. Less than 1 percent have a score of seven or eight, and the percentage with nine or ten is even smaller—on the order of 0.1% (one in a thousand). In one four-week period in 2014, all three of the killers I interviewed had scores of 10. In this they are typical of so many I have listened to over the past twenty years. Their accumulation of adverse childhood experiences is stunning, and they often have one or more of the Sameroff risk factors as well (most notably, racism and low educational attainment of parents). The accumulation of risk matters developmentally. But the same is true of positive influences.

Standing against the accumulation of risk are the number of developmental assets in a child's life and the components of resilience. Research conducted by the Search Institute has identified forty developmental assets— positive characteristics of family, school, neighborhood, peers, culture, and belief systems. As these assets accumulate, the likelihood that a child or adolescent will demonstrate good health habits, good grades at school, tolerance of others, and delay of gratification to meet important goals increases.

By contrast, as the number of assets decreases, the odds increase that a child or adolescent will use drugs or alcohol, become sexually active before age fifteen, reject others who are different from themselves, and be engaged in antisocial violence. The rate at which kids have such problems with aggression declines as the number of assets increases, from 61 percent for kids with zero to ten assets to 6 percent for kids with thirty-one to forty. Although research has yet to demonstrate conclusively that it is possible to reduce a child's or an adolescent's risk of violent behavior by increasing the number of assets in his or her life, it is clearly a preventive strategy that merits increased investment and attention. I was hard pressed to identify very many developmental assets in Barry's sad life. My best guess put him in the zero-to-ten range, and in that he is typical of the killers to whom I have listened over the past two decades.

ASSET ACCUMULATION PREDICTS RESILIENT RESPONSE TO STRESS AND CHALLENGE

If we ask, "Does absence of a parent produce long-lasting negative developmental effects?" the answer is, as Sameroff's research demonstrates, "It depends." That's always the answer *in general*. But we can move beyond that if we know what else a particular child is facing—risk factors like poverty, drug abuse in a parent, child abuse, racism, or too many siblings, as well as developmental assets such as a trio of supportive nonparental adults who care, a supportive school, involvement in artistic and/or athletic activities, a strong sense of having a positive purpose in life. The more we know, the more we can move closer to "Yes, probably" or "No, probably not." And one important influence on the developmental impact of these contingencies is always the temperament of the child.

Each child offers a distinctive emotional package, a temperament. Each child shows up in the world with a different package of characteristics. Some are more sensitive; others are less so. Some are very active; some are lethargic. Why are these differences important? For one thing, they affect how much and in what direction the world around them will influence how they think and feel about things. And this brings us back to resilience.

At least at the lower range of risk accumulation, what one child can tolerate, another will experience as highly destructive. What will be overwhelming to one child will be a minor inconvenience to another. Knowing a child's temperament goes a long way toward knowing how vulnerable that child will be in the world, particularly in the range of stressful life situations that are common in the lives of American children (e.g., for the 88% of kids with ACE scores between zero and three). Alexander Thomas and Stella Chess's classic research on temperament in the United States reported that while about 70 percent of "difficult" babies exhibited serious adjustment problems by the time they entered elementary school, for "easy" babies the figure was 10 percent.

In my prison interviews, I have listened to many adolescents and adults who were "difficult babies." Again, the point is not that they suffer from "resilience deficiency disorder," but rather that as human beings they grow and develop in a context defined by the interaction of what they bring to each encounter with life and what highly adverse childhood experiences life brings to them.

As I said before, although it is defined in numerous ways, *resilience* generally refers to an individual's ability to stand up to adverse experiences, to avoid long-term negative effects, or to otherwise overcome developmental threats. We see this in the pioneering work of Norman Garmezy, Emmy Werner, Michael Rutter, and others. As is pointed out in a collection of research and programmatic-intervention reports on resilience edited by Suniya Luthar, "At the heart of much resilience research is the desire to uncover salient protective and vulnerability processes that, if targeted in interventions, would substantially improve at-risk children's odds of doing well in life."

Many of us know a child whose life is a testament to resilience. The concept of resilience rests on the research finding that although there is a positive correlation between specific negative experiences and specific negative outcomes, in *most* situations—principally in that "normal" range of ACE scores of zero to three, for example—a majority (perhaps 60 to 80 percent) of children will not display a significant negative outcome. All children have some capacity to deal with adversity, but some have more than others and are thus more "resilient," while others are more "vulnerable" in difficult times. But some children face relatively easy lives, while others face mountains of difficulty with few allies and resources. And resilience is not absolute. Every child has a "breaking point" or an upper limit on "stress absorption capacity." Kids are "malleable" rather than "resilient," in the sense that each threat costs them something—and if the demands are too heavy, the child may experience a kind of psychological bankruptcy.

Virtually all the children within some highly stressful and threatening environments demonstrate their negative effects. We must remember the Chicago data presented by psychologist Patrick Tolan, in which *none* of the minority, adolescent males—living in both highly dangerous, threatening low-income neighborhoods and low-resource, high-stress families—was resilient at age fifteen. ("Resilience" was indicated by a continuous two-year period of neither being more than one grade level behind in school nor having mental health problems sufficient to warrant professional intervention.) This finding has led Tolan to question the usefulness and validity—indeed, the resilience—of the concept of resilience. His view is that what people call "resilience" is really just unexplained variation, variation that would be explained if we included more variables in our analyses. It's a good point. If you pile up enough risk factors, there comes a point when the context is so hostile to humans that the casualty rate is 100 percent. I can illustrate this point with the following example.

It seems clear that individuals who go to the gym and work out, doing aerobic exercises, are generally more fit than couch potatoes who do not work out. We can think of the aerobic workout group as having "more resilient breathing." But what will happen if we put both groups, the aerobic exercisers and the couch potatoes, on the surface of the moon? The lunar environment will be fatal to both groups; no one will demonstrate resilient breathing on the surface of the moon. My point is that many of the people I interview in murder cases have grown up on the moon, socially and psychologically speaking.

What is more, resilience in gross terms (e.g., absence of incarceration and ability to maintain employment) may obscure real psychic costs to the individual. Some children manage to avoid succumbing to the risk of "social failure" as defined by poverty and criminality, but nonetheless experience real harm in the form of diminished capacity for successful intimate relationships. Even apparent social success—performing well in the job market, avoiding criminal activity, and creating a family—may obscure some of the costs of being resilient in a socially toxic environment of the kind faced by millions of children—from whose ranks most killers are recruited.

I think of this often when I speak with or read the statements of the siblings of the killers I interview. Of course, sometimes they too are incarcerated (often for crimes less serious than murder, to be sure, like Barry's brother John) or suffer from debilitating mental health problems that force them into repeated institutionalizations (like Barry's sister Suzanne). But sometimes these siblings appear to be much more socially functional than their incarcerated brother (or sister). Still, the inner lives of these children may be fraught with emotional damage—to self-esteem and intimacy, for example. Many have mental health problems that plague them and the people around them. Though resilient in social terms, these kids may be severely wounded souls.

. . .

Understanding and preventing killing in America hinges on adopting an ecological perspective in looking at the lives of the killers themselves, directing our attention not to a laundry list of "problems" in America, but rather to the actual accumulation of developmental risks and assets in the lives of the kids who walk down the pathway to acts of lethal violence. Robert Zagar's work in developing predictors of murder in early experience testifies to this. Educators, social service workers, police, and mental health professionals must be aware of, and pay attention to, this dynamic in childhood and early adolescence, and not wait until violent reality has answered the questions of resilience in a negative manner. This is not because a particular child or teenager suffers from "resilience deficiency disorder," but because he (or she) is embedded in a context in which resilience would be miraculous, not expected. This understanding alone could help us focus resources on the kids who are being overcome by the world they inhabit, and bring more coherence to intervention programs in schools and communities.

FELONY CHARGES FOR A CHEESEBURGER?

Fourteen-year-old Bruce Warner* was rather pathetic as he sat in his jail cell, awaiting trial for murdering another teenager seven months earlier, in a dispute over a stolen bicycle that got out of hand and ended in a shooting. We spent the whole morning talking about his life and the events that led up to the murder charges that brought us together. Noon came, and I left with the promise that I would come back in the afternoon to continue. As I was leaving, Bruce asked where I was going for lunch. I told him. It was a small town, so he knew the place I mentioned. "I used to go there all the time," he said, with a mournful look on his face. He continued, "It's been seven months since I had one of their cheeseburgers. They're really good, nothing like what we get here at the jail."

Sitting in the restaurant eating my veggie burger, I made a rash decision. "One cheeseburger to go," I said to the waitress. It wasn't a big deal to bring it back to the jail in my bag, since I had been there in the morning and had been cleared to return. And it wasn't death row, just the county jail. When I presented it to Bruce, the look on his face was priceless, a boy with a brief respite of normality in the terrible reality that had become his day-to-day life. He thanked me profusely as he chomped down on what for him was the ultimate comfort food, given the situation. The interview continued.

After I left the jail that day and headed home to write my report, I didn't think much more about the cheeseburger. In particular, I didn't think to put together the fact that I had done a kindness for a lonely, scared kid and the fact that the interview had been taped. A week after returning home, I received a phone call from the boy's lawyer, who had, not surprisingly, listened to the tape, and heard Bruce thanking me and eating the cheeseburger. I should say that there were some very strange rumors about this lawyer floating around the small town where all this was happening (for example, he was said to have bought drugs from the older brother of the boy Bruce killed). In any case, the gist of the call was that I had committed "felony contraband smuggling" by bringing the illicit cheeseburger into the jail. He fired me from the case and told me that if I ever set foot in the state, he would have me arrested. I didn't go back for years (at least until the statute of limitations expired), and I never smuggled anything into a prison again. But really? "Felony contraband smuggling charges" for bringing a lonely, hungry kid a cheeseburger? Where's the sense in that?

I raise the case of my impulsive, and somewhat foolish, smuggling of a cheeseburger because it speaks to an important feature of institutional life in prisons that contributes to the larger problem of killing in America. This problem is the way our treatment of juveniles comes back to haunt us later, when they become adults. A report from the federal government indicates that 67 percent of murderers had an arrest record before they killed someone, in most cases as juveniles. As I said before, the racist application of drug laws that has resulted in the widespread incarceration of Black and Brown men sets the stage for this link.

Looking at the broader pool of "violent felons" that feeds the ranks of killers, a 2010 Bureau of Justice Statistics report indicates that 36 percent had an active criminal justice status *at the time of their arrest*. This included 18 percent on probation, 12 percent on release pending disposition of a prior case, and 7 percent on parole. Overall, 70 percent of violent felons had a prior arrest record, and 57 percent had at least one prior arrest for a felony. The majority of murderers (and those who commit violent assaults that *could* be fatal) have been detained before they kill, ordinarily *not* because of an earlier murder (or attempted murder). Many of them started down the path that led eventually to killing someone by doing something criminal that landed them in jail, usually as a juvenile, and often involving the illicit drug trade.

As I have noted before, psychologist Craig Haney looked at the evidence and concluded that the younger individuals are when incarcerated, the more likely they will develop severe adjustment reactions to prison life that will impede normal development of social skills and appropriate values and codes of behavior. This sets them up for committing a violent felony upon release and speeds their return to prison. The odds go down if they experience transformative education and prosocial socialization. The odds go up if they experience traumatic victimization and socialization to hardcore criminality while in prison.

Some of this flows from the dynamic in which troubled childhoods lead to early detention and incarceration, of course. Obviously, even among Black and Brown kids who are targeted by the Drug War, kids do not get sent to prison at random. The accumulation of risks on one hand and developmental assets on the other is related to the larger picture of life in the slice of America in which they live. In their America, the legacy of racism and economic inequality manifests acutely in the lives of kids. Although the "psychological poverty" of risk accumulation and the "psychological affluence" of developmental asset accumulation are not completely congruent with one's place in society and the economy, they are sadly correlated.

But some of the adverse impact of incarceration on future violent behavior flows from the kind of dehumanizing institutional mind-set in which bringing a cheeseburger to a lonely kid is "felony contraband smuggling." Let me be clear on this: I know that many staff members go out of their way to show kindness and respect the dignity of inmates. I have seen it firsthand and hear about it often. But acts of deliberate hostility designed to degrade exist too, of course.

Given who they house and their legal mandate to protect society (and themselves) from criminals, I am sympathetic to the challenges of prison administration. I acknowledge the need for rules and procedures to keep everyone as safe as possible in prison. I am not naive on that point, and I thank the guards who have kept me safe in my many visits to prisons around the country. But this cannot be the whole story if we want prison to be part of the solution and not just a magnifier of the problem. In reviewing the files of one young man, I found he had received a disciplinary write-up for "possession of anything not authorized . . . being in an unauthorized area, getting too much orange juice." Too much orange juice? Really?

. . .

As head of mental health services for a Massachusetts prison, psychiatrist James Gilligan was able to organize this prison around a "culture of respect."

This led to a dramatic reduction in violence between inmates, violence against themselves, and violence directed at guards. This can only help reduce recidivism and lethal violence, because it means that more young offenders will get better and fewer will get worse. Fewer will be traumatized by their prison experience, and more will have a chance to mature, gain insight, accumulate socially useful skills and knowledge, and thus reduce the odds that they will become killers after they are released. That's my point: a respect-based culture in prisons (and youth detention centers) is a crucial component of a national effort to reduce killing.

THE CHALLENGE OF KNOWING THE WHOLE STORY

When I serve as an expert witness, I ordinarily rely on documents to augment my interview with the defendant. These include school reports, police reports, psychiatric assessments, prison records, and other sources of information. I usually don't interview family members, relying on the social worker who prepares the defendant's "social history" to do that.

Once in a while, though, I do talk with a defendant's family members. In the case of Robert Smith*, it happened that the defendant's mother was visiting the defense lawyer's office on the day that I was there to interview her son, so I seized the opportunity to talk with her. We spoke for a while about the family situation when her son was a child in the U.S. Virgin Islands. She reported a great deal of family conflict and violence, which had eventually caused her to flee her rural village with her two sons and relocate to the mainland United States, in an attempt to escape her abusive husband.

At some point, I asked her about what her son was like as a baby. In the midst of talking about her son as an infant, she made a rather startling, but offhand, admission. "When he was a baby," she said, "the only way he would fall asleep was if I sat in a chair with my feet up on another chair and laid him on my legs. That was the only way that baby child would fall asleep." She laughed. "Sometimes I would fall asleep and he would fall off and hit his head on the floor."

"How often did this happen?" I asked. "Oh, I don't know," she replied, "maybe once a week." Knowing a bit about her son's social and intellectual problems—the usual issues of executive function and emotional regulation—I immediately thought this could be a clue to possible neurological damage, and wondered why tests for such damage did not appear in the records I had reviewed prior to meeting with her. "Have you told anyone else about this?" I asked. "Oh no," she said, again laughing. "No one ever asked about it before."

When we were finished, I reported the conversation to the lead lawyer assigned to the case. He ordered a neurological exam that revealed substantial brain damage in his client, and this figured prominently in testimony for the penalty phase of the trial. His brain damage became a mitigating factor in the defense's attempt to persuade the jury to spare his life.

It is disturbing to think that in a situation in which the stakes involved are so high (execution or life in prison), such random events as Robert's mother coincidentally being in the lawyer's office on the one day that I was there can prove crucial to the case. I'm not one to put much stock in divine intervention in my work, but this certainly had a whiff of it.

The larger point is that the process of understanding killers must be exhaustive and often requires an exhaustive (and exhausting) gathering of information from multiple sources. Moreover, everyone involved must be up to the task of making sense of it all. Unfortunately, not everyone is.

Often I am called to testify in hearings to determine whether a defendant deserves a new trial—"a habeas hearing." The grounds for requesting a new trial are usually that the representation in the original trial was so ineffective as to constitute a violation of the constitutional right to a fair trial. Russell Stetler and W. Bradley Wendel have laid out the ways in which defense lawyers typically fail to meet the standards set by the American Bar Association for defending clients in death penalty cases. Usually, the claim of "ineffectiveness" involves the lawyers directly (as in cases where the lawyer fails to offer an opening statement in the penalty phase of the trial, which would give the jury guidance on the meaning of mitigation and how it applies to the defendant they have found guilty). But another basis for arguing inadequate representation is to show that the quality of expert-witness testimony in the original trial was insufficient (usually in the sense that at the time of the trial, more sophisticated expertise was available than that which was presented, and if that other expertise had been presented, it could have affected the verdict and the sentencing). That's where I come in.

In preparing for a recent hearing of this sort, I was asked to look at the information available at the time of the first trial, six years earlier, and offer what I would have said if I had been called for that trial. At issue in the case were not the facts of the murder, but rather the significance of the mitigating factors in the young man's life. A psychologist had testified at the trial about the defendant's many negative life experiences—family disruption and hostility from parents and stepparents. But no unifying concept was presented to organize this information (and some that should have been introduced but wasn't) into something more than a litany of unhappy and unfortunate events. In thinking about this, I was drawn to a metaphor, which I offered to the court in my testimony at the habeas hearing. I share it here because I believe it captures something very important about how powerful concepts can be in understanding what at first may seem like "random" facts in the life of a killer.

Consider the following numbers: 3, 5, 7, 11, and 17. I can tell you that these numbers are taken from a series of numbers that have something in common. For those who have no mathematical concepts at their disposal, they are just numbers. But for those who are a bit more sophisticated, it is clear that the list may not be just a set of random numbers. Anyone with a rudimentary knowledge of mathematics would offer the hypothesis that they are "odd" numbers. True enough. They are odd numbers. But that is not the whole story, because I can tell you that the number 2 (an even number) is part of this sequence but the number 15 (an odd number) is not. This disproves the hypothesis that this is simply a list of odd numbers. End of story?

No. For those with a still more sophisticated knowledge of mathematics, this list represents a higher-order concept: each is a prime number (i.e., a whole number divisible only by itself and by the number 1). Knowing this, you can know that the number 13 was skipped in the list I provided and that following 17 are the numbers 19 and 23 (and so on). Still more sophisticated mathematicians know that there are, in fact, numerous kinds of prime numbers (as a cursory web search will demonstrate).

It is for this reason that I resonate with the way Russell Stetler summarized the value of the conceptual framework that expert witnesses can offer in a 2014 analysis titled "Mental Health Evidence and the Capital Defense Function." As he sees it after decades of experience, "Lay witnesses on their own are unlikely to recognize the significance of the symptoms and behaviors they describe, and only an expert is likely to be able to provide an overview of the factors that shaped the client over the course of his life and to offer an empathic framework for understanding the resultant disorders and disabilities."

I cringe when I read the transcript of an expert witness and don't see some higher-order concepts to organize the litany of bad life experiences into a compelling narrative that can render the defendant's childhood and adolescent suffering and deprivation into a story that makes developmental sense to a jury, not just a litany of diagnoses (antisocial personality disorder, bipolar disorder, borderline personality disorder, etc.).

I cringed when I reviewed the case of Dennis Stetson*, who was sentenced to death in a double murder when he was nineteen. Seven years later, I read the testimony of the psychologist presenting the case for mitigation, and the devastating cross-examination by the prosecutor. I wondered how the guy managed to make such a mess of it (for it later became clear that there was a powerful and persuasive case to be made). When I asked the attorney handling the appeal about it, her answer was simple and blunt: "He's a hack." Having interviewed the defendant myself and reviewed the records available to him when he testified in the first trial, I had to agree. But it is more than a matter of simple incompetence.

As I said earlier, the key to the ecological perspective is knowing that when the question is "Does x cause y?" the best answer is "It depends." But this is only the beginning, because the more we know, the more we can move from a generic "It depends" to a more informative "yes" or "no." Usually, the accumulation of information moves us along the path from a generic "It depends" to a more specific understanding of how one individual life has gone so wrong. Sometimes one fact—like repeated head trauma because an infant fell on his head once a week—allows us to leap ahead on that journey.

It did in the case of twenty-two-year-old Texan Jerry Williams*, who beat his four-year-old stepson to death because he defied him about eating his dinner. To find the key, I had to read through a thousand pages of his phone text messages. Amid the banal details of life—"Pizza for dinner?" "Yo, what's up?" "Where are you?" "Who won the game yesterday?"—was a series of messages between the defendant and the little boy's mother in which he displayed the extreme narcissism, the bloated sense of self-importance and entitlement that often arises as a compensation for early prolonged trauma and a pervasive lack of genuine self-worth and self-esteem. It was this grandiosity of Jerry's that allowed him to define the normal behavior of a four-year-old as an insulting and intolerable provocation.

Once that was clear, it became possible to see the defendant's history with his pathologically indulgent mother and cold, absent father as a story that led to the little boy's death. It didn't excuse it. Nothing could. But it made human sense of the horror, of the young man who killed a defenseless little boy because he wouldn't eat his beans and threw the dinner plate on the floor.

. . .

It is possible to see the patterns, and thus to put the information together to tell the story. But it requires an expensive mix of time, energy, and accumulated knowledge about how human development works.

MAKING THE INVESTMENT TO UNDERSTAND

One of the weak spots in the whole legal process is that the allocation of resources to understanding killers often does not begin until the killing is over. As the research conducted by Zagar and his colleagues (outlined at the end of chapter 4) makes clear, it is possible to know which kids are most at risk for becoming killers (with 97 percent accuracy in his study). Other work by Zagar demonstrated that by intervening to divert high-risk youths from this predictable pathway, lives and money could be saved. In Chicago, a program that invested in jobs, mentoring, and anger management programs for youths identified as at high risk for becoming killers resulted in a 43 percent reduction in the number of shootings and a 77 percent drop in the number of assaults (compared to what would have occurred if the investment were not made in the kids identified by Zagar's predictive model).

Where can the money for such preventive efforts come from? The cost–benefit analysis presented by Zagar's research offers one clear answer: for every dollar invested in diverting a high-risk kid from the pathway that leads to murder, more than six dollars are saved in the future monetary costs associated with killing. This figure parallels what prenatal home visits by health professionals save by preventing child abuse and neglect, according to research conducted by David Olds, John Eckenrode, and their colleagues.

Part of this economic argument lies in the fact that the costs of death penalty cases are so high—$1.6 million, on average—that they may "starve" the rest of the system. An analysis in California by the Death Penalty Information Center found that if there were no death penalty cases (and all the existing convictions were commuted to life without parole), the savings would be on the order of $171 million a year. That money could fund better assessment and treatment of troubled individuals before they reach the end of the line by committing a murder.

However, what are we to make of the fact that although these hard facts were available when California's citizens were given a chance in 2012 to vote on Proposition 34, which would have abolished the death penalty, they turned it down: 53 percent voted no, despite advocacy by a broad coalition of groups that outspent opponents of the repeal by a factor of six to one. I spoke earlier in this book about "cultural insanity." Apparently it exists even in a generally "smart" state like California. The death penalty was affirmed in Proposition 34, and the march of costly death penalty cases goes forward.

Given the high stakes in death penalty cases, courts generally approve funding for a team of lawyers, mitigation specialists, mental health professionals, and others who can shed light. I have worked on capital cases with psychiatrists, psychologists, neurologists, anthropologists, and even historians. That's to the good, of course. But the extraordinary expenditures on death penalty cases often seem an unnecessary waste of money, compared with simply forgoing that process and taking execution off the table. That would allow a reallocation of resources where they might do more good.

I should add that this might even bring more closure to victims, because a sentence of life (especially when it is life without parole) is usually the final legal word in a murder case. By contrast, a death penalty sentence is only the beginning of a process that lasts years, perhaps decades. The process of appeals before the "closure" of execution can be had is incredible: I recently met a man who has been on death row since my thirty-five-year-old daughter was born.

. . .

If we know enough, almost every killing "makes sense," no matter how senseless it appears at first, before there has been a deep exploration of the killer's life. I use the guidance provided by psychiatrist Harry Stack Sullivan: "Human beings are more simply human than otherwise." The more we know, the better our potential response. The earlier we know it, the more likely we are to be empowered to act preventively. The more we drain resources in the misguided effort to seek death sentences and then validate them through the various levels and venues of the appeals process (which justice demands), the less there is for the productive work of understanding individuals on the path to murder and intervening before they get there.

Most murder cases involve a team working for the defense. There are the lawyers, of course (usually a pair), the mitigation specialist (usually a social worker), and an investigator (often a former police officer). There is often a psychiatrist or clinical psychologist or neurologist to do standardized testing of one sort or another, when there are issues of brain damage, severe mental illness, or some other diagnosable condition that could prove relevant in explaining the defendant's behavior to a judge and jury. Usually, I work in parallel with these other professionals; we may talk on the phone, but we rarely meet in person before the trial, if at all. In the case of Jonathan Brown*, however, it happened that the psychiatrist on the case, Dr. Smith, was present in the public defender's office on the same day that I was. The defendant's brother and sister were there to be interviewed, so we took the opportunity to interview them together, hoping to get a better perspective on the defendant's family experience.

We spent forty minutes with the pair, going over details of their mutual childhood experiences with Jonathan. The interview came to a head when the brother was asked about his relations with his extended family. "I hate them all," he said. "In fact," he continued, "I have a hit list." "A hit list?" Dr. Smith replied. "What do you mean by a hit list?" The brother calmly explained, "The hit list is the order in which I plan to kill them. I revise it every month. If they are good to me that month they get moved down on the list. If they treat me bad, they get moved up." The psychiatrist nodded sagely, and we finished up the interviews, thanked the brother and sister for their time, and watched as they left the office. I remember thinking of the brother, "This is the guy who *isn't* in jail!"

Soon after, Dr. Smith and I sat down to discuss the case in the office of the public defender, who turned to him and asked, "Doctor, based upon the interview, what's your professional opinion of Jonathan's brother?" "My professional opinion?" he replied. "He's fucking crazy!"

As I said in chapter 1, the legal system has a hard time adopting a reasonable standard of "mental illness" in its deliberations. The definition of "insanity" is so narrow that it does not match up well with the mental health realities of those accused of murder—being so out of touch with reality that the killer doesn't know that what he is doing is wrong or feels an irresistible compulsion to kill. But those who come at the issue from the mental health side of things see a much broader issue beyond what this narrow definition of insanity suggests. Russell Stetler's review of mental health issues in mitigation proceedings makes this clear.

In 2006, the federal Bureau of Justice Statistics estimated that more than half of all prison inmates have a diagnosable mental illness (and studies of incarcerated youths have reported even higher estimates, as I pointed out in chapter 5). On the basis of their research, psychiatrist Dorothy Lewis and her colleague, neurologist Jonathan Pincus, concluded that *all* the killers (and other violent individuals) they studied were mentally "damaged." I agree.

No one who studies this issue seriously is suggesting that these mental health problems justify a verdict of "innocent" in the courts. What they are saying is that the current line between "legally sane" and "legally insane" is unrealistic, inadequate, and dangerous to the individual and the community.

· · ·

Preventing murder requires early and sustained intervention for individuals traumatized by abuse or significant head injuries that might lead to problems with brain function and thus put them at risk for engaging aggressive themes in our culture and becoming violent. These individuals may not be legally insane, but their moral and emotional development has been compromised by their terribly adverse childhood experiences. Thus, child-abuse prevention is murder prevention. Trauma treatment is murder prevention. This applies to children, adolescents, and adults.

I think this line of reasoning is more to the point than the impetus to organize mitigation around "diagnosable" psychiatric conditions. A diagnosis-driven assessment simply groups together ways in which an individual functions emotionally and cognitively. It doesn't really tell a developmental story, which is essential to persuade jurors and judges of the need to show compassion. It usually doesn't say much about how the conditions that make up the diagnosis arose from the interaction of life experience and temperament. Also, diagnoses tend to "stick," in the sense that they become permanent labels rather than names for the individual's current package of behaviors and attributes. Once you have a diagnosis of antisocial personality disorder it is hard to shake, no matter what process of rehabilitation and transformation you undergo. Finally, diagnoses are often "in the eye of the beholder" to some extent. When the same individual is seen from a variety of perspectives, in a variety of contexts, by different professionals, and at different points in life, the result may be different diagnoses. Reviewing the case files of many defendants in murder cases, I often find multiple diagnoses—sometimes incompatible diagnoses. I think it is generally better to focus on how the various packages of behaviors and attributes reflect the diverse ways in which individuals adapt to and cope with experiences of trauma, adversity, and social deprivation, always with an eye to the cultural context in which they are doing this coping and adapting.

THE DARK SIDE OF SHOPPING

Tyrone Johnson* killed a police officer. The story was sad from start to finish. His father was long gone by the time he was born, and his mother abandoned him when he was thirteen, which put him out on the streets to fend for himself. Tyrone survived, at first by scrounging food from people who felt sorry for him, and even from dumpsters behind local restaurants. Eventually, he clawed and fought his way into the local drug-dealing business. That changed his life. By the time he was seventeen, he had plenty of money and everything that went with it—sharp clothes, a car, girlfriends, respect. All that came to an end one summer's night when he was stopped by a police officer. Tyrone was carrying both a gun and a lot of drugs, so he tried to get away. When the officer tried to stop him, Tyrone pulled his gun and shot the officer dead. The state sought the death penalty, but the jury responded positively to the litany of mitigating factors in Tyrone's history. However, after the judge told him he would be sentenced to life imprisonment rather than the death penalty, Tyrone said, "I am going to kill myself." "Why?" he was asked. "Because I'm never going to the mall again," he replied. I guess when spiritually and psychologically you have nothing, the only thing that seems worth anything in this crass consumer culture of ours is shopping.

Tyrone's is an extreme case, to be sure, but America teaches its kids, by word and deed, the big lie that shopping is an existential affirmation. This feeds the problem of narcissism that is evident in the lives of many killers—as a self-deluding effort to compensate for deep feelings of worthlessness and low self-esteem or as the result of indulgent parenting that plants the seeds of bloated ego early.

Psychologists Jean Twenge and Keith Campbell have been studying this link and have reported several findings that are relevant to the issue of lethal violence among vulnerable individuals. They conclude that thirty years of data tell the story that as youths embrace materialism (in the sense that they place a high priority on money and possessions), they are more likely to exhibit a variety of problems, including depression and anxiety. Twenge and Campbell conclude that "when family life and economic conditions are unstable, youth may turn to material things for comfort. And when our society funds large amounts of advertising, youth are more likely to believe that 'the good life' is 'the goods life.'"

This consumerist materialism is bad enough when it occurs among kids who have the resources and opportunities to indulge their materialism—it contributes to rising rates of self-centeredness and narcissism among affluent young people. But it is directly linked to many instances of lethal violence among the many kids whose lives are loaded up with the unstable family life and economic conditions that make it difficult, if not impossible, to participate in that materialistic culture without making money illicitly.

These kids are drawn to "things" because their lives are socially and psychologically impoverished, and the advertiser's promise—"Have this and feel good"—is seductive. Their version of the American Dream of affluence runs through the world of drug dealing and robbery. And that world provides a shortcut to murder in many cases.

Violence is the currency of the world of drug dealing as much as the cash that changes hands. I recall sitting with two homicide detectives in Baltimore twenty years ago as we took a break from the seminar on "youth crime" in which the three of us were participating. They told me that when their colleagues in the vice squad "got lucky"—meaning they seized more than their usual monthly haul of illicit drugs—it meant that the homicide division had extra work in the next month. Why? Because someone had to pay for the lost drugs, either by killing someone else to replace the lost merchandise or by being killed as an example to other employees to be more careful in the future.

Beyond the special dynamics of the illegal drug economy, the American economic problem that ultimately underlies so much of the murder problem is as much inequality as it is poverty. There are several approaches to measuring economic inequality. Timothy Smeeding and his colleagues have used Luxembourg Income Study data to compare the ratio of incomes for the top 10 percent of the population with that of the bottom 10 percent. These comparisons were made after taxes and income transfers were taken into account.

That's because a society's economy may generate inequality, but its political system can seek to reduce that inequality by income redistribution programs that supplement the incomes of the poor directly and/or fund public services like education, health care, and recreation so that family income becomes less of a factor in the quality of life for children.

Using this approach, the study revealed that among industrialized "rich" countries, the United States had the worst ratio, about six to one, while Sweden had the best, about two to one (with Canada at four to one and no country other than the United States above four to one). Other research has validated this result: among modern, industrialized rich countries, the United States has a very high degree of income inequality. One of the important statistical measures of this inequality is the Gini Index. The World Bank uses it to compare a country's divergence from complete income inequality. For example, if each 10 percent of the population receives 10 percent of the income, the Gini score is zero; if the top 10 percent controls all the income, the score is 100. Scandinavian countries usually report the lowest Gini indices—Denmark's score is 24—and most industrialized nations have scores of about 30. The countries with the most inequality have scores in the 60s (e.g., South Africa). The United States has a score of about 45—and rising.

The greater the level of economic inequality, the more likely it is that individuals at the bottom will feel some mixture of shame and rage about their situation, and that is a dangerous combination when it comes to violence. For example, Ichiro Kawachi and his colleagues at the Harvard School of Public Health have found, in a study of thirty-three countries, that the degree of economic inequality is correlated with the homicide rate (accounting for about 60 percent of the variation). This reminds me of a boy I once interviewed in prison who posed an insightful but disturbing question. He asked me, "When you were coming up, were you poor or regular?"

. . .

Poor or regular. If that is the choice, then being poor means you are "irregular." That's the message America sends kids. In such a world, why would you choose to work at a fast-food restaurant for minimum wage and be deprived of the products essential for a "normal" life, when by selling drugs or committing robberies you can buy and own what "normal" people buy and own?

What would it take to overcome the danger in this culturally grounded path to delusion and violence? It would take extraordinary "good character" to choose the minimum wage job. That's one reason why any national effort to prevent killing must include a comprehensive and in-depth commitment to character education in schools, in families, and in communities (for a sample of what this means, take a look at http://charactercounts.org/). David Brooks has written persuasively on this point in *The New York Times,* in an essay titled "The Character Factory." And such efforts should include the kind of jobs program that Robert Zagar and his colleagues found reduced murders in Chicago, because good character cannot operate in an economic void.

And it must include a deeper analysis of the value of shallow materialism in American life that erodes meaningfulness and spirituality for young people. That's why efforts to reduce the cultural foundation for killing must include emphasis on the kind of spiritual development that buffers kids from the socially toxic messages that abound in our culture, spirituality that emphasizes loving acceptance of self and others, peaceful resolution of conflicts instead of angry revenge, and, above all else, the practice of compassion that builds social trust.

MAKING IT HARDER TO KILL

What makes killing possible, and what can we change? There are some obvious avenues of change. For example, if we were a society without guns, killing would decline. Of course, people would die because they were stabbed, beaten, or poisoned. But guns are so damnably efficient. Stabbing someone to death usually requires sustained effort; rarely does one cut kill, and few people can sustain the emotions needed to complete the job. I have interviewed men and boys who did it, but what awful emotional power it took to fuel the sustained attack necessary.

Beating someone to death usually requires a prolonged attack—rarely do one or two punches do the job. Poisoning is also hard to accomplish (that's why most suicide attempts using poison are physiologically clumsy and thus fail). But guns do the job with minimal emotional investment, with little effort, and with little technique required. Much of America doesn't want to hear that message, but it rings true nonetheless. No matter how "impractical" it is in our gun-drenched society, with its profit- and fear-driven "gun culture," disarmament is a key element to murder (and suicide) prevention (and to the larger problem of serious assault that damages and maims so many of those who are shot but do not die).

Another avenue of prevention is a national commitment to understand violence. Most murders seem senseless to us. But they are not senseless to killers, at least at the time they act violently. Murders happen in a context—a social, cultural, and psychological place—that makes violence feel like logical necessity. Every time we think of murder as senseless, and of a killer as a crazy or evil monster who needs to be extracted from society for our collective safety, we prime the pump for more murder of the same kind. I sit and listen to killers. I get inside their heads and find out what brought them to a place where killing felt like a reasonable option, or perhaps the only option.

Implementing the process of "making sense of senseless violence" takes many forms. Mobilizations for peace in high-violence communities are one example (e.g., www.cureviolence.org). These programs seek to enlist community members to support and control aggressive individuals, particularly youths, who are on a path that will likely lead to murder. The Ceasefire/Boston Gun Project mentioned in chapter 7 is another example: by focusing on getting guns out of the hands of teenagers, it achieved a remarkable reduction in fatal youth violence over a period of years.

The Centers for Disease Control and Prevention start from the idea that violence is a public health issue and have amassed a large inventory of programs and policies that offer a reduction in aggressive behavior and, ultimately, a reduction in killing in America (www.cdc.gov/violenceprevention/).

BUILDING A SOCIAL AND PSYCHOLOGICAL FOUNDATION FOR NONVIOLENCE

In addition to the many other strategies that make sense and are being applied in communities around the country, I see several especially productive paths to building the social and psychological foundations for nonviolence: promoting competent emotional regulation for traumatized youths, building meaning in the midst of despair, enhancing empathy in the face of fear and rage, and careful management of the peer process.

Emotional Regulation Issues for Traumatized Youths

Self-medication in the form of illicit drug use (including alcohol) is a significant issue for many at-risk youths around the world. This "need" cannot be ignored or simply punished. Traumatized youths need alternative tactics and strategies for dealing with the arousal issues associated with trauma. The use of consciousness-orienting approaches such as insight meditation and mindfulness exercises should be part of any comprehensive program (perhaps, in some cases, combined with psychiatric use of psychoactive drugs to permit the youths to stabilize emotions while processing trauma).

Techniques that permit processing of traumatic memories without the debilitating emotional "flooding" that can overwhelm the cognitive functions needed to make sense of the traumatic experience can be part of this effort. Eye-movement desensitization and reprocessing (EMDR) was developed by Francine Shapiro some twenty-five years ago as a way to provide the psychological "space" to process traumatic memories by protecting the traumatized individual from being overwhelmed by reexperiencing the symptoms of post-traumatic stress disorder. Numerous studies have validated its effectiveness for victims of trauma, including youths. For example, in their 2009 review of the evidence, Eldra Solomon and her colleagues confirmed the effectiveness of EMDR in helping to move trauma victims to a place of emotional health, a feeling of safety, and insight. In fact, anything that encourages stabilization of emotions so that cognitive processing can move forward will help victims of trauma.

Building Meaning

The various crises in "meaningfulness" experienced by chronically traumatized youths require special attention. Cooperative, prosocial projects can assist in this and also allow violent youths *to be seen* as engaged in restorative justice efforts that help the community and themselves. Spiritual development activities such as insight meditation and prayer groups can also be useful in this effort. Studying Matthieu Ricard's teachings on "happiness" as the result of meditative practice can be transformative.

Efforts to involve traumatized and violent youths in caregiving (e.g., with plants, animals, and other dependent beings) can enhance a sense of meaningfulness (but, of course, must be undertaken with adequate adult supervision to prevent harm to the dependent beings involved in the project). These efforts stand in contrast to "get tough" approaches exemplified in the militaristic "boot camp" model (I was involved in one such pilot alternative effort, called "From Boot Camp to Monastery," outlined in my book *Lost Boys*).

Enhancing Empathy

Some adolescent rehabilitation programs have involved "victim awareness" programming to build empathy for those affected by the behavior of violent youths. One of the problems of many violent individuals is that their compensatory narcissism leads them to focus on how others hurt them, rather than vice versa. Efforts to promote victim awareness can be helpful, but only after the victimization experienced by the traumatized and violent youths has been acknowledged and processed. As one incarcerated youth said after completing his *tenth* go-through of his facility's victim awareness program, "I'll be damned if I am going to focus on the victimization of those I have hurt until someone acknowledges the hurt I experienced at the hands of my father."

An important caveat in any effort to promote empathy comes from programs attempting to teach "empathy skills" to adult inmates. As psychologists Marnie Rice and her colleagues showed in their 1992 research report, while "normal" inmates profit from this learning experience (e.g., improving relationships), psychopaths approach such programs as an opportunity to improve their "manipulation skills." Vernon Quinsey, Grant Harris, Marnie Rice, and their colleagues have taken this insight to heart in their efforts to guide practice and policy (see *Violent Offenders: Appraising and Managing Risk*, published by the American Psychological Association in 2006).

Understanding the depth of any psychopathy in youths and adults involved in programming is essential to avoid such problems, but sophisticated psychiatric and psychological assessments are required, in order to avoid the pitfalls of making things worse. As Marnie Rice and her colleagues summarized their 1992 work: "The present study was a retrospective evaluation of the efficacy of a maximum security therapeutic program in reducing recidivism among mentally disordered offenders, some of whom were psychopaths. . . . The results showed that, compared to no program (in most cases prison), treatment was associated with lower recidivism (especially violent recidivism) for nonpsychopaths and higher violent recidivism for psychopaths." That's right. The psychopaths got worse, while the "normals" got better.

Careful Management of Peer Process

In a similar vein, efforts to rehabilitate "delinquent" youths can be counterproductive if they fall into one or both of the following traps. First, according to research conducted by Ronald Feldman and his colleagues, if such programs rely on a peer process for influence and change in groups in which a significant minority (perhaps 30 percent) are exhibiting antisocial beliefs, rhetoric, and behavior, the net effect is likely to be a worsening of the less delinquent youths (rather than an improvement in the most delinquent youths), because the more delinquent youths form a powerful social force demonstrating negative behavior in the way they talk and behave that encourages the nondelinquent youths to emulate them. The principal antidote to this problem, according to a review conducted by Thomas Dishion, Joan McCord, and Francois Poulin in an article titled "When Interventions Harm," is some mixture of powerful control of group process and language by prosocial adults, and systematic group composition that limits the disproportionate involvement of the most delinquent youths.

Second, intervention can be counterproductive if it focuses on "lecture" models, particularly when these lectures involve emotionally intense and threatening rhetoric. A prime example is "Scared Straight" (and similar programs used across the United States), which employs "hardcore" adult criminals to lecture delinquent and "predelinquent" youths (often accompanied by threatening language and gestures). Research by Anthony Petrosino and his colleagues revealed that this approach makes things worse rather than better. It may indeed "scare" more prosocial and sensitive youths (who are not at risk for long-term patterns of serious delinquent behavior) but serves to increase the severity of antisocial behavior of youths already involved in delinquent behavior (and thus at heightened risk for more serious delinquent behavior).

These youths tend to interpret the intense messages from the adult criminals *not* as "I am scared of the consequences of my current activities, so I will curtail my delinquent behavior," but rather as "I am going to have to be even more tough to survive in prison." Succeeding with youths at risk for violent behavior is essential for any national effort to reduce killing in America.

Successful programs exist. For example, in Texas, the Giddings State School offers its Capital Offenders Program to violent youths often described as "the worst of the worst." Kathleen Heide has reviewed this (and other intensive treatment programs) and found it sound and successful. By exploring the roots of violence in the adaptation to childhood abuse, and then focusing on cognitive restructuring and emotional rebuilding, the Capital Offenders Program has achieved a remarkable level of success—a 10 percent recidivism rate, compared with the more typical 70 percent reported for simple incarceration.

John Hubner, who explored this process and its outcomes in his 2008 book *Last Chance in Texas,* included a caveat: as others who have taken on this population have found, true psychopaths do not benefit from the program. Once identified, they are precluded from participation (and sent on to regular prison to serve their full terms). It's a sad truth, but a truth nonetheless, that true psychopaths come to the human community with a fundamental disconnection that cannot be repaired by any conventional means, if by any means at all.

FINAL THOUGHTS

In her 1963 book on the war-crimes trial of Nazi exterminator Adolf Eichmann, Hannah Arendt spoke of how, as she sat in the courtroom observing him, she was struck by what she called "the banality of evil." I do understand that. Reading the letters I receive from inmates whom I have gotten to know and keep in touch with, I am struck often by the human ordinariness in which their "crazy" violent behavior is embedded. But there is more to be heard and seen in America's killers.

The ordinariness of their aspirations and, sometimes, their goodwill stand alongside the fact that they have taken a human life in a shooting or a brutal knife attack or beating. They have to live with that duality, but so do we. It is part of the human condition. It starts with refusing to disconnect from the humanity of anyone, killer or victim. I want to return to the case of Nathaniel Brazill (from chapter 2) here, because it carries an important message.

Recall that Nathaniel was thirteen years old on May 26, 2000, when he shot and killed his English teacher, his favorite teacher, thirty-five-year-old Barry Grunow, on the last day of school in Lake Worth, Florida. Nathaniel had been suspended earlier in the day for throwing a water balloon and sent home. Once there, angry and frustrated that he would not have a chance to say goodbye to a girl in his class with whom he was infatuated (and who took the bus to a home distant from where Nathaniel lived), he retrieved a gun that a member of his family kept there, and returned to Lake Worth Middle School. Despite the fact that the boy said he only meant to threaten the teacher, there was no doubt that he committed the crime—the shooting was captured on the school's video security cameras.

The murdered teacher was known in his community as "The Gandhi of Lake Worth." To call someone the "Gandhi" of anyplace is quite a tribute. He must have been a wonderful person, to evoke the spirit of the man who is known throughout the world as the liberator of India and whose ideas about nonviolent resistance to oppression became the inspiration for Martin Luther King. India's Gandhi was himself murdered, and it is clear what he would have wanted for his assailant. He would have wanted the man held, cared for, and understood—and, if possible, returned to the community to do whatever good he was capable of, as a way to make amends to the community, to his victim, and to his better self. I think we can assume that the Gandhi of Lake Worth would have wanted much the same for his young student, Nathaniel Brazill. But not in America, it would seem.

While the death penalty was off the table because of Nathaniel's age, life in prison without the possibility of parole was an option for the court. The prosecutors argued for convicting Nathaniel of first-degree murder to invoke this option. I was there in the courtroom at the request of attorney Robin Shellow, waiting to testify about Nathaniel's life and times, when family members (but not his widow) and friends of Barry Grunow expressed their feelings on the matter. They argued for Nathaniel to receive the maximum penalty for what he did. Speaking to the press, one of Grunow's friends said he wanted the boy to go to prison and be raped and tortured every day for the rest of his life. For killing the Gandhi of Lake Worth.

I can understand their pain and their rage at the snuffing out of a life that was precious to them. But "raped and tortured every day for the rest of his life"? It would make the Gandhi of India sad to hear those words—and as compassionate for the person who said them as for the boy whose murderous actions evoked them. For every Gandhi, anywhere and anytime, and for anyone who pledges allegiance to his spirit, there must be sadness and hope for enlightenment for everyone who has turned his back on compassion to angrily pursue retribution. The moral philosophy of nonviolence to which Gandhi devoted his life is captured in the famous reworking of the Biblical principle of revenge into a cautionary message of compassion: "An eye for an eye will only make the whole world blind."

· · ·

The cartoon character Pogo famously said, "We have met the enemy and he is us." And when it comes to the enemy within—the would-be killers among us—we need to couple that understanding with healing, rather than leap to the conclusion that only violence can prevent violence.

When all is said and done, what I have learned most reliably from my work as a psychological expert witness in murder cases over the past twenty years is that to understand killers, you must resist the temptation to dissociate from them. Inside most killers is an untreated traumatized child. The emotional problems and stunted morality of these "children" haunt the actions of the scary adults they inhabit. Inside some killers is a mind that has lost its lucidity (or, in some rare cases, never had it to begin with) and cannot understand the primary social contract, "Thou shalt not kill."

Inside still others is a soul so poisoned by the social toxicity of its experience in our society that it no longer lives and breathes love for others, but only sees others as instruments for gratifying the lust for financial reward, sexual conquest, and personal power. But inside every one of these killers is a bit of the human condition, a piece of our collective humanity. To disconnect from them out of fear and loathing is to miss the opportunity to understand ourselves better and to live in a more peaceful world. That is the bottom line. That is what I have learned from listening to killers for the past twenty years. That is the lesson we can use to prevent killing in the next twenty.

APPENDIX

Zagar's Model

Zagar and Grove (2010) improved the accuracy of predicting homicide from records of up to 12 years of early childhood and youth risks in a sample of 1,127 youths to 91% (as expressed as "Area under the Curve [AUC] = 0.91"). Using a similar procedure, among 1,595 adults, using Shao's bootstrapped logistic regression procedure (Shao, 1996), the predictive power was 99%. The predictive equations in a combined adult and youth sample of 2,722 were correct 97% of the time. The accuracy of these results is noteworthy because most literature attempting to predict recidivism or violence has been in the region from 69% to 76%. Thus, the bootstrapped logistic regression represents a considerable improvement in predictive accuracy, providing a sound empirical basis for risks that consistently and reliably predict future violent criminal activity. These risks include poor executive functioning (decision making and related abilities), lower social maturity, weapons possession conviction, violent family, gang membership or participation, male gender, academic underachievement, serious illness, prior court contact or arrest, low socioeconomic status, substance abuse, previous neurological disorder, alcohol abuse, head injury, and truancy/ suspension or expulsion.

Several tests were chosen, after an exhaustive review of the research on the sensitivity and specificity of actuarial evaluations for "return-to-court" or fitness-for-duty uses. Tests with high reliability and validity, simplicity, and relatively short time of administration were chosen. For receptive vocabulary the Ammons Quick Test has the quickest test administration time, with test–retest reliability of 0.8–0.9 and concurrent validity with other measures of ability of 0.7–09. The Beck Suicide Scale was chosen for similar reasons, short test time, test retest reliability of 0.8–0.9, and concurrent validity coefficients with other measures of depression of 0.7–0.9. The Minnesota Multiphasic Personality Inventory (MMPI) Second Edition (MMPI-2) or the Adolescent Edition (MMPI-A) has 19,000 empirical studies attesting to its reliability and validity in a variety of populations. Raven's Advanced Progressive Matrices is a measure of visual, nonverbal problem solving that has been normed in more than 54 countries. The Standard Predictor (SP) has the best sensitivity and specificity of any instrument measuring violence potential. Standard Predictor (SP) is an assessment of violence potential for adults, with 98 true–false or multiple-choice format items. The Standard Predictor for Adolescents (SP) has 139 items. The SP evaluates specific, historical self-descriptions and requires 15 minutes to complete. The SP has no items from any of the other tests and is a free-standing instrument with 98 or 137 independent items distinct from the other tests. This measure was successful in discriminating randomly selected violent offenders (1,595 adults and 1,127 adolescents) from matched controls with 96% success in a combined adult and adolescent version based on a sample of 2,722 (Zagar and Grove, 2010). This is noteworthy because most tests in the literature attempting to predict criminal recidivism or "return to court" have success rates from 70% to 80%.

This carefully selected set of tests was administered either by paper and pencil or over the Internet, with a total test time of 110 minutes for 823 items. In the Internet format, tests with automated reports cost 70% to 80% less than current paper-and-pencil versions. The MMPI and other tests in this study can assess employees in airlines, military, nonprofits/religious organizations, power generation industries, police and fire public safety, trucking and ports, veterans, worker compensation and personal injury insurance clients, native Americans, and also prisoners.

REFERENCES

Alexander, M. (2012) The new Jim Crow. New York, NY: New Press.

Ambrogi, R. (2011) Two more states adopt Daubert rule, bringing total to 32. Blog entry, October 7. www.ims-expertservices.com/bullseye-blog/october-2011/two-more-states-adopt-daubert,-bringing-total-to-32/

American Bar Association (No date) The history of juvenile justice. www.americanbar.org/content/dam/aba/migrated/publiced/features/DYJpart1.authcheckdam.pdf

American Civil Liberties Union (No date) The school-to-prison pipeline. www.aclu.org/school-prison-pipeline

American Psychiatric Association (2000) Diagnostic and statistical manual of mental disorders, 4th ed., text revision [DSM-IV-TR]. Washington, DC: American Psychiatric Association.

American Psychiatric Association (2000) Diagnostic criteria for shared psychotic disorder 297.3. In Diagnostic and Statistical Manual of Mental Disorders, 4th ed., text revision [DSM-IV-TR]. Washington, DC: American Psychiatric Association.

Amnesty International (2008) Death penalty and race. www.amnestyusa.org/our-work/issues/death-penalty/us-death-penalty-facts/death-penalty-and-race

Anderson, E. (2000) Code of the street: decency, violence, and the moral life of the inner city. Boston, MA: Norton.

Annie E. Casey Foundation (2011) Reducing youth incarceration in the United States. www.aecf.org/resources/no-place-for-kids-full-report/

Arendt, H. (2006) Eichmann in Israel: a report on the banality of evil. New York, NY: Penguin. [Originally published in 1963.]

Arluke, A. and Sanders, C. (1996) Regarding animals. Philadelphia, PA: Temple University Press.

Armstrong, K. (2009) The case for God. New York, NY: Knopf.

Armstrong, K. (2010) Twelve steps to a compassionate life. New York, NY: Knopf.

Arnet, J. (2000) Emerging adulthood: a theory of development from the late teens through the twenties. American Psychologist, 55, 469–480.

Ashton, P. (2011) Gaming the system: how the political strategies of private prison companies promote ineffective incarceration policies. Washington, DC: Justice Policy Institute. June 22. www.justicepolicy.org/research/2614

Bales, W., Bedard, L., Quinn, S., Ensley, D., Holley, G., Duffee, A. and Sanford, S. (2003) Recidivism: an analysis of public and private state prison releases in Florida. www.dc.state.fl.us/pub/recidivismfsu/RecidivismStudy2003.PDF

Bartolomeo, L. (2012) Gun control and gun rights: legislation, policy and influence. Sunlight Foundation. December 17. http://sunlightfoundation.com/blog/2012 /12/17/gun-legislation-policy-influence/

Batson, C. (2011) Altruism in humans. Oxford Scholarship Online. May 2011 [published in print 2010]. www.oxfordscholarship.com/view/10.1093/acprof: oso/9780195341065.001.0001/acprof-9780195341065

Beauregard, M. and O'Leary, D. (2009) The spiritual brain: a neuroscientist's case for the existence of the soul. New York, NY: Harper-Collins.

Beck, A. (2008). The evolution of the cognitive model of depression and its neurobiological correlates. American Journal of Psychiatry, 165, 969–977.

Berkowitz, L., and LePage, A. (1967) Weapons as aggression-eliciting stimuli. Journal of Personality and Social Psychology, 7, 202–207.

Bernet, W., Vnencak-Jones, C., Farahany, N. and Montgomery, S. (2007) Bad nature, bad nurture, and testimony regarding MAOA and SLC6A4 genotyping at murder trials. Journal of Forensic Science, 52, 1362–1371.

Bishop, D., Frazier, C., Lanza, L., Kaduce, L. and Winner, L. (1996) The transfer of juveniles to criminal court: does it make a difference? Crime & Delinquency, 42, 171–191.

Bloom, P. (2013) The baby in the well: the case against empathy. The New Yorker, May 20.

Boyle, G. (2011) Tattoos on the heart: the power of boundless compassion. New York, NY: Free Press.

Braga, A., Kennedy, D., Piehl, A. and Waring, E. (2000) Boston Gun Project: impact evaluation findings. Research report submitted to the U.S. National Institute of Justice, Washington, DC, May 17.

Bronfenbrenner, U. (1970) Two worlds of childhood: US and USSR. New York, NY: Sage.

Bronfenbrenner, U. (1979) The ecology of human development: experiments by design and nature. Cambridge, MA: Harvard University Press.

Brooks, D. (2014) The character factory. The New York Times, August 1, A23.

Brower, M. and Price, B. (2001) Neuropsychiatry of frontal lobe dysfunction in violent and criminal behaviour: a critical review. Journal of Neurological Neurosurgery and Psychiatry, 71, 720–726.

Brumfield, B. (2014) After decades in prison over murders, DNA evidence frees 2 New York men. CNN Justice. www.cnn.com/2014/02/08/justice/new-york-convicted-men-released/

Buettner, R. (2013) Mentally ill, but insanity plea is long shot. The New York Times, April 3, A23.

Buka, S., Stichick, T., Birdthistle, I. and Earls, F. (2001) Youth exposure to violence: prevalence, risks, and consequences. American Journal of Orthopsychiatry, 71, 298–310.

Bureau of Alcohol, Tobacco, Firearms, and Explosives (2006) Oversight of the Bureau of Alcohol, Tobacco, Firearms and Explosives Part 2: Gun Show Enforcement: Hearings before the House Subcommittee on Crime, Terrorism, and Homeland Security, 109th Congress, 2nd Session, February 28.

Bureau of Justice Statistics (2010) Recidivism. Washington, DC: Department of Justice. www.ojp.usdoj.gov

Bureau of Justice Statistics (2013) Recidivism. www.bjs.gov/index.cfm?ty=tp&tid =17

Burgess, E. (1928) Factors determining success or failure on parole. In Bruce, A., Harno, A., Burgess, E. and Landesco, J. (Eds.), The workings of the indeterminate-sentence law and parole system in Illinois (pp. 221–234). Springfield, IL: State Board of Parole.

Burstow, B. (2005) A critique of posttraumatic stress disorder and the DSM. Journal of Humanistic Psychology, 45, 429–445.

Butterfield, F. (2008) All God's children: the Bosket family and the American tradition of violence. New York, NY: Vintage.

Calhoun, G., Glaser, B., Stefurak, B. and Bradshaw, C. (2000) Preliminary validation of the Narcissistic Personality Inventory—juvenile offender. International Journal of Offender Therapy and Comparative Criminology, 44, 564–580.

Campbell, J., Webster, D. and Glass, N. (2009) The danger assessment: validation of a lethality risk assessment instrument for intimate partner femicide. Journal of Interpersonal Violence, 24, 653–674.

Capote, T. (1966) In cold blood. New York, NY: Random House.

Caspi, A., McClay, J., Moffitt, T., Mill, J., Martin, J., Craig, I., Taylor, A. and Poulton, R. (2002) Role of genotype in the cycle of violence in maltreated children. Science, 297, 851–854.

Cavanaugh, W. (2009) The myth of religious violence: secular ideology and the roots of modern conflict. New York, NY: Oxford University Press.

Centers for Disease Control and Prevention (2011) Seat belts: every person, every seat, every trip. www.cdc.gov/Features/VitalSigns/SeatbeltSafety/

Centers for Disease Control and Prevention (2013) Trends in homicide rates among persons ages 10–24 years, by sex, United States, 1994–2010. www.cdc.gov /violenceprevention/youthviolence/stats_at-a_glance/hr_trends_sex.html

Children's Defense Fund (2012) Protect children not guns. Washington, DC: Children's Defense Fund.

Clément, M. and Bouchard, C. (2005) Predicting the use of single versus multiple types of violence towards children in a representative sample of Quebec families. Child Abuse & Neglect, 29, 1121–1139.

Cohen, D., Nisbett, R., Bowdle, F. and Schwarz, N. (1996) Insult, aggression, and the southern culture of honor: an "experimental ethnography." Journal of Personality and Social Psychology, 70, 945–959.

Cook, M. (2008) Chasing justice: my story of freeing myself after two decades on death row for a crime I didn't commit. New York, NY: William Morrow.

Crime in America.Net (2010) Percent of released prisoners returning to incarceration. September 29. www.crimeinamerica.net/2010/09/29/percent-of-released-prisoners-returning-to-incarceration/

Dalai Lama (1997) The power of compassion. New York, NY: Thorsens.

Davidson, J. and Smith, R. (1990) Traumatic experiences in psychiatric outpatients. Journal of Traumatic Stress Studies, 3, 459–475.

Davidson, R., Putnam, K. and Larson, C. (2000) Dysfunction in the neural circuitry of emotion regulation—a possible prelude to violence. Science, 289, 591–594.

Day, A., Casey, S. and Gerace, A. (2010) Interventions to improve empathy awareness in sexual and violent offenders: conceptual, empirical, and clinical issues. Aggression and Violent Behavior, 15, 201–208.

Death Penalty Focus (No date) Arbitrariness in the application of the death penalty. www.deathpenalty.org

Death Penalty Information Center (2014) Costs of the death penalty. www.deathpenaltyinfo.org/costs-death-penalty

Death Penalty Information Center (2014) Murder rates nationally and by state. www.deathpenaltyinfo.org/murder-rates-nationally-and-state

Desilver, D. (2013) A minority of Americans own guns but just how many is not clear. Pew Research Center. June 4. http://pewrsr.ch/Zj1vd8

DeSteno, D. (2012) Compassion made easy. The New York Times Sunday Review, July 14. www.nytimes.com/2012/07/15/opinion/sunday/the-science-of-compassion.html?_r=0&adxnnl=1&adxnnlx=1383709047–1BQY+zd1UUEdu RC7gYcifA

Dickert, S. and Slovic, P. (2009) Attentional mechanisms in the generation of sympathy. Judgment and Decision Making, 4, 297–306.

Dieter, R. (2013) How a minority of counties produce most death cases at enormous cost to all. www.deathpenaltyinfo.org

Dilulio, J. (1995) The coming of the super-predators. Weekly Standard, 1(11), 23.

Dishion, T., McCord, J. and Poulin, F. (1999) When interventions harm: peer groups and problem behavior. American Psychologist, 54, 755–764.

Dodge, K. (2003) Do social information processing patterns mediate aggressive behavior? In Lahey, B., Moffitt, T. and Caspi, A. (Eds.), Causes of conduct disorder and juvenile delinquency (pp. 254–274). New York, NY: Guilford Press.

Dodge, K., Pettit, G., Bates, J. and Valente, E. (1995) Social information-processing patterns partially mediate the effect of early physical abuse on later conduct problem. Journal of Abnormal Psychology, 104, 632–643.

Doidge, N. (2007) The brain that changes itself. New York, NY: Penguin.

Downey, G. and Feldman, S. (1996) Implications of rejection sensitivity in intimate relationships. Journal of Personality and Social Psychology, 70, 1327–1343.

Drutman, L. (2012) Explaining the power of the National Rifle Association, in one graph. December 17. http://sunlightfoundation.com/

Fagan, J. (1996) The comparative advantage of juvenile versus criminal court sanctions on recidivism among adolescent felony offenders. Law & Policy, 18, 77–114.

Fagan, J. et al. (2012) [Brief in the U.S. Supreme Court.] www.americanbar.org /content/dam/aba/publications/supreme_court_preview/briefs/10–9647_ petitioner_amcu_fagan_etal.authcheckdam.pdf

Falk, P. (1996) Novel theories of criminal defense based upon the toxicity of the social environment: urban psychosis, television intoxication, and Black rage. North Carolina Law Review, 74, 731.

Farrington, D., Loeber, R. and Van Kammen, W. (1990) Long-term criminal outcomes of hyperactivity–impulsivity–attention deficit and conduct problems in childhood. In Robins, L. and Rutter, M. (Eds.), Straight and devious pathways to adulthood (pp. 62–81). New York, NY: Cambridge University Press.

Federal Bureau of Investigation (2012) Crime in the United States 2011. www.fbi .gov/about-us/cjis/ucr/crime-in-the-u.s./2011/crime-in-the-u.s.-2011/index-page

Feldman, R., Caplinger, T. and Wodarski, J. (1983) The St. Louis conundrum: the effective treatment of antisocial youths. Englewood Cliffs, NJ: Prentice-Hall.

Feldman, S. and Downey, G. (1994) Rejection sensitivity as a mediator of the impact of childhood exposure to family violence on adult attachment behavior. Development and Psychopathology, 6, 231–247.

Feletti, V., Anda, R., Nordenberg, D., Williamson, D., Spitz, A., Edwards, E., Koss, M. and Marks, J. (1998) Relationship of childhood abuse and household dysfunction to many of the leading causes of death in adults: the adverse childhood experiences (ACE) study. American Journal of Preventive Medicine, 14, 245–258.

Finkelhor, D. (1979) What's wrong with sex between adults and children? American Journal of Orthopsychiatry, 49, 692–697.

Foster, J., Campbell, W. and Twenge, J. (2003) Individual differences in narcissism: inflated self-views across the lifespan and around the world. Journal of Research in Personality, 37, 469–486.

Fox, J. (1996) Trends in juvenile violence. Washington, DC: U.S. Department of Justice, Bureau of Justice Statistics.

Freud, S. (1962) The neuro-psychoses of defense. In Strachey, J. (Ed. and Trans.), The standard edition of the complete works of Sigmund Freud (vol. 3, pp. 45–61). London, UK: Hogarth Press. [Original work published 1894.]

Garbarino, J. (1976) A preliminary study of some ecological correlates of child abuse: the impact of socioeconomic stress on mothers. Child Development, 47, 178–185.

Garbarino, J. (1994) Raising children in a socially toxic environment. San Francisco, CA: Jossey-Bass.

Garbarino, J. (1999) Lost boys: why our sons turn violent and how we can save them. New York, NY: Free Press.

Garbarino, J., Dubrow, N., Kostelny, K. and Pardo, C. (1992) Children in danger: coping with the consequences of community violence. San Francisco, CA: Jossey-Bass.

Garbarino, J., Guttman, E. and Seeley, J. (1986) The psychologically battered child. San Francisco, CA: Jossey-Bass.

Garbarino, J. and Kostelny, K. (1990) The ecology of infant mortality in Chicago neighborhoods. Chicago, IL: Erikson Institute.

Garbarino, J. and Kostelny, K. (1996) The impact of political violence on the behavioral problems of Palestinian children. Child Development, 67, 33–45.

Garbarino, J., Kostelny, K. and Dubrow, N. (1991) No place to be a child: growing up in a war zone. New York, NY: Lexington Books.

Garland, S. (2013) When class became more important to a child's education than race. The Atlantic, August 28. www.theatlantic.com/national/archive/2013/08/when-class-became-more-important-to-a-childs-education-than-race/279064/

Garmezy, N. and Rutter, M. (Eds.) (1988) Stress, coping, and development in children. Baltimore, MD: Johns Hopkins University Press.

Gelman, A., Fagan, J. and Kiss, A. (2007) An analysis of the New York City Police Department's "Stop-and-Frisk" policy in the context of claims of racial bias. Journal of the American Statistical Association, 102, 813–823.

Gibbs, R., Jr. (2005) Embodiment and cognitive science. New York, NY: Cambridge University Press.

Gibbs, S. (2005) Islam and Islamic extremism: an existential analysis. Journal of Humanistic Psychology, 45, 156–203.

Gilligan, J. (1997) Violence: reflections on a national epidemic. New York, NY: Vintage.

Gladwell, M. (2010) Drinking games. The New Yorker, February 15.

Goleman, D. (1995) Emotional intelligence: why it can matter more than IQ. New York, NY: Bantam.

Gopnik, A. (2012) The caging of America. The New Yorker, January 30.

Grant, J. (1993) Gun ownership as a risk factor for homicide in the home. New England Journal of Medicine, 329, 1084–1091

Gross, J. and Thompson, R. (2009) Emotion regulation: conceptual foundations. In Gross, J. (Ed.), Handbook of emotion regulation, 497–512. New York, NY: Guilford Press.

Grossman, D. (1996) On killing: the psychological cost of learning to kill in war and society. Boston, MA: Back Bay Books.

Grossman, D. and Christensen, L. (2004) On combat. New York, NY: PPCT.

Grubel, J. (2013) Australia's gun controls a political template for the U.S. Reuters, April 3.

GunPolicy.org (No date) United States—gun facts, figures and the law. www.gunpolicy.org/firearms/region/united-states

Haney, C. (2001) The psychological impact of incarceration: implications for post-release adjustment. http://aspe.hhs.gov/hsp/prison2home02/haney.htm

Hare, R. (1999) Without conscience: the disturbing world of the psychopaths among us. New York, NY: Guilford Press.

Harris, A., Thomas, S., Fisher, G. and Hirsch, D. (2002) Murder and medicine: the lethality of criminal assault 1960–1999. Homicide Studies, 6, 128–166.

Harris, S. and Picchioni, M. (2013) A review of empathy in violence risk in mental disorders. Aggression and Violent Behavior, 18, 335–342.

Harvard School of Public Health (2014) Means matter. www.hsph.harvard.edu /means-matter/

Heath, D. (2000) Drinking occasions: comparative perspectives on alcohol and culture. Philadelphia, PA: Taylor and Francis.

Heide, K. (2013) Understanding parricide: when sons and daughters kill parents. New York, NY: Oxford University Press.

Heide, K. and Solomon, E. (2006) Biology, childhood trauma, and murder: rethinking justice. International Journal of Law & Psychiatry, 29, 220–233.

Heide, K. and Solomon, E. (2009) Female juvenile murderers: biological and psychological dynamics leading to homicide. International Journal of Law & Psychiatry, 32, 244–252.

Heide, K., Spencer, E., Thompson, A. and Solomon, E. (2001) Who's in, who's out, and who's back: follow-up data on 59 juveniles incarcerated for murder or attempted murder in the early 1980s. Behavioral Sciences and the Law, 19, 97–108.

Herman, J. (1992) Trauma and recovery. New York, NY: Basic Books.

Heyman, G. (2010) Addiction: a disorder of choice. Cambridge, MA: Harvard University Press.

Hobbes, T. (2012) Leviathan. New York, NY: Penguin. [Originally published in 1651.]

Howell, J. (2009) Preventing and reducing juvenile delinquency. New York, NY: Sage.

Hubner, J. (2008) Last chance in Texas: the redemption of criminal youth. New York, NY: Random House.

Hughes, V. (2010) Science in court: head case. Nature, 464, 340–342.

Human Rights Watch (2001) No escape: male rape in US prisons. www.hrw.org /reports/2001/prison/report1.html

Human Rights Watch (2011) US: an attack on human dignity. www.hrw.org /news/2011/10/10/us-attack-human-dignity

Justice Policy Institute (2011) Gaming the system: how the political strategies of private prison companies promote ineffective incarceration policies. Washington, DC: Justice Policy Institute.

Kagan, J. (2004) The long shadow of temperament. New York, NY: Belknap Press.

Kasser, T. (2003) The high price of materialism. Cambridge, MA: MIT Press (Bradford Books).

Kassin, S., Meissner, C. and Norwick, R. (2005) "I'd know a false confession if I saw one": a comparative study of college students and police investigators. Law and Human Behavior, 29, 211–227.

Kawachi, I., Kennery, B. and Wilkinson, R. (1999) Income inequality and health: a reader. New York, NY: New Press.

Kellermann, A. and Reay, D. (1986) Protection or peril? An analysis of firearm-related deaths in the home. New England Journal of Medicine, 314, 1557–1560.

Kellermann, A., Rivara, F., Rushforth, N., Banton, J., Reay, D., Francisco, J., Locci, A., Prodzinski, J., Hackman, B. and Somes, G. (1998) Injuries and deaths due to firearms in the home. Journal of Trauma, Injury Infection, and Critical Care, 45, 263–267.

Kerby, S. (2012) Ten top most startling facts about people of color and criminal justice in the United States. Center for American Progress. www.americanprogress .org/issues/race/news/2012/03/13/11351/the-top-10-most-startling-facts-about-people-of-color-and-criminal-justice-in-the-united-states/

Kiehl, K., Smith, A., Hare, R. and Liddle, P. (2000) An event-related potential investigation of response inhibition in schizophrenia and psychopathy. Biological Psychiatry, 48, 210–221.

Kim-Cohen, J., Caspi, A., Taylor, A., Williams, B., Newcombe, R., Craig, I. and Moffitt, T. (2006) MAOA, maltreatment, and gene-environment interaction predicting children's mental health: new evidence and a meta-analysis. Molecular Psychiatry, 11, 903–913.

Kogut, T. and Ritov, I. (2005) The "identified victim" effect: an identified group, or just a single individual? Journal of Behavioral Decision Making, 18, 157–167.

Korbin, J. (1990) Hana 'Ino: child maltreatment in a Hawaiian-American community. Pacific Studies, 13(3), 7–23.

Kubrin, C. and Stewart, E. (2006) Predicting who reoffends: the neglected role of neighborhood context in recidivism studies. Criminology, 44, 165–197.

Lewis, D. (2009) Guilty by reason of insanity. New York, NY: Random House.

Lilienfeld, S. (2005) Scientifically unsupported and supported interventions for childhood psychopathology: a summary. Pediatrics, 115, 761–764.

Lilienfeld, S., Lynn, S., Ruscio, J. and Beyerstein, B. (2010) 50 great myths of population psychology: shattering widespread misconceptions about human behavior. Malden, MA: Wiley-Blackwell.

Lisak, D. (1994) The psychological impact of sexual abuse: content analysis of interviews with male survivors. Journal of Traumatic Stress, 7, 525–548.

Loeber, R. and Farrington, D. (Eds.) (1998) Serious and violent juvenile offenders: risk factors and successful interventions. New York, NY: Sage.

Loeber, R. and Farringon, D. (2011) Young homicide offenders and victims: risk factors, prediction, and prevention. New York, NY: Springer.

Lord, C., Ross, L. and Lepper, M. (1979) Biased assimilation and attitude polarization: the effects of prior theories on subsequently considered evidence. Journal of Personality and Social Psychology, 37, 2098–2109.

Luthar, S. (2003) Resilience and vulnerability: adaptation in the context of childhood adversities. New York, NY: Cambridge University Press.

Lynch, M. and Haney, C. (2011) Looking across the empathic divide: racialized decision making on the capital jury. Michigan State Law Review 573.

MacAndrew, C. and Edgerton, R. (2003) Drunken comportment: a social explanation. Toronto, ON: Percheron Press.

Maccoby, E. and Martin, J. (1983) Socialization in the context of the family: parent–child interaction. In Mussen, P. and Hetherington, E. (Eds.), Handbook of child psychology, vol. 4: socialization, personality, and social development, 4th ed. (pp. 1–101). New York, NY: Wiley.

Mann, R. and Barnett, G. (2012) Victim empathy intervention with sexual offenders: rehabilitation, punishment, or correctional quackery? Sexual Abuse, 25, 282–301.

Marshall, G., Schell, T., Elliott, M., Berthold, S. and Chun, C. (2005) Mental health of Cambodian refugees 2 decades after resettlement in the United States. JAMA, 294, 571–579.

Masters, J. (1997) Finding freedom: writings from death row. San Francisco, CA: Padma.

Masters, J. (2009) That bird has my wings. New York, NY: Harper-Collins.

Mauer, M. (2011) Addressing racial disparities in incarceration. Prison Journal, Supplement to 91(3), 87S–101S.

McCrory, E., De Brito, S., Sebastian, C., Mechelli, A., Bird, G., Kelly, P. and Essi Viding, E. (2011) Heightened neural reactivity to threat in child victims of family violence. Current Biology, 21, R947–R948.

McKean, L. and Ransford, C. (2004) Current strategies for reducing recidivism. Chicago, IL: Center for Impact Research.

Mednick, S. and Kandel, E. (1988) Genetic and perinatal factors in violence: biological contributions to crime causation. NATO ASI Series, 40, 121–131.

Messner, S. and Tardiff, K. (1986) Economic inequality and levels of homicide: an analysis of urban neighborhoods. Criminology, 24, 297–316.

Moore, S. (2009) Number of life terms nears record. The New York Times, July 22. www.nytimes.com/2009/07/23/us/23sentence.html?pagewanted=all&_r=0

NAACP Legal Defense Fund (2012) Death row USA. www.naacpldf.org/death-row-usa

National Child Traumatic Stress Network (No date) Psychological first aid. www.nctsn.org/content/psychological-first-aid

National Institute of Justice (2001) Reducing gun violence: the Boston Gun Project's Operation Ceasefire. www.ncjrs.gov/pdffiles1/nij/188741.pdf

National Public Radio (2012) Guns 101: what we know and what we don't. August 8. www.npr.org/2012/08/08/158433081/guns-101-what-we-know-and-what-we-dont

Nellis, A. and King, R. (2009) No exit: the expanding use of life sentences in America. Washington, DC: Sentencing Project.

New York State Parole Board (2013) Recidivism. www.doccs.ny.gov/Research/annotate.asp#recid

Newman, J. and Lorenz, A. (2003) Response modulation and emotion processing: implications for psychopathy and other dysregulatory psychopathology. In Davidson, R., Scherer, K. and Goldsmith, H. (Eds.), Handbook of affective sciences (pp. 1043–1067). New York, NY: Oxford University Press.

Nisbett, R. and Cohen, D. (1996) Culture of honor: the psychology of violence in the South. New York, NY: Westview.

Odgers, C., Burnette, M., Chauchan, M., Moretti, M. and Repucci, D. (2005) Misdiagnosing the problem: mental health profiles of incarcerated juveniles. Canadian Child and Adolescent Psychiatry Review, 14, 26–29.

Olds, D., Eckenrode, J., Henderson, C., Kotzman, H., Powers, J., Cole, R., Sidora, K., Morris, P., Pettit, L. and Luckey, D. (1997) Long-term effects of home visitation on maternal life course and child abuse and neglect: 15 year follow-up of a randomized trial. Journal of the American Medical Association, 278, 637–643.

Olive, M. (2009) Narrative works. UMKC Law Review, 77, 989–1020.

Olive, M. and Stetler, R. (2008) Using the supplementary guidelines for the mitigation function of defense teams in death penalty cases to change the picture in post-conviction. Hofstra Law Review, 36, 1067–1093.

Palmer, B. (2013) Which is safer: city streets or prison? Prison. Slate, June 19. www.slate.com/articles/news_and_politics/explainer/2013/06/murder_rate_in_prison_is_it_safer_to_be_jailed_than_free.html

Patrick, C. (2007) Handbook of psychopathy. New York, NY: Guilford Press.

Patton, D. (2013) Navigating the streets: African American adolescent males describing experiences with community violence. In Harris, M. (Ed.), African American perspectives: family dynamics, health care issues and the role of ethnicity, 55–63. Hauppauge, NY: Nova Science.

PBS-Frontline. Insanity Defense FAQs. www.pbs.org/wgbh/pages/frontline/shows/crime/trial/faqs.html

Perez, M., Vohs, K. and Joiner, T. (2005) Discrepancies between self- and other-esteem as correlates of aggression. Journal of Social and Clinical Psychology, 24, 607–620.

Perry, B. (1997) Incubated in terror: neurodevelopmental factors in the "cycle of violence." In Osofsky, J. (Ed.), Children, youth and violence: the search for solutions (pp. 124–148). New York, NY: Guilford Press.

Petrosino, A., Turpin-Petrosino, C., Hollis-Peel, M. and Lavenberg, J. (2013) 'Scared Straight' and other juvenile awareness programs for preventing juvenile delinquency. Cochrane Database of Systematic Reviews, 4, article CD002796.

Piaget, J. (1952) The origins of intelligence in children. New York, NY: International University Press.

Pujara, M., Motzkin, J., Newman, J., Kiehl, K. and Koenigs, M. (2014) Neural correlates of reward and loss sensitivity in psychopathy. Social Cognitive and Affective Neuroscience, 6, 794–801.

Putnam, R. (2001) Bowling alone. New York, NY: Simon and Schuster.

Quinsey, V., Harris, G., Rice, M. and Cormier, C. (2006) Violent offenders: appraising and managing risk, 2nd ed. Washington, DC: American Psychological Association.

Raine, A., Meloy, J., Bihrle, S., Stoddard, J., Lacasse, L. and Buchsbaum, M. (1998) Reduced prefrontal and increased subcortical brain functioning assessed using positron emission tomography in predatory and affective murderers. Behavioral Sciences and the Law, 16, 319–332.

Ramachandran, V. (2011) The tell-tale brain: a neuroscientist's quest for what makes us human. New York, NY: Norton.

Rastogl, S., Johnson, T., Hoeffel, E. and Dremery, M. (2011) The Black population: 2010. Washington, DC: U.S. Census Bureau.

Rattan, A., Levine, C., Dweck, C. and Eberhardt, J. (2012) Race and the fragility of the legal distinction between juveniles and adults. PLoS ONE, 7, e36680.

Ricard, M. (2007) Happiness: a guide to life's most important skill. Boston, MA: Little, Brown.

Rice, M., Harris, T. and Cormier, C. (1992) An evaluation of a maximum security therapeutic community for psychopaths and other mentally disordered offenders. Law and Human Behavior, 16, 399–412.

Richo, D. (1999) Shadow dance. Boston, MA: Shambhala.

Roberts, A., Zgoba, K. and Shahidullah, S. (2007) Recidivism among four types of homicide offenders: an exploratory analysis of 336 homicide offenders in New Jersey. Aggression and Violent Behavior, 12, 493–507.

Roberts, D. (2012) Fatal intervention: how science, politics, and big business re-create race in the twenty-first century. New York, NY: New Press.

Rohner, R., Khaleque, A. and Cournoyer, D. (2005) Parental acceptance–rejection: theory, methods, cross-cultural evidence, and implications. Ethos, 33, 299–334.

Ronson, J. (2012) The psychopath test. New York, NY: Riverhead Trade.

Rutter, M. (1989) Pathways from childhood to adult life. Journal of Psychology and Psychiatry, 30, 25–51.

Rutter, M., Moffitt, T. and Caspi, A. (2006) Gene–environment interplay and psychopathology: multiple varieties but real effects. Journal of Child Psychology and Psychiatry, 47, 226–261.

Saigh, P., Yasik, A., Mitchell, P. and Abright, A. (2011) The psychological adjustment of a sample of New York City preschool children 8–10 months after September 11, 2001. Psychological Trauma: Theory, Research, Practice, and Policy, 3, 109–116.

Sameroff, A., Seifer, R., Barocas, R., Zax, M. and Greenspan, S. (1987) Intelligence quotient scores of 4-year-old children: socio-environmental risk factors. Pediatrics, 79, 343–350.

Savulescu, J., Sinnott-Armstrong, W., Levy, N. and Fulford, B. (No date) Free will and addiction. Oxford Centre for Neuroethics. www.neuroethics.ox.ac.uk/research/area_3#wrapper

Schelling, T. (1968) The life you save may be your own. In Chase, S. (Ed.), Problems in public expenditure analysis, 127–162. Washington, DC: Brookings Institute.

Schweitzer, N., Saks, M., Murphy, E., Roskies, A., Sinnott-Armstrong, W. and Gaudet, L. (2011) Neuroimages as evidence in a mens rea defense: no impact. Psychology, Public Policy, and Law, 17, 357–393.

Search Institute (1990) 40 Developmental Asssets. www.search-institute.org/research/developmental-assets

Secret, M. (2011) States prosecute fewer teenagers in adult court. The New York Times, March 6, A1.

Sellman, D. (2010) The 10 most important things known about addiction. Addiction, 105, 6–13.

Seppala, E. and Akhtar, M. (2012) Compassion behind bars. Palo Alto, CA: Stanford University Center for Compassion and Altruism Research and Education.

Shao, J. (1996) Bootstrap model selection. Journal of the American Statistical Association, 91, 655–665.

Shapiro, J., Dorman, R., Burkey, W. and Welker, C. (1997) Development and factor analysis of a measure of youth attitudes towards guns and violence. Journal of Clinical Child Psychology, 26, 311–320.

Silton, R. (2013) Personal communication, Loyola University, Chicago, IL.

Small, D., and Loewenstein, G. (2003) Helping a victim or helping the victim: altruism and identifiability. Journal of Risk and Uncertainty, 26, 5–16.

Small, D., Loewenstein, G. and Slovic, P. (2006) Sympathy and callousness: the impact of deliberative thought on donations to identifiable and statistical victims. Organizational Behavior and Human Decision Processes, 102, 143–153.

Smeeding, T. and Grodner, A. (2000) Changing income inequality in OECD countries: updated results from the Luxembourg Income Study (LIS). In Hauser, R. et al. (Eds.), The personal distribution of income in an international perspective (pp. 205–224). New York, NY: Springer.

Smith, A. (2012) Private vs. public facilities, is it cost effective and safe? June 6. www.corrections.com

Solomon, E. and Heide, K. (1999) Type III trauma: toward a more effective conceptualization of psychological trauma. International Journal of Offender Therapy and Comparative Criminology, 43, 202–210.

Solomon, E., Solomon, R. and Heide, K. (2009) EMDR: an evidence-based treatment for victims of trauma. Victims & Offenders, 4, 391–397.

Squeglia, L., Jacobus, B. and Tapert, S. (2009) The influence of substance use on adolescent brain development. Clinical EEG Neuroscience, 40, 31–38.

Starr, D. (2013) The interview: do police interrogation techniques produce false confessions? The New Yorker, December 9, 42–49.

Starr, S. (2014) Sentencing, by the numbers. The New York Times, August 11, A17.

Stein, S. and Blumenthal, P. (2012) The gun lobby: why the NRA is the baddest force in politics. Huffington Post, December 18. www.huffingtonpost.com/2012/12/17/gun-lobby-nra_n_2317885.html

Steinberg, L. and Scott, E. (2003) Less guilty by reason of adolescence: developmental immaturity, diminished responsibility and the juvenile death penalty. American Psychologist, 58, 1009–1018.

Sterling, J. and Amaya-Jackson, L. (2008) Understanding the behavioral and emotional consequences of child abuse. Pediatrics, 122, 667–673.

Stetler, R. (2014) Mental health evidence and the capital defense function: prevailing norms. 82 UMKC L. Rev. 407 (April 7). Available at SSRN: http://ssrn.com/abstract=2422159

Stetler, R. and Wendell, W. (2014) The ABA guidelines and the norms of capital defense representation. Hofstra Law Review, January 17. www.hofstralawreview.org/tag/volume-41/

Stockdale, L. (2014) Empathy and violent video games. PhD dissertation, Loyola University Chicago, Chicago, IL.

Streib, V. (2002) Gendering the death penalty: countering sex bias in a masculine sanctuary. Ohio State Law Journal, 63, 433–474.

Struckman-Johnson, C. and Struckman-Johnson, D. (2000) Sexual coercion rates in seven midwestern prison facilities for men. Prison Journal, 80, 379–390.

Sullivan, H. (1953) The interpersonal theory of psychiatry. New York, NY: Norton.

Teplin, L., Abram, K., McClelland, G., Dulcan, M. and Mericle, A. (2002) Psychiatric disorders in youth in juvenile detention. Archives of General Psychiatry, 59, 1133–1143.

Terr, L. (1991) Childhood trauma: an outline and overview. American Journal of Psychiatry, 148, 10–20.

Thomas, A. and Chess, S. (1977) Temperament and development. New York, NY: Brunner/Mazel.

Thomas, L., De Bellis, M., Reiko, G. and LaBar, K. (2007) Development of emotional facial recognition in late childhood and adolescence. Developmental Science, 10, 547–558.

Tolan, P. (1996) How resilient is the concept of resilience? Community Psychologist, 29, 12–15.

Trope, Y. and Bassok, M. (1982) Confirmatory and diagnosing strategies in social information gathering. Journal of Personality and Social Psychology, 43, 22–34.

Twenge, J. and Campbell, K. (2009) The narcissism epidemic. New York, NY: Simon and Schuster.

Uggen, C. (2000) Work as a turning point in the life course of criminals: a duration model of age, employment, and recidivism. American Sociological Review, 65, 529–546.

UNESCO (No date) What do we mean by "youth"? www.unesco.org/new/en/social-and-human-sciences/themes/youth/youth-definition/

U.S. Census Bureau (2010) The Black population: 2010. www.census.gov/prod/cen2010/briefs/c2010br-06.pdf

U.S. Census Bureau (2013) Distribution of households by race. www.census.gov/

U.S. Department of Justice, Office of Justice Programs, Bureau of Justice Statistics (2006) Special Report State Court Processing Statistics, 1990–2002. Violent Felons in Large Urban Counties. NCJ 205289.

van der Kolk, B., MacFarlane, A. and Weisaeth, L. (2006) Traumatic stress: the effects of overwhelming experience on mind, body and society. New York, NY: Guilford Press.

Vera Foundation (2012) The price of prisons: California. www.vera.org/files/price-of-prisons-california-fact-sheet.pdf

Vieth, V. (2004) When words hurt: investigating and proving a case of psychological maltreatment. Reasonable Efforts, 2 (1).

Vygotsky, L. and Kozulin, A. (1986) Thought and language. Cambridge, MA: MIT Press.

Wall Street Journal (2013) Murder in America [database]. http://projects.wsj.com/murderdata/?mg=inert-wsj#view=all

Wallace, L. (2010) Are all murderers mentally ill? The Atlantic, December 3.

Ward, K., Longaker, A., Williams, J., Naylor, A., Rose, C. and Simpson, C. (2013) Incarceration within American and Nordic prisons: comparison of national and international policies. www.dropoutprevention.org/engage/incarceration-within-american-and-nordic-prisons/

Weinberger, D., Elvevag, B. and Giedd, J. (2005) The adolescent brain. Washington, DC: National Campaign to Prevent Teen Pregnancy.

Werner, E. (2000) Protective factors and individual resilience. In Shonkoff, J. and Meisels, S. (Eds.), The handbook of early intervention. Cambridge, UK: Cambridge University Press.

West Coast Poverty Center (2010) Families and poverty in the United States. http://depts.washington.edu/wcpc/sites/default/files/poverty%20basics/US_Family_2009.pdf

Wilson, J. (1995) Crime and public policy. In Wilson, J. and Petersilia, J. (Eds.), Crime. San Francisco, CA: Institute of Contemporary Studies.

Winner, L., Lanza, C., Kaduce, L., Bishop, D. and Frazier, C. (1997) The transfer of juveniles to criminal court: reexamining recidivism over the long term. Crime & Delinquency, 43, 548–563.

World Bank (2013) GINI index. http://data.worldbank.org/indicator/SI.POV.GINI

World Health Organization (1999) Programming for adolescent health and development. http://whqlibdoc.who.int/trs/WHO_TRS_886_(p1-p144).pdf

Wright, E. (1978) Race, class, and income inequality. American Journal of Sociology, 83, 1368–1397.

Yurgelun-Todd, D. (2007) Emotional and cognitive changes during adolescence. Current Opinion in Neurobiology, 17, 251–257.

Zagar, R. and Grove, W. (2010) Violence risk appraisal of male and female youth, adults, and individuals. Psychological Reports, 107, 983–1009.

Zagar, R., Kovach, J., Ferrari, B., Grove, W., Busch, K., Hughes, J. and Zagar, A. (2013) Applying best treatments by using a regression equation to target violence-prone youth: a review. Comprehensive Psychology, 2, article 7.

Zagar, R., Zagar, A., Bartikowski, B. and Busch, K. (2009) Cost comparisons of raising a child from birth to 17 years among samples of abused, delinquent, violent, and homicidal youth using victimization and justice system estimates. Psychological Reports, 104, 309–338.

Zagar, R., Zagar, A., Bartikowski, B., Busch, K. and Stark, R. (2009) Accepted legal applications of actuarial testing and delinquency interventions: examples of savings in real life situations. Psychological Reports, 104, 339–362.

Zagar, R., Zagar, A., Busch, K., Grove, W., Hughes, J., Arbit, J., Bartikowski, B., Isbell, S. and Stark, R. (2009) Predicting and preventing homicide: a cost effective empirical approach from infancy to adulthood. Psychological Reports, 104, 1–377.

Zeier, J., Baskin-Sommers, A., Racer, H. and Newman, K. (2012) Cognitive control deficits associated with antisocial personality disorder and psychopathy. Personality Disorders: Theory, Research, and Treatment, 3, 283–293.

INDEX

abandonment, 23–24, 111, 249. *See also* father abandonment; rejection sensitivity

abuse excuse, the, 12, 115, 134

academic achievement: abused male children and, 131; PTSD (post-traumatic stress disorder) and, 118; race and, 68; "Risk and Opportunity in Children and Adolescence" essay and, 43–44; as risk factor, 234; Zagar's model and, 142, 261. *See also* education; schools

ACE (adverse childhood experiences), 233–34, 235, 236

actuarial model (Zagar), 141–43, 182–84, 185, 191, 261–62

acute trauma, 117, 194

Adams, Brenda, 8, 9

Addiction: A Disorder of Choice (Heyman), 29

addictions, 29–32. *See also* alcohol use; drugs; substance abuse

adolescence. *See* teenagers

adulthood, as legal line, 27. *See also* trials, juvenile vs. adult status

Advanced Progressive Matrices, Raven's, 261–62

adverse childhood experiences (ACE), 233–34, 235, 236

affective murderers, 109, 170

African Americans: Black on Black crime, 90; charter schools and, 98–99; criminal justice status, pre-murder and, 239; culture of honor and, 90–91; Felicia Morgan case, 7–11; homicide rates and, 61, 90; incarceration rates and, 62, 228; narcissism and, 23; police relationships and, 67; rage and, 11, 62; risk factors and, 68–69; single-parent homes and, 68. *See also* racism

Alabama, Miller v. (2012), 176, 180

Alcoholics Anonymous, 186

alcohol use, 70, 106, 142, 173–75, 234. *See also* addictions; substance abuse

Alexander, Michelle, 62, 64, 68, 184, 232

Alexis, Aaron, 211

Alito, Samuel A., Jr., 176, 180

All God's Children (Butterfield), 89–90, 151

Amaya-Jackson, Lisa, 136

American Academy of Child and Adolescent Psychiatry, 136

American Bar Association, 150, 242

American Civil Liberties Union, 62

American Dream, 42, 250

American gun culture: fear and, 214–15, 218, 252; government mistrust and, 215–16, 217; gun lobby and, 215–16, 220–21; home safety and, 203–7, 208–9; innocents killing innocents and, 221–22; international standards and, 203–4, 209, 212–14, 216–17; NRA (National Rifle Association) and, 154, 207, 216, 219–220; ownership data, 203, 204; profits and, 218, 252; sales and, 210–11; weapons effect and, 205–6. *See also* guns; school shootings

American Psychiatric Association, 115–16, 161
American Psychological Association, 255
American Psychologist, 156
Ammons Quick Test, 261
Amnesty International, 2, 61
amygdala, 86, 121, 169. *See also* brains; neuroscience
Anda, Robert, 233
Anderson, Elijah, 40–41, 83
Andrew Dirkson case, 134–39, 215
Andy Williams case, 159–160
Angleson, Jonny, 23
animals, human treatment of, 77–78
Annie E. Casey Foundation, 153
anti-social personality disorder, 101, 142, 187–88, 248
appeals, execution, 3, 75, 246
Arendt, Hannah, 257
Arizona, 34, 36, 186
Arizona, Miranda v. (1966), 34, 36
Arluke, Arnold, 77
Armstrong, Dan, 160–64, 168, 210
Armstrong, Karen, 78
Arnet, Jeffrey, 156
artistic activities, 235
assaults: Danny Samson case and, 1, 101; guard, 155; guns and, 212, 252; incarceration rates and, 3–4; interventions and reductions in, 245; nonlethal, 75, 87, 214; preemptive, 84, 95
assault weapons, 214
assets, developmental, 234–35
ATF (Bureau of Alcohol, Tobacco, Firearms and Explosives), 207, 210
athletic activities, 235
attachment relations. *See* rejection sensitivity
Aurora, Colorado movie theater massacre, 210, 211, 215, 227
Australia, 212, 216–17

Baby Lollipops Case, 7
Bankovic, Tim, 24, 25, 103–4
Banks, Tyrone, 38–41
Banner, Marquan, 124–27
Barrington, Nate, 23
Barry Lodi case, 227–28, 233, 234–35

Bartolomeo, Liz, 220
Batson, C. Daniel, 49
Beauregard, Mario, 108
Beck Suicide Scale, 261
Bedard, Claire, 26, 147
behavioral genetics, 127–130
Benson, Marvin, 222–25
Berkowitz, Leonard, 205
Bernet, William, 129–130
Berns, Joyce, 124
Berthson, Shawn, 23
bigotry, 63. *See also* racism
Billy Bob Wilson case, 45–48, 75
Bishop, Donna, 175
Black on Black crime, 90. *See also* African Americans
Black rage, 11, 62. *See also* African Americans
blind, gun permits and the, 207–8
Bloom, Paul, 49
Blumstein, Al, 152
Bobbs, Ronald, 41
boot camp model, 254
bootstrapped logistic regression, 261
Bosket, Willie, 151–52
Boston Gun Project/Operation Ceasefire, 170–71, 218–19, 253
Bouchard, Camil, 232
Bowlby, John, 102
Bowling Alone (Putnam), 217
Boyle, Gregory, 80
Brady Campaign to Prevent Gun Violence, 220
Braga, Anthony, 171, 218
brain injuries, 142, 171–72, 193, 248, 261
brains: addiction and the, 30, 31; adolescent and teenage, 28, 88–89, 169; amygdala of the, 86, 121, 169; childhood development of the, 116; culture of honor and the, 94; emotional regulation and the, 15; frontal cortex of the, 169; genes and the, 127–130; injuries to, 142, 171–72, 193, 248, 261; neuroscience, 20, 30, 85–86, 108–10; prefrontal cortex of the, 109, 121; war zones and the, 84–86. *See also* executive function
Brain That Changes Itself, The (Doidge), 108
Braveheart (film), 90

Brazill, Nathaniel, 60–61, 257–58
Bronfenbrenner, Urie, 5, 108, 195, 231
Bronson, Lasalle, 82
Brooks, David, 252
Brown, James, 55–56
Brown, Jonathan, 247
Brown, Michael, 64
Bruce Walters case, 52–53
Bruce Warner case, 238–39
Bryant, Fred, 43
Bryant, Martin, 216–17
Buddhism, 52–53, 57, 77
Buettner, Robert, 22
Buka, Stephen, 86
bullying, 84, 123, 159
Bureau of Alcohol, Tobacco, Firearms and Explosives (ATF), 207, 210
Bureau of Justice Statistics, 176, 239, 248
Burgess model, 180
Burstow, Bonnie, 116
Butterfield, Fox, 89–90, 151

Calhoun, Georgia, 23
Calhoun, John C., 92
California, 245–46
Cambodia, 9, 33, 79, 120
campaign contributions, 154
Campbell, Jacqueline, 38
Campbell, Keith, 250
Canada, 212–13, 217, 232, 251
Capital Offenders Program, Giddings State School, 256–57
capital punishment, 75, 165. See also death penalty; death row; executions
Capote, Truman, 183–84
Cardona, Ana Maria, 7
Cared Straight program, 80
caregiving, 254
Carey, Hugh, 152
caring, circle of, 26–27, 76–78, 79
Carranza, Audrey, 59
"Case Against Empathy, The" (Bloom), 49
Caspi, Avshalom, 85, 127, 128, 129
Casson, Derrick, 221
Cavanaugh, William, 79
CDC (Centers for Disease Control and Prevention): gun control and the, 207; murder rates and the, 3, 153; National

Center for Injury Prevention and Control, 87; risk accumulation approach and the, 233; violence as public health issue and the, 253
Center for Compassion and Altruism Research and Education, Stanford University, 80
Center for Impact Research, 184–85
Centers for Disease Control and Prevention. See CDC (Centers for Disease Control and Prevention)
CEOs (Chief Executive Officers), 25
"Character, Factory, The" (Brooks), 252
character education, 252
character model, addictions and the, 29
Charles Smith case, 121–24
charter schools, 98–99
Chasing Justice (Cook), 56
C. Henry Kempe Award, 5
Chess, Stella, 235
Chicago: children and youth killed in, 87–88; intervention programs and, 236, 245; James Jackson case and, 97; Patrick Tolan research and, 131, 236; "Risk and Opportunity in Childhood and Adolescence" (course), 43–44; urban war zones of, 8, 9
Chicago Tribune, 87–88
child abuse: Andrew Dirkson case, 134–39; Baby Lollipops case and, 7; Billy Bob Wilson case and, 46–47; Capital Offenders Program, Giddings State School and, 256; Charles Smith case and, 121–24; C. Henry Kempe Award and, 5; child murder, 7, 69–71, 115, 244–45; chronic trauma and, 117, 119–121, 194–95; conduct disorder and, 192–93; disassociation and, 69–70; Duke Jimenez case and, 105–6; home visit interventions and, 245; James Jackson case and, 97–98; Junior Mercedez case and, 19, 69–71; juries and, 65; Malcolm Jones case and, 58–59; MAOA gene, aggression and, 128–29; Marquan Banner case and, 125–26; negative social cognition and, 231; prevention as murder prevention, 248; psychological elements of, 133; psychopathy and, 25; as

child abuse *(continued)*
  risk factor, 182, 191, 233; Ron Richardson case and, 112–14; single mothers
  and, 232; social cues and, 32; Tim Bankovic case and, 103–4; Zagar model and,
  142. *See also* child maltreatment; children, as murder witnesses; sexual abuse
Child Development journal, 5
childhood trauma. *See* trauma, childhood
child maltreatment, 8, 56, 131–39, 232, 233.
  See also child abuse; children, as murder
  witnesses; sexual abuse
child murder, 7, 69–71, 115, 244–45. *See
  also* child abuse
children, as murder witnesses: Billy Bob
  Wilson case, 46; Charles Smith case,
  122; data on, 87; James Jackson case, 97;
  Jorge Susindo case, 71; Malcolm Jones
  case, 58–59; Melvin Grandjean case,
  41–42; Stephen Walton case, 202
*Children in Danger: Coping with the Conse-
  quences of Community Violence* (Garbarino, Dubrow, Kostelny, Pardo), 9, 87
China, 79
choices: addiction and, 30–32; contexts of,
  37; criminal justice system and, 15,
  19–20; environments and, 44; external
  issues and, 20; false confessions and, 36;
  geographic effect and, 33; good vs. bad,
  28–29; informed consent and, 36–37;
  internal issues and, 20; social, cultural
  environments and, 33–34; typology of
  killing, 22–24; violence over nonviolence, 2
Christianity, 53, 76, 78–79
Christianson, John, 76, 147–150, 165–66,
  206
Christopher Simmons, Missouri v. (2005),
  164, 176
chromosomes, X, Y, 128, 129
chronic trauma, 117, 119–121, 194–95. *See
  also* trauma, childhood
circle of caring, 26–27, 76–78, 79
Clément, Marie-Eve, 232
Clemons, Christopher, 82
Cleveland-Marshall Law School, 11
code of the street, 83. *See also* honor,
  culture of

cognitive behavioral therapy, 33
cognitive competence, 231
Cohen, Dov, 90–91, 93
Colorado, 13–15, 210, 211, 215, 227
Colorado v. Rivas (1995), 13
Columbine High School shooting: disassociation and the, 227; FBI (Federal
  Bureau of Investigation) conference
  post, 212; gun control and the, 208; gun
  sales post, 215; Martin Teffler case and
  the, 157–58, 168; peer reporting and the,
  170; shared psychotic disorder and the,
  161; Youth Violence Panel post, 219
combat, 54–55, 86, 96–97, 130–31, 211
community violence: *Children in Danger:
  Coping with the Consequences of Community Violence* (Garbarino, Dubrow,
  Kostelny, Pardo), 9, 87; children's play
  and, 87–88; as chronic trauma, 194–95;
  community members, programs and,
  253; Marquan Banner case and, 126;
  murder witnesses and, 86–87; Robert
  Tallman case and, 83–84; smoking and,
  33; St. Louis, Missouri, 38–39; violence
  as moral imperative and, 83. *See also*
  children, as murder witnesses; domestic
  violence; gangs
comorbidity, 29
compassion: character education and, 252;
  Dalai Lama and, 43, 76–77; as defense
  strategy, 51; intellectual commitment
  and, 81; lucidity and, 42; research on,
  49; spiritual integrity and, 79; for
  untreated traumatized child, 15. *See also*
  empathy
conduct disorder, 32, 33, 166, 192–93, 194
confessions, 34–36
confirmatory bias, 28, 63
constitutional rights: Eighth Amendment,
  177; Felicia Morgan case and, 10; Fifth
  Amendment, 34; Fourteenth Amendment, 66; Second Amendment, 208,
  216, 220
consumerist materialism, 249–250, 252.
  See also economic inequality
Convention on the Rights of the Child,
  United Nations, 164
Cook, Kerry Max, 56

Cornell University, 5, 116
corrections.com, 154–55
Corrections Corporation of America, 154
corrections officers, 79, 155
Coulter, Marshall, 221
covert rejection, 139
crack cocaine epidemic, 152
Creighton McFarland case, 171–73, 174, 175, 193–97
Criminal Gangs Anonymous, 186
criminal justice status, killers pre-murder, 239
criminal justice system, 15, 19–20, 61–69, 89. *See also* trials, juvenile vs. adult status
criminal practicality, 24
criminal responsibility, age of, 150–52, 155–56, 164. *See also* trials, juvenile vs. adult status
cruel and unusual punishment, Eighth Amendment, 177
culture, Hawaiian vs. haole, 232
culture of honor. *See* honor, culture of
culture of respect or shame, 240–41
cureviolence.org, 253
curiosity or thrill killing, 24, 103

Dalai Lama, 43, 76–77
Dalton, Simon, 23–24, 27
Dan Armstrong case, 160–64, 168, 210
Daniel Wellington case, 23, 91–92
Danny Samson case, 1, 101
Daubert rule, 6, 14, 174
Daubert v. Merrell Dow Pharmaceuticals (1993), 6
Davidson, Jonathan, 118
Davidson, Richard, 109, 110
Davis, Jordan, 65
death penalty: age of criminal responsibility and the, 164; appeals process and the, 3, 246; confirmatory bias study and the, 28; costs, 245–46; defense standards and the, 242; federal government and the, 75; *Fisher v. The United States* (1946) and the, 12–13; males vs. females and the, 2; *Missouri v. Christopher Simmons* (2005) and the, 164, 176; Proposition 34 (California) and the,

246; race and the, 61–62; states and the, 3, 4, 75. *See also* executions
Death Penalty Focus, 3
Death Penalty Information Center, 3, 245
Deathpenalty.org, 3
death row, 3, 57, 124. *See also* death penalty; executions
death sentences. *See* death penalty
Denmark, 251
Dennis Stetson case, 244
depression, 129, 134, 233–34
Descartes, René, 77–78
DeSteno, David, 49
deterrence, 167–68, 170–71
developmental assets, 234–35
developmental depth psychology, 2, 8
developmental factors, 28, 248–49
developmental pathways, 11, 12, 14, 104
developmental theory, Piaget, 119
DeVore, Quintin, 208
Diagnostic and Statistical Manual-IV (American Psychiatric Association), 161
Dickey, John, 222, 224
Dieter, Richard, 3
Dilulio, John, 152
Dirkson, Andrew, 134–39, 215
disease model, addictions as, 29
Dishion, Thomas, 256
disinhibition model, alcohol, 173–74
disassociation, 69–70, 113–14, 117–18, 122, 226
dissociative amnesia, 37–38, 53
District Attorneys Association, 133
DNA evidence, 35, 36
Dodge, Kenneth, 32, 231
Doidge, Norman, 108
domestic violence: Andrew Dirkson case, 134; brain studies, children and, 86; child abuse and, 232; guns and, 206, 221; John Mendoza case and, 84; recidivism rates and, 176–77; rejection sensitivity and, 23, 38, 138; as risk factor, 233
Downey, Geraldine, 23, 138, 139
drugs: as adulthood outcome, 233–34; choices and, 32; consumerist materialism and, 250, 251; Daniel Wellington case and, 23; decision making and, 31; John Christianson case and, 148; Mar

Johnson case and, 249; U.S. Census Bureau data on, 111

FBI (Federal Bureau of Investigation), 155–56, 208, 212

Federal Rule of Evidence 702 (1975), 6

Feldman, Ronald, 255–56

Feldman, Scott, 139

Feletti, Vincent, 233

Felicia Morgan case, 7–11, 12, 199

felons, violent, 239, 240

felony convictions, 184

females, 2, 7, 23, 27, 166

Ferguson, Missouri, 64

Fifth Amendment, 34

Figuero, Lazaro, 7

Finding Freedom: Writings from Death Row (Masters), 57

Finkelhor, David, 37

Firearm Amendment Acts, United Kingdom, 216

Fish, Susan, 13, 14

Fisher v. The United States (1946), 12–13

Florida, 7, 14, 60, 75, 175–76

Florida v. Graham (2010), 4, 165, 176, 180

forensic developmental psychology, 13

Fortune, James and Jennifer, 91–92

Foster, Joshua, 23

Fourteenth Amendment, 66

Fox, James, 152

Frankfurter, Felix, 12

Frederick Hill case, 178–79, 200–201

Freud, Sigmund, 107

"From Boot Camp to Monastery" program, 254

frontal cortex, 169. *See also* brains; neuroscience

Frye v. United States (1923), 6

"Gaming the System: How the Political Strategies of Private Prison Companies Promote Ineffective Incarceration Policies" (Justice Policy Institute), 154

gangs: Bobbs, Ronald, 41; Boston Gun Project/Operation Ceasefire and, 170–71, 218–19, 253; Chicago, 8; Criminal Gangs Anonymous, 186; James Jackson case and, 98; Jane Montero case and, 59–60; John Christianson case and, 148; Jorge Susindo case and, 71; Leonel Rivas case and, 13–15; Mannie Townsend case and, 186–87; Melvin Grandjean case and, 39–41; as parole risk factor, 184; power and, 23; prison, 198–99; as protection and identity, 88; as risk factor, 261; Robert Navarro case and, 229–230; Zagar model and, 142

Garbarino, James: *Children in Danger: Coping with the Consequences of Community Violence* (Garbarino, Dubrow, Kostelny, Pardo), 9, 87; as expert witness, 4–5, 15, 242–43; Felicia Morgan case and, 9; *No Place to Be A Child: Growing Up in a War Zone* (Garbarino, Kostelny, Dubrow), 9; parole questions and, 191–92; *Psychologically Battered Child, The,* 132–33; *Raising Children in a Socially Toxic Environment,* 12. *See also Lost Boys* (Garbarino)

Gargoni, Flavio, 103

Garland, Sarah, 68

Garmezy, Norman, 236

Garner, Ronald, 24

Gelman, Andrew, 67

gender, 3, 128, 231, 261. *See also* females; males

"Gene–environment interplay and psychopathology: multiple varieties but real effects" (Rutter), 110

genetics vs. environments, 85, 109–11, 127–130

genital mutilation, 33–34

genotyping, 129

geographic effect, 33

Get On Up (film), 55–56

Ghandi, 258

Gibb, Scott, 78

Giddings State School, 256–57

Gilligan, James, 23, 101, 240–41

Gini Index, 251

Gladwell, Malcolm, 173

Glasgow, Scotland, 95

Goleman, Daniel, 140

good cop/bad cop interrogation technique, 36

Goulee, Michael, 9

Graham, Florida v. (2010), 4, 165, 176, 180

LaPierre, Wayne, 216
Last Chance in Texas (Hubner), 257
Latin Avengers, 59
Latinos, 59, 61, 68–69. *See also* Hispanics
Law and Human Behavior journal, 28
lecture models, intervention, 256
legal appeals, execution, 3, 75, 246
legal insanity, 20–22, 247–48
Leonel Rivas case, 13–15, 22
LePage, Anthony, 205
"Less Guilty by Reason of Adolescence"
  (Steinberg, Scott), 94
Leviathan (Hobbes), 199
Levine, Cynthia, 66
Lewis, Dorothy, 248
life imprisonment: as best legal outcome, 3;
  expert witnesses and, 2; *Florida v.
  Graham* (2010) and, 176; incarceration
  damage and, 73; juveniles and, 4, 165,
  176, 180; prison paths and, 198–200;
  states and, 4
Lima-Marin, Rene, 72–73
Lisak, David, 27
lobbying, 154. *See also* gun lobby
Lodi, Barry, 227–28, 233, 234–35
Loeber, Rolf, 33, 141, 192–93
Lord, Charles, 28
Los Angeles, 59, 71, 88, 148
Lost Boys (Garbarino): "From Boot Camp
  to Monastery" program and, 254; circle
  of caring and, 26, 77; Creighton McFar-
  land case and, 171; letters and, 76,
  80–81, 178; superpredators and, 152
lucidity, 42
Luthar, Suniya, 236
Luxembourg Income Study, 250–51
Lynch, Mona, 64–65

MacAndrew, Craig, 174
Maccoby, Eleanor, 231
Making Sense of Senseless Youth Violence
  Project, 26
Malcolm Jones case, 58–59
males, 2, 23, 128, 166, 261
Mannie Townsend case, 186–88, 193,
  199–200
manslaughter, 3–4
MAOA gene, 127–130

Marquan Banner case, 124–27
Marshall, Grant, 120
Martin, Trayvon, 14, 64–65
Martin Teffler case, 157–59, 160
Marvin Benson case, 222–25
Marvin Tolman case, 37–38, 53–54
Masters, Jarvis, 57, 199
materialism, consumerist, 249–250, 252
maternal responsiveness, 231
Mauer, Mark, 61
McCord, Joan, 256
McCrory, Eamon, 86
McFarland, Creighton, 171–73, 174, 175,
  193–97
McFarland, Loretta, 195–96
McKean, Lisa, 184–85
Means Matter Project, Harvard School of
  Public Health, 209
media, 11, 226. *See also* television
medical experiments, prisoners, 37
medical trauma technology, 75, 211–12, 214
meditation, 80, 254
Mednick, Sarnoff, 110
Melvin Grandjean case, 38–41
Mendoza, John, 84
mens rea (guilty mind), 150
mental defect or disease insanity defense,
  21–22
mental health, 29, 51, 163, 166–67, 184.
  See also rehabilitation; treatment
"Mental Health Evidence and the Capital
  Defense Function" (Stetler), 243
mental illness, 21–22, 139–140, 247–48.
  See also narcissism; personality
  disorders; psychopathy; sociopathy
Mercedez, Junior, 19, 69–71
Merrell Dow Pharmaceuticals, Daubert v.
  (1993), 6
Mexico, 213
Michigan, 197
Miller v. Alabama (2012), 176, 180
Milwaukee Journal Sentinel, 199
mindfulness exercises, 254
Minnesota Multiphasic Personality Inven-
  tory (MMPI), 261, 262
minorities. *See* African Americans; His-
  panics; Latinos; race; racism
Miranda v. Arizona (1966), 34, 36

mirror neurons, 48–49

Missouri, 38–39, 64, 164, 176

Missouri v. Christopher Simmons (2005), 164, 176

mitigation factors: death penalty cases and, 244, 246; defense teams and, 247; juries and, 242; mental health as, 248; narratives as framework for, 2, 51; psychiatric diagnoses and, 248

MMPI (Minnesota Multiphasic Personality Inventory), 261, 262

Moffitt, Terrie, 85, 127

Montero, Jane, 59–60

Moore, Solomon, 3, 73

morals: behavior code and, 25–26; chronic trauma and, 120; death penalty and, 75; moral imperative violence, 83; murders and, 109; parole and, 198; psychopathy and, 24, 25–26; racism and, 62–63, 64; as risk factor, 104; sociopathy and, 101–2; Tim Bankovic case and, 103–4

Morgan, Felicia, 7–11, 12–13, 199

Morse, Stephen, 94

mother abandonment, 111, 249

Mozambique, 9

multisystemic therapy, 153

murders: affective vs. predatory, 109; African Americans and, 61, 90; age groupings and rates of, 155–56; current imprisonment for, 3–4; guns and, 212, 217, 221; of inmates, 75; medical trauma technology and, 75, 211–12, 214; prevention of, 252; prior criminal justice status and, 239; rates of, 89, 213–14, 251; recidivism rates and, 176–77, 185; southern states and, 89; United States, annual, 3; Whites and, 61–62; youth rates decline of, 153; Zagar's model and, 141–43, 261–62

murder victims, 9, 61. *See also individual cases*

murder witnesses, 86–87. *See also* children, as murder witnesses

Murphy, William Francis "Frank," 12

myopia model, alcohol, 173–74

narcissism: African Americans and, 23; consumerist materialism and, 249, 250; females and, 23; Jerry Williams case and, 244; males and, 23; Nate Barrington case and, 23; racism and, 68; trauma and, 117; victim awareness and, 255

"Narrative Works" (Oliver), 51

Nathaniel Brazill case, 60–61, 257–58

National Child Protection Training Center, 133

National Child Traumatic Stress Network, 121

National Conference on Child Abuse and Neglect, 5

National Institute of Mental Health, 21–22

National Public Radio (NPR), 208, 215–16

National Rifle Association (NRA), 154, 207, 216, 219–220

nature vs. nurture. *See* genetics vs. environments

Navarro, Robert, 229–230

Navy Yard shooting, Washington D.C., 211

negative arousal, 116

negative cognition, 116

neighborhoods: abused male children and violent, 131; conduct disorder and, 193; as developmental asset, 234; geographic effect and, 33; infant mortality, poverty and, 232; resilience and, 236; social toxicity of, 38

Nellis, Ashley, 190

neuroplasticity, 108–9

neuroscience, 20, 30, 85–86, 108–10. *See also* brains

New England Journal of Medicine, The, 206, 208–9

New Jim Crow, The (Alexander), 62, 184

Newman, Joseph, 102

New York City, 67

New Yorker magazine, 49, 173

New York State Division of Criminal Services, 22

New York State Parole Board, 177

New York Times, The, 3, 153, 181, 252

New Zealand, 95

Nicaragua, 9

9/11 attacks, 119

Nisbett, Richard, 90–91

non-negligent manslaughter, 3–4

nonparental adults, 235
No Place to Be A Child: Growing Up in a War Zone (Garbarino, Kostelny, Dubrow), 9
Nordic vs. U.S. prison policy, 74
North Carolina Law Review, 11
northerners, culture of honor and, 93–94
Northwestern University, Innocence Project, 35
Norway, 74, 213
novel scientific evidence, 6, 174
"Novel Theories of Criminal Defense Based Upon the Toxicity of the Social Environment: Urban Psychosis, Television Intoxication, and Black Rage" (Falk), 11
NPR (National Public Radio), 208, 215–16
NRA (National Rifle Association), 154, 207, 216, 219–220

Olds, David, 232, 245
Olive, Mark, 51
On Combat (Grossman), 131, 211
On Killing (Grossman), 96
Operation Ceasefire/Boston Gun Project, 170–71, 218–19, 253
overt rejection, 139

Palestinian–Israeli conflict, 8, 9, 120
Palmer, Brian, death penalty and, 75
panic, 24
Pardo, Carol, 9
parental absence, 233, 235. *See also* father abandonment; mother abandonment; single-parent homes
parental rejection, 111, 227. *See also* father abandonment; mother abandonment
parole: *Alabama, Miller v.* (2012) and, 176; childhood trauma and, 194–95; Creighton McFarland case and, 193–97; decision making and, 181–82, 185, 188–89; life sentences and, 3, 4, 165, 176, 190; Mannie Townsend case and, 186–88; moral issues and, 198; post release conditions and, 184–85; prison paths and, 198–200; risk assessment and, 179–185; risk factors and, 182–83; risk questions and, 191–92; Robert Harris

case and, 189–190; superpredators model and, 152; years served and possibility of, 74
Patrick, Christopher, 103
Patton, Desmond, 98–99
PBS (Public Broadcasting System), 21–22, 208
peers, 169–170, 171, 234, 253, 255–56
Perry, Bruce, 84, 85, 118, 121
personality disorders, 23, 101, 187–88, 248. *See also* narcissism; psychopathy; sociopathy
Petrosino, Anthony, 256
Piaget, Jean, 119
Picchioni, Marco, 140
Pincus, Jonathan, 248
Pisano, Ricky, 103
Pittsburgh Youth Study, 141
play, 87, 118
plea bargains, 22
police, 28, 35–36, 64, 66–67, 112
political influence, for-profit prisons, 154
Pol Pot, 120
Pope Francis, 43, 76, 78
Port Arthur, Tasmania mass shooting, 216–17
post-traumatic stress disorder (PTSD), 10, 115–16, 117, 118, 120
Poulin, Francois, 256
poverty, 4, 68, 181, 233. *See also* economic inequality
Powder (film), 205
power, 22–23, 203
Pratt, Larry, 216
prayer groups, 254
predatory murderers, 109, 170
preemptive violence, 23, 25, 84, 96, 101
prefrontal cortex, 109, 121. *See also* brains; neuroscience
Preventing and Reducing Juvenile Delinquency (Howell), 152
prison administration, 51
prison furlough programs, 50–51
'prisonization,' 73, 149
Prison Journal, The, 100
prison policies, U.S. vs. Nordic, 74
prisons. *See* incarceration
prisons, for-profit, 154–55

prison sex, 100. *See also* homosexual rape

Project on Human Development, 86

Proposition 34 (California), 246

prosecutions, trend away from juveniles as adults, 153

prosocial projects, 254

prostitution, 33, 112

psychiatric diagnoses, 248–49. *See also* personality disorders

psychiatric disorders, incarceration and, 166–67

psychiatry, adult vs. adolescent, 167

psychic annihilation, 23, 100

psychoanalysis, 107–8

Psychologically Battered Child, The (Garbarino), 132–33

psychological maltreatment, 132–34. *See also* child maltreatment

psychology, law and, 12–13

psychology of second chances, 43

Psychopath Test, The (Ronson), 25

psychopathy: anti-social personality disorder and, 102, 187–88; curiosity or thrill killing and, 24, 103; definitions of, 25, 101–3; empathy and, 255; frontal cortex and, 169; as parole risk factor, 183; rehabilitation program exclusion and, 255, 257; Tim Bankovic case and, 103–4; war zone mentality social maps and, 95

PTSD (post-traumatic stress disorder), 10, 115–16, 117, 118, 120

Public Broadcasting System (PBS), 21–22, 208

purpose, as developmental asset, 235

Putnam, Robert, 217

Quinsey, Vernon, 255

race, 3, 61–62, 64–69, 181, 233. *See also* African Americans; Hispanics; Latinos; racism

racism: criminal justice system and, 61–69; drug laws and, 239; incarceration and, 228, 239; Marquan Banner case, 126; as risk factor, 232, 233, 234, 240; as social factor, 4; as social toxin, 11. *See also* race

rage, 11, 62, 117, 140, 195

Raine, Adrian, 109, 110, 170

Raising Children in a Socially Toxic Environment (Garbarino), 12

Ramachandran, V. S., 48–49

Ransford, Charles, 184–85

rape: Bruce Walters case, 52–53; current imprisonment for, 3–4; homosexual, 99–101, 192, 195; Marquan Banner case and, 125, 126; recidivism rates and, 176

Rattan, Aneeta, 66

Raven's Advanced Progressive Matrices, 261–62

recidivism: adult court, Florida juveniles and, 175–76; Capital Offenders Program and, 256; employment and, 192; incarceration culture and, 241; murderers and, 176–77; neighborhoods and, 192; Nordic vs. U.S., 74; private vs. public prisons and, 154–55; program elements that reduce, 184–85; psychopathy and, 255; Zagar's Model and, 261–62

Regarding Animals (Arluke, Sanders), 77

Register, The, 208

rehabilitation: adolescent, 255; Capital Offenders Program, Giddings State School, 256–57; lecture models and, 256; Nordic vs. U.S. policies and, 74; peer process and, 255–56; Rene Lima-Marin case and, 72–73. *See also* interventions; treatment

rejection sensitivity, 23–24, 25, 38, 68, 138–39

religion, 78–79

Rene Lima-Marin case, 72–73

reoffending, 167. *See also* recidivism

resilience, 130–31, 196, 229–230, 235–38

respect or shame culture, incarceration and, 240–41

restorative justice projects, 254

reverse waiver hearing, 163

Ricard, Matthieu, 42, 254

Rice, Marnie, 255

Richards, Mannie, 147

Richardson, Ron, 24, 112–14, 120

Richo, Dave, 79

Richtel, Murray, 14

"Risk and Opportunity in Childhood and Adolescence" course, 43–44

Shriner, Texas sexual abuse case, 21
Silton, Rebecca, 108
Simms, Lamar, 13
Simpson, Robert, 115
single-parent homes, 68, 97–98, 111, 142.
    See also father abandonment; mother
    abandonment
SLC6A4 gene, 127–130
Slovic, Paul, 50
Small, Deborah, 50
Smeeding, Timothy, 250
Smith, Adrian, 154–55
Smith, Charles, 121–24
Smith, Rebecca, 118
Smith, Robert, 241–42
Snake River Correctional Institution,
    1, 45
social cues, 32, 169
social maps, 32, 94, 95–96
social policy, 51
social toxins, 11–12, 38
social workers, 3, 70, 217, 241, 247
Society for the Study of Emerging Adult-
    hood, 156–57
socioeconomic status, 261. *See also* eco-
    nomic inequality
sociopathy, 25, 95, 103–4, 188
soldiers, 54–55, 86, 88, 96–97, 130–31.
    See also combat
Solomon, Eldra, 117, 118, 119, 254
southern states, 89–91, 93–94
Soviet Union, Communist, 79
Spacey, Kevin, 220
Spiritual Brain, The (Beauregard), 108
spirituality, 108, 252, 254
spiritual conversions, 57
Squeglia, L. M., 31
stable vs. unstable families, 110, 114–15
Standard Predictor (SP), 261–62
stand your ground defense, 14
Stanford University, 80
Starr, Douglas, 35
Starr, Sonja, 181
*State of Tennessee v. Davis Bradley Wal-
    droup, Jr.* (2009), 129–130
states: criminal responsibility, age of and,
    155; death penalty and, 3, 75; life sen-
    tences, parole and, 4; murder in south-

ern, 89; trials, juvenile vs. adult status
    and, 151
statistics, parole and, 181–82, 185
Steinberg, Laurence (Larry), 28, 89, 94, 168,
    169
Stephen Walton case, 202, 203
Sterling, John, 136
Stetler, Russell, 51, 242, 243, 248
Stetson, Dennis, 244
Sting, Jim, 199
St. Lawrence University, 5
Stockdale, Laura, 140, 196
stop and frisk program, 67
Struckman-Johnson, Cindy and David, 100
substance abuse: adolescent violence and,
    173–75; Andrew Dirkson case and, 134;
    Barry Lodi case and, 227; Creighton
    McFarland case and, 172, 194; emerging
    adulthood and, 156; Nordic prisons,
    treatment and, 74; recidivism and, 184;
    as risk factor, 183, 184, 233, 261; Zagar's
    model and, 142. *See also* alcohol use;
    drugs
Sudan, 33–34
suicide: as adulthood outcome, 233–34;
    Beck Suicide Scale, 261; children and,
    114, 129; Dan Armstrong case and,
    161–62; Germans and rates of, 208–9;
    guns and, 206, 208–10, 217, 221;
    inmate, 75
Sullivan, Harry Stack, 246
Sunlight Foundation, 220
superpredators, 95, 152–53
Supreme Court. *See* U.S. Supreme Court
survival, as typology choice, 22
Susindo, Jorge, 20, 71–72
Sweden, 74, 251
Switzerland, 204

Tallman, Robert, 19, 82–84, 86, 87, 100
Tasmania, 216–17
Tattoos on the Heart (Boyle), 80
teachers: Andrew Dirkson case and, 136–
    37, 139; guns and, 208; Nathaniel Brazill
    case and, 60, 257–58; Ron Richardson
    case and, 113; zone of proximal develop-
    ment and, 119
Teebee, Roberta, 31–32, 74, 105, 190